3

31
1

CAMBRIDGE BOOK OF
ENGLISH VERSE
1939–1975

CAMBRIDGE
BOOK OF
ENGLISH VERSE
1939–1975

Edited by
ALAN BOLD

CAMBRIDGE UNIVERSITY PRESS

CAMBRIDGE

LONDON · NEW YORK · MELBOURNE

Published by the Syndics of the Cambridge University Press
The Pitt Building, Trumpington Street, Cambridge CB2 IRP
Bentley House, 200 Euston Road, London NW1 2DB
32 East 57th Street, New York, NY 10022, USA
296 Beaconsfield Parade, Middle Park, Melbourne 3206, Australia

Library of Congress catalogue card number: 75-10239

hard covers ISBN: 0 521 20391 0
paperback ISBN: 0 521 09840 8

First published 1976

Printed in Great Britain
at the
University Printing House, Cambridge
(Euan Phillips, University Printer)

ACKNOWLEDGEMENTS

The editor and publisher would like to express their thanks as follows for permission to reprint copyright material:

WILLIAM EMPSON – to Chatto and Windus and the poet for the poems from *Collected Poems of William Empson*.

ROBERT GRAVES – to the poet for 'Mid-winter Waking', 'The Door', 'Through Nightmare', 'She Tells her Love While Half Asleep', 'To Juan at the Winter Solstice', 'The Survivor', 'Counting the Beats', 'Questions in a Wood', 'Dialogue on the Headland', 'Spoils', 'Call it a Good Marriage', 'The Face in the Mirror', 'The Visitation', 'Hedges Freaked with Snow' from *Collected Poems 1965*; 'The Glutton' from *Collected Poems 1955*, and 'Song: Dew-drop and Diamond', 'Fact of the Act' and 'Within Reason' from *Collected Poems 1965–1968*.

THOM GUNN – to Faber and Faber Ltd for 'The Wound' from *Fighting Terms*; 'On the Move' and 'Vox Humana' from *The Sense of Movement*; 'In Santa Maria del Popolo', 'The Byrnies' and 'My Sad Captains' from *My Sad Captains*; 'The Goddess', 'Touch' and 'Pierce Street' from *Touch*; and 'Rites of Passage', 'The Messenger' and 'Sunlight' from *Moly*.

TED HUGHES – to Faber and Faber Ltd for 'Hawk Roosting' and 'An Otter' from *Lupercal*; 'Second Glance at a Jaguar', 'Gog' and 'Skylarks' from *Wodwo*; 'A Childish Prank', 'Song for a Phallus' and 'Lovesong' from *Crow*.

– to Faber and Faber Ltd and Harper and Row, Publishers, Inc., for 'Roarers in a Ring' from *The Hawk in the Rain* Copyright © 1956 by Ted Hughes.

– to the poet for 'Song of Woe'.

PHILIP LARKIN – to Faber and Faber Ltd for 'Toads Revisited', 'Mr Bleaney', 'Love Songs in Age', 'The Whitsun Weddings', 'Ambulances', 'Reference Back', and 'Afternoons' from *The Whitsun Weddings*; and for 'Vers de Société', 'The Explosion' and 'The Building' from *High Windows*.

– to The Marvell Press, England, for 'Church Going', 'Lines on a Young Lady's Photograph Album' and 'Toads' from *The Less Deceived*.

HUGH MACDIARMID – the poems 'The Glen of Silence', 'Ballad of Aun, King of Sweden', 'Scotland Small?' and 'The

Glass of Pure Water' are reprinted with permission of Macmillan Publishing Co., Inc. from *Collected Poems of Hugh MacDiarmid* © Christopher Murray Grieve 1948, 1962.

– to the poet for 'Third Hymn to Lenin', 'Facing the Chair', lines from 'In Memoriam James Joyce' and 'Bracken Hills in Autumn'.

EDWIN MUIR – to Faber and Faber Ltd for poems from *Collected Poems of Edwin Muir*.

SYLVIA PLATH – apart from 'Lesbos', the poems by Sylvia Plath are from *Ariel*, published by Faber and Faber Ltd © 1965 by Ted Hughes; 'Lesbos', from *Winter Trees*, published by Faber and Faber Ltd © Ted Hughes, 1971.

DYLAN THOMAS – to J. M. Dent and Sons Ltd and the Trustees for the Copyrights of the late Dylan Thomas for the poems from *Collected Poems of Dylan Thomas*.

CHARLES TOMLINSON – to Oxford University Press for 'Steel: the night shift' and 'The Gossamers' from *A Peopled Landscape* © Oxford University Press 1963; for 'The Weathercocks' from *American Scenes* © Oxford University Press 1966; for 'Swimming Chenango Lake', 'Prometheus', 'Assassin', 'Against Extremity', and 'The Fox Gallery' from *The Way of a World* © Oxford University Press 1969; for 'On Water', 'Mackinnon's Boat', 'The Compact: At Volterra', 'Over Elizabeth Bridge' and 'During Rain' from *Written on Water* © Oxford University Press 1972; and for 'The Way In' from the volume *The Way In* published by Oxford University Press in 1974.

– to the poet for 'The Crane'.

CONTENTS

CONTENTS ix

PREFACE

In the preface to the *Cambridge Book of English Verse 1900–1939* Allen Freer and John Andrew said their anthology was intended for the general reader, for use in the upper forms of school, for students – including foreign students – studying English poetry in the twentieth century. This anthology is addressed to the same audience and tells, or rather *is*, the story of English verse since the end of the Second World War. It is, of course, difficult to select ten poets from the dozens who have distinguished themselves in the postwar period, particularly when so few contemporary reputations are settled. But the ten poets represented in the following pages all share a technical mastery of English verse and a broad enough thematic concern to make them worthy of the attention of a wide audience.

Naturally manner and matter were not the only criteria. There was also a conscious desire to demonstrate the variety of postwar English poetry, to indicate how one island could contain the volcanic energy of Dylan Thomas, the poignant observations of Philip Larkin, the mythical quest of Edwin Muir. There has been no bias towards any 'school' of poetry but, instead, an emphasis on the individual development of each poet. Hence the substantial selection of work from each poet, hence the extended biographical data, hence the technical details and points of information in the notes. My main intention in the editorial commentary has been to isolate the technical microstructure and the thematic macrostructure of each poet's work.

Where I have differed from Freer and Andrew is in giving each poet equal space. I decided on this principle because it seemed invidious to imply quality by quantity. I have also tried to be fair in the presentation of each poet. It is now for the reader to assess each poet on his or her own terms.

Finally, I would like to express my warm appreciation for the co-operation of the poets involved. Hugh MacDiarmid, Philip Larkin, Charles Tomlinson, Thom Gunn and Ted Hughes all patiently and painstakingly answered questions I put to them. Ted Hughes was exceptionally generous in breaking his own rule of placing a limitation of six poems per anthology: I am most grateful to him for his willingness to take the scope and structure of the anthology into account. I am also very grateful to William Empson, who through his publishers, Chatto and Windus, similarly made an exception to his normal rule and has allowed me to use a substantial number of his poems so that the principle on which the whole anthology is based could be preserved.

ALAN BOLD

EDWIN MUIR

Edwin Muir was born in the Folly, his father's rented farm in Deerness parish, Orkney, on 15 May 1887, the youngest of six children. When Muir was two the family moved to the tiny Orkney island of Wyre and the six idyllic years spent there were to give Muir his vision of Eden.

The Muirs were driven out of Wyre by their landlord and, in 1901, moved to Glasgow. Later he looked back on this period as the Fall into a nightmarish labyrinth from which at times there seemed no escape. Muir had to work in an office, a beer-bottling factory, a bone factory and a shipbuilding office, and he was psychologically shattered by a series of personal tragedies: his father died of a heart-attack, his brother Willie of consumption, his brother Johnnie from a brain tumour, and his mother from an internal disease.

In 1918 he married Willa Anderson, a classics graduate of St Andrews then working as a lecturer in a women's college in London. Muir was thirty-two, with no qualifications and little money. It was an inauspicious beginning, yet with Willa, Edwin Muir was to recover his mental stability and eventually find a way back to his childhood Eden. As he said: 'My marriage was the most fortunate event in my life.'

In London Muir got a part-time job with *The New Age* and some freelance reviewing, but he still suffered from the mental torment inflicted by the events in Glasgow. The size of London intimidated him as 'the vast solidity of my surroundings and my own craving emptiness threw me into a slightly feverish state, drove fear up into my throat, and made my lips dry'. He agreed to undergo a course of psychoanalysis to alleviate his troubles and as part of the treatment was encouraged to record his dreams. This had literary importance, as many of his poems, for example 'The Combat', are based on dream experiences.

By 1921 the Muirs were ready to leave London to spend four years abroad: in Czechoslovakia, Germany, Italy and Austria. In Prague Muir felt physically and mentally well for the first time in many years. Then, at last, in Dresden and the nearby garden-city of Hellerau, Muir began to write poetry at the age of thirty-five. Not surprisingly he felt 'too old to submit myself to contemporary influences' but forced to rely on 'the rhythms of English poetry on the one hand, the images in my mind on the other'. Perhaps because of this late start he did not reach his peak as a poet until he was in his fifties.

Muir knew he could not survive on verse alone so, after his return to London in 1925, he and his wife worked at German translations producing the definitive versions of the novels of Kafka (with whose images of life Muir could identify).

On the outbreak of war (which deprived the Muirs of income from their German translations) Edwin, lacking paper qualifications, had to take a job in the Food Office in Dundee, while Willa took a teaching post. After the war, Muir went to Prague as the Director of the British Council Institute there until the Communist coup of 1948. Horrified, Muir left Prague and went as Director of the British Council Institute to Rome where for the first time in his life he knew 'that Christ was born in the flesh and had lived on earth'. Henceforth he was to remain sympathetic to Roman Catholicism though he could never join one particular religious denomination.

Muir had by now attained inner peace, a conviction that through imaginative effort he could regain his childhood Paradise with an informed innocence due to experience. Life, he felt, was not a story but a fable – the first version of his autobiography was called *The Story and the Fable* (1940) – and that 'the life of every man is an endlessly repeated performance of the life of man'. The publication of *The Labyrinth* in 1949 established him as an important writer and he returned to Scotland in 1950 to spend five years as the Warden of Newbattle Abbey, an adult education college outside Edinburgh.

Muir enjoyed his work with staff and students but was irritated by the pettiness of committees, and was relieved when an offer to deliver the 1955–6 Charles Eliot Norton lectures at Harvard (published as *The Estate of Poetry* in 1962) gave him an opportunity to retire from Newbattle. With the money earned in America Muir was able to buy, on his return to Britain, a cottage in Swaffham Prior outside Cambridge. He died in Addenbrooke's Hospital, Cambridge, on 3 January 1959 and on his tombstone in Swaffham Prior churchyard are lines from his sonnet 'Milton':

> his unblinded eyes
> Saw far and near the fields of Paradise.

FURTHER READING

Muir, Edwin. *An Autobiography*. The Hogarth Press, 1954. (Paperback, Methuen, 1965.)
Butter, P. H. *Edwin Muir*. 'Writers and Critics' Series, Oliver and Boyd, 1962.
Butter, P. H. *Edwin Muir: Man and Poet*. Oliver and Boyd, 1966.
Muir, Willa. *Belonging*. The Hogarth Press, 1968.

The Wayside Station

Here at the wayside station, as many a morning,
I watch the smoke torn from the fumy engine
Crawling across the field in serpent sorrow.
Flat in the east, held down by stolid clouds,
The struggling day is born and shines already   5
On its warm hearth far off. Yet something here
Glimmers along the ground to show the seagulls
White on the furrows' black unturning waves.

But now the light has broadened.
I watch the farmstead on the little hill,   10
That seems to mutter: 'Here is day again'
Unwillingly. Now the sad cattle wake
In every byre and stall,
The ploughboy stirs in the loft, the farmer groans
And feels the day like a familiar ache   15
Deep in his body, though the house is dark.
The lovers part
Now in the bedroom where the pillows gleam
Great and mysterious as deep hills of snow,
An inaccessible land. The wood stands waiting   20
While the bright snare slips coil by coil around it,
Dark silver on every branch. The lonely stream
That rode through darkness leaps the gap of light,
Its voice grown loud, and starts its winding journey
Through the day and time and war and history.   25

The Little General

Early in spring the little General came
    Across the sound, bringing the island death,
And suddenly a place without a name,
    And like the pious ritual of a faith,

Hunter and quarry in the boundless trap,   5
    The white smoke curling from the silver gun,
The feather curling in the hunter's cap,
    And clouds of feathers floating in the sun,

While down the birds came in a deafening shower,
    Wing-hurricane, and the cattle fled in fear.   10
Up on the hill a remnant of a tower
    Had watched that single scene for many a year,

Weaving a wordless tale where all were gathered
    (Hunter and quarry and watcher and fabulous field),
A sylvan war half human and half feathered,   15
    Perennial emblem painted on the shield

Held up to cow a never-conquered land
Fast in the little General's fragile hand.

The Transmutation

That all should change to ghost and glance and gleam,
And so transmuted stand beyond all change,
And we be poised between the unmoving dream
And the sole moving moment – this is strange

Past all contrivance, word, or image, or sound,   5
Or silence to express, that we who fall
Through time's long ruin should weave this phantom ground
And in its ghostly borders gather all.

There incorruptible the child plays still,
The lover waits beside the trysting tree,   10
The good hour spans its heaven, and the ill,
Rapt in their silent immortality,

As in commemoration of a day
That having been can never pass away.

In Love for Long

I've been in love for long
With what I cannot tell
And will contrive a song
For the intangible
That has no mould or shape,   5
From which there's no escape.

It is not even a name,
Yet all is constancy;
Tried or untried, the same,
It cannot part from me;   10
A breath, yet as still
As the established hill.

It is not any thing,
And yet all being is;
Being, being, being,   15
Its burden and its bliss.
How can I ever prove
What it is I love?

This happy happy love
Is sieged with crying sorrows,   20
Crushed beneath and above
Between to-days and morrows;
A little paradise
Held in the world's vice.

And there it is content   25
And careless as a child,
And in imprisonment
Flourishes sweet and wild;
In wrong, beyond wrong,
All the world's day long.   30

This love a moment known
For what I do not know
And in a moment gone
Is like the happy doe
That keeps its perfect laws   35
Between the tiger's paws
And vindicates its cause.

The Labyrinth

Since I emerged that day from the labyrinth,
Dazed with the tall and echoing passages,
The swift recoils, so many I almost feared
I'd meet myself returning at some smooth corner,
Myself or my ghost, for all there was unreal   5
After the straw ceased rustling and the bull
Lay dead upon the straw and I remained,
Blood-splashed, if dead or alive I could not tell
In the twilight nothingness (I might have been
A spirit seeking his body through the roads   10
Of intricate Hades) – ever since I came out
To the world, the still fields swift with flowers, the trees
All bright with blossom, the little green hills, the sea,
The sky and all in movement under it,
Shepherds and flocks and birds and the young and old,   15
(I stared in wonder at the young and the old,
For in the maze time had not been with me;
I had strayed, it seemed, past sun and season and change,
Past rest and motion, for I could not tell
At last if I moved or stayed; the maze itself   20
Revolved around me on its hidden axis
And swept me smoothly to its enemy,
The lovely world) – since I came out that day,
There have been times when I have heard my footsteps
Still echoing in the maze, and all the roads   25
That run through the noisy world, deceiving streets
That meet and part and meet, and rooms that open
Into each other – and never a final room –
Stairways and corridors and antechambers
That vacantly wait for some great audience,   30
The smooth sea-tracks that open and close again,
Tracks undiscoverable, indecipherable,
Paths on the earth and tunnels underground,
And bird-tracks in the air – all seemed a part
Of the great labyrinth. And then I'd stumble   35
In sudden blindness, hasten, almost run,
As if the maze itself were after me
And soon must catch me up. But taking thought,

I'd tell myself, 'You need not hurry. This
Is the firm good earth. All roads lie free before you.'   40
But my bad spirit would sneer, 'No, do not hurry.
No need to hurry. Haste and delay are equal
In this one world, for there's no exit, none,
No place to come to, and you'll end where you are,
Deep in the centre of the endless maze.'   45
I could not live if this were not illusion.
It is a world, perhaps; but there's another.
For once in a dream or trance I saw the gods
Each sitting on the top of his mountain-isle,
While down below the little ships sailed by,   50
Toy multitudes swarmed in the harbours, shepherds drove
Their tiny flocks to the pastures, marriage feasts
Went on below, small birthdays and holidays,
Ploughing and harvesting and life and death,
And all permissible, all acceptable,   55
Clear and secure as in a limpid dream.
But they, the gods, as large and bright as clouds,
Conversed across the sounds in tranquil voices
High in the sky above the untroubled sea,
And their eternal dialogue was peace   60
Where all these things were woven, and this our life
Was as a chord deep in that dialogue,
As easy utterance of harmonious words,
Spontaneous syllables bodying forth a world.

That was the real world; I have touched it once,   65
And now shall know it always. But the lie,
The maze, the wild-wood waste of falsehood, roads
That run and run and never reach an end,
Embowered in error – I'd be prisoned there
But that my soul has birdwings to fly free.   70

Oh these deceits are strong almost as life.
Last night I dreamt I was in the labyrinth,
And woke far on. I did not know the place.

The Transfiguration

So from the ground we felt that virtue branch
Through all our veins till we were whole, our wrists
As fresh and pure as water from a well,
Our hands made new to handle holy things,
The source of all our seeing rinsed and cleansed   5
Till earth and light and water entering there
Gave back to us the clear unfallen world.
We would have thrown our clothes away for lightness,
But that even they, though sour and travel stained,
Seemed, like our flesh, made of immortal substance,   10
And the soiled flax and wool lay light upon us
Like friendly wonders, flower and flock entwined
As in a morning field. Was it a vision?
Or did we see that day the unseeable
One glory of the everlasting world   15
Perpetually at work, though never seen
Since Eden locked the gate that's everywhere
And nowhere? Was the change in us alone,
And the enormous earth still left forlorn,
An exile or a prisoner? Yet the world   20
We saw that day made this unreal, for all
Was in its place. The painted animals
Assembled there in gentle congregations,
Or sought apart their leafy oratories,
Or walked in peace, the wild and tame together,   25
As if, also for them, the day had come.
The shepherds' hovels shone, for underneath
The soot we saw the stone clean at the heart
As on the starting-day. The refuse heaps
Were grained with that fine dust that made the world;   30
For he had said, 'To the pure all things are pure.'
And when we went into the town, he with us,
The lurkers under doorways, murderers,
With rags tied round their feet for silence, came
Out of themselves to us and were with us,   35
And those who hide within the labyrinth
Of their own loneliness and greatness came,
And those entangled in their own devices,

The silent and the garrulous liars, all
Stepped out of their dungeons and were free.   40
Reality or vision, this we have seen.
If it had lasted but another moment
It might have held for ever! But the world
Rolled back into its place, and we are here,
And all that radiant kingdom lies forlorn,   45
As if it had never stirred; no human voice
Is heard among its meadows, but it speaks
To itself alone, alone it flowers and shines
And blossoms for itself while time runs on.

But he will come again, it's said, though not   50
Unwanted and unsummoned; for all things,
Beasts of the field, and woods, and rocks, and seas,
And all mankind from end to end of the earth
Will call him with one voice. In our own time,
Some say, or at a time when time is ripe.   55
Then he will come, Christ the uncrucified,
Christ the discrucified, his death undone,
His agony unmade, his cross dismantled –
Glad to be so – and the tormented wood
Will cure its hurt and grow into a tree   60
In a green springing corner of young Eden,
And Judas damned take his long journey backward
From darkness into light and be a child
Beside his mother's knee, and the betrayal
Be quite undone and never more be done.   65

The Combat

It was not meant for human eyes,
That combat on the shabby patch
Of clods and trampled turf that lies
Somewhere beneath the sodden skies
For eye of toad or adder to catch.   5

And having seen it I accuse
The crested animal in his pride,
Arrayed in all the royal hues

Which hide the claws he well can use
To tear the heart out of the side.   10

Body of leopard, eagle's head
And whetted beak, and lion's mane,
And frost-grey hedge of feathers spread
Behind – he seemed of all things bred.
I shall not see his like again.   15

As for his enemy, there came in
A soft round beast as brown as clay;
All rent and patched his wretched skin;
A battered bag he might have been,
Some old used thing to throw away.   20

Yet he awaited face to face
The furious beast and the swift attack.
Soon over and done. That was no place
Or time for chivalry or for grace.
The fury had him on his back.   25

And two small paws like hands flew out
To right and left as the trees stood by.
One would have said beyond a doubt
This was the very end of the bout,
But that the creature would not die.   30

For ere the death-stroke he was gone,
Writhed, whirled, huddled into his den,
Safe somehow there. The fight was done,
And he had lost who had all but won.
But oh his deadly fury then.   35

A while the place lay blank, forlorn,
Drowsing as in relief from pain.
The cricket chirped, the grating thorn
Stirred, and a little sound was born.
The champions took their posts again.   40

And all began. The stealthy paw
Slashed out and in. Could nothing save
These rags and tatters from the claw?

Nothing. And yet I never saw
A beast so helpless and so brave.   45

And now, while the trees stand watching, still
The unequal battle rages there.
The killing beast that cannot kill
Swells and swells in his fury till
You'd almost think it was despair.   50

The Good Town

Look at it well. This was the good town once,
Known everywhere, with streets of friendly neighbours,
Street friend to street and house to house. In summer
All day the doors stood open; lock and key
Were quaint antiquities fit for museums   5
With gyves and rusty chains. The ivy grew
From post to post across the prison door.
The yard behind was sweet with grass and flowers,
A place where grave philosophers loved to walk.
Old Time that promises and keeps his promise   10
Was our sole lord indulgent and severe,
Who gave and took away with gradual hand
That never hurried, never tarried, still
Adding, subtracting. These our houses had
Long fallen into decay but that we knew   15
Kindness and courage can repair time's faults,
And serving him breeds patience and courtesy
In us, light sojourners and passing subjects.
There is a virtue in tranquillity
That makes all fitting, childhood and youth and age, 20
Each in its place.

            Look well. These mounds of rubble,
And shattered piers, half-windows, broken arches
And groping arms were once inwoven in walls
Covered with saints and angels, bore the roof,   25
Shot up the towering spire. These gaping bridges
Once spanned the quiet river which you see
Beyond that patch of raw and angry earth
Where the new concrete houses sit and stare.

Walk with me by the river. See, the poplars   30
Still gathering quiet gazing on the stream.
The white road winds across the small green hill
And then is lost. These few things still remain.
Some of our houses too, though not what once
Lived there and drew a strength from memory.   35
Our people have been scattered, or have come
As strangers back to mingle with the strangers
Who occupy our rooms where none can find
The place he knew but settles where he can.
No family now sits at the evening table;   40
Father and son, mother and child are *out*,
A quaint and obsolete fashion. In our houses
Invaders speak their foreign tongues, informers
Appear and disappear, chance whores, officials
Humble or high, frightened, obsequious,   45
Sit carefully in corners. My old friends
(Friends ere these great disasters) are dispersed
In parties, armies, camps, conspiracies.
We avoid each other. If you see a man
Who smiles good-day or waves a lordly greeting   50
Be sure he's a policeman or a spy.
We know them by their free and candid air.

It was not time that brought these things upon us,
But these two wars that trampled on us twice,
Advancing and withdrawing, like a herd   55
Of clumsy-footed beasts on a stupid errand
Unknown to them or us. Pure chance, pure malice,
Or so it seemed. And when, the first war over,
The armies left and our own men came back
From every point by many a turning road,   60
Maimed, crippled, changed in body or in mind,
It was a sight to see the cripples come
Out on the fields. The land looked all awry,
The roads ran crooked and the light fell wrong.
Our fields were like a pack of cheating cards   65
Dealt out at random – all we had to play
In the bad game for the good stake, our life.
We played; a little shrewdness scraped us through.
Then came the second war, passed and repassed,

And now you see our town, the fine new prison,   70
The house-doors shut and barred, the frightened faces
Peeping round corners, secret police, informers,
And all afraid of all.

          How did it come?
From outside, so it seemed, an endless source,   75
Disorder inexhaustible, strange to us,
Incomprehensible. Yet sometimes now
We ask ourselves, we the old citizens:
'Could it have come from us? Was our peace peace?
Our goodness goodness? That old life was easy   80
And kind and comfortable; but evil is restless
And gives no rest to the cruel or the kind.
How could our town grow wicked in a moment?
What is the answer? Perhaps no more than this,
That once the good men swayed our lives, and those   85
Who copied them took a while the hue of goodness,
A passing loan; while now the bad are up,
And we, poor ordinary neutral stuff,
Not good or bad, must ape them as we can,
In sullen rage or vile obsequiousness.   90
Say there's a balance between good and evil
In things, and it's so mathematical,
So finely reckoned that a jot of either,
A bare preponderance will do all you need,
Make a town good, or make it what you see.   95
But then, you'll say, only that jot is wanting,
That grain of virtue. No: when evil comes
All things turn adverse, and we must begin
At the beginning, heave the groaning world
Back in its place again, and clamp it there.   100
Then all is hard and hazardous. We have seen
Good men made evil wrangling with the evil,
Straight minds grown crooked fighting crooked minds.
Our peace betrayed us; we betrayed our peace.
Look at it well. This was the good town once.'   105

These thoughts we have, walking among our ruins.

One Foot in Eden

One foot in Eden still, I stand
And look across the other land.
The world's great day is growing late,
Yet strange these fields that we have planted
So long with crops of love and hate.   5
Time's handiworks by time are haunted,
And nothing now can separate
The corn and tares compactly grown.
The armorial weed in stillness bound
About the stalk; these are our own.   10
Evil and good stand thick around
In the fields of charity and sin
Where we shall lead our harvest in.

Yet still from Eden springs the root
As clean as on the starting day.   15
Time takes the foliage and the fruit
And burns the archetypal leaf
To shapes of terror and of grief
Scattered along the winter way.
But famished field and blackened tree   20
Bear flowers in Eden never known.
Blossoms of grief and charity
Bloom in these darkened fields alone.
What had Eden ever to say
Of hope and faith and pity and love   25
Until was buried all its day
And memory found its treasure trove?
Strange blessings never in Paradise
Fall from these beclouded skies.

The Horses

Barely a twelvemonth after
The seven days war that put the world to sleep,
Late in the evening the strange horses came.
By then we had made our covenant with silence,

But in the first few days it was so still   5
We listened to our breathing and were afraid.
On the second day
The radios failed; we turned the knobs; no answer.
On the third day a warship passed us, heading north,
Dead bodies piled on the deck. On the sixth day   10
A plane plunged over us into the sea. Thereafter
Nothing. The radios dumb;
And still they stand in corners of our kitchens,
And stand, perhaps, turned on, in a million rooms
All over the world. But now if they should speak,   15
If on a sudden they should speak again,
If on the stroke of noon a voice should speak,
We would not listen, we would not let it bring
That old bad world that swallowed its children quick
At one great gulp. We would not have it again.   20
Sometimes we think of the nations lying asleep,
Curled blindly in impenetrable sorrow,
And then the thought confounds us with its strangeness.
The tractors lie about our fields; at evening
They look like dank sea-monsters couched and waiting.   25
We leave them where they are and let them rust:
'They'll moulder away and be like other loam.'
We make our oxen drag our rusty ploughs,
Long laid aside. We have gone back
Far past our fathers' land.   30
                          And then, that evening
Late in the summer the strange horses came.
We heard a distant tapping on the road,
A deepening drumming; it stopped, went on again
And at the corner changed to hollow thunder.   35
We saw the heads
Like a wild wave charging and were afraid.
We had sold our horses in our fathers' time
To buy new tractors. Now they were strange to us
As fabulous steeds set on an ancient shield   40
Or illustrations in a book of knights.
We did not dare go near them. Yet they waited,
Stubborn and shy, as if they had been sent
By an old command to find our whereabouts
And that long-lost archaic companionship.   45

In the first moment we had never a thought
That they were creatures to be owned and used.
Among them were some half-a-dozen colts
Dropped in some wilderness of the broken world,
Yet new as if they had come from their own Eden.   50
Since then they have pulled our ploughs and borne our loads,
But that free servitude still can pierce our hearts.
Our life is changed; their coming our beginning.

'I see the image'

I see the image of a naked man,
He stoops and picks a smooth stone from the ground,
Turns round and in a wide arc flings it backward
Towards the beginning. What will catch it,
Hand, or paw, or gullet of sea-monster?   5
He stoops again, turns round and flings a stone
Straight on before him. I listen for its fall,
And hear a ringing on some hidden place
As if against the wall of an iron tower.

HUGH MACDIARMID

Hugh MacDiarmid was born Christopher Murray Grieve in the little Border town of Langholm, Dumfriesshire, on 11 August 1892, the son of a rural postman. The family lived in the post office building underneath the local library and young Grieve had constant access to a collection of some 12,000 books which he claims to have read by the age of fourteen. When he was not out playing with other children in the rich Border landscape Grieve would 'fill a big washing-basket with books' and gradually master them.

Grieve attended Langholm Academy, went to Edinburgh to train as a schoolteacher but, when his father died in 1911, soon abandoned all idea of a steady career. As he explains in *Lucky Poet*: 'I was very early determined that I would not "work for money", and that whatever I might have to do to earn my living, I would never devote more of my time and my energies to remunerative work than I did to voluntary and gainless activities.'

In the 1914–18 War Grieve served with the Royal Army Medical Corps and was invalided home from Salonika suffering from cerebral malaria. In 1918 he married Margaret Skinner and the couple moved to Montrose where Grieve became the chief reporter of the weekly *Montrose Review*, the father of two children, a Labour Member of the Town Council, a J.P., and a founder of the Scottish Centre of P.E.N., the National Party of Scotland, and two magazines. The first of these, *Northern Numbers*, was a fairly conventional Georgian publication. However, as the editor of *The Scottish Chapbook*, C. M. Grieve introduced his readers, in 1923, to the work of 'Hugh MacDiarmid', a writer of poetry in vernacular Scots – or 'Lallans' (Lowland Scots). The heather was about to be set on fire.

Impressed by MacDiarmid's energy Compton Mackenzie invited him to London in 1929 to edit *Vox*, a radio magazine which collapsed after three months. The poet almost went down with it. He left his wife in London while he found a job as a Publicity Officer in Liverpool. After an unhappy year there he returned to London to be divorced in 1932. Since those distressing years in England MacDiarmid has been 'desperately anxious not to leave Scotland again'. Significantly, too, *Who's Who* has always listed his hobby as 'Anglophobia'.

After his divorce MacDiarmid married a Cornish girl, Valda Trevlyn, and, with their baby Michael, the family moved to an abandoned cottage on the Shetland island of Whalsay in 1933. On arrival the poet was, he recounts in *Lucky Poet*, 'absolutely down-and-out . . . with no money behind me at all, broken down in health, unable to secure remunerative employment of any kind, and wholly concentrated on projects in poetry and other literary fields which could bring no monetary return whatever'.

Nevertheless he remained on Whalsay until 1941 and it was in this period of isolation that he abandoned both lyrics and Lallans to work on a new kind of epic poetry in which English was extended by the use of technical and scientific terms and enriched by phrases from foreign languages. To the adherents of his poetry in Scots it was apostasy but MacDiarmid was not interested in easy popularity.

When he did leave Whalsay, at the age of forty-nine, it was to do a war job: 'hard manual labour' at a Clydeside factory.

When the war ended MacDiarmid was technically unemployed again – though his literary output was as prolific as ever – and his difficult circumstances were only momentarily relieved when the Duke of Hamilton offered him a house on his Lanarkshire estate. Soon after the MacDiarmids had moved in, the National Coal Board took over the estate and the poet and his wife had to go, in 1951, to a derelict, rent-free cottage on a hill-farm near Biggar, Lanarkshire. Thanks to voluntary work by students and members of the Young Communist League the cottage was modernised and the poet felt that 'after about twenty years' tough struggle we were very comfortably ensconced in a house of our own with every likelihood that it would prove a per-manency'. In 1950 MacDiarmid was awarded a Civil List pension.

In 1957 Edinburgh University made MacDiarmid an honorary LLD though by rejoining the Communist Party that same year – *and* in favour of the Russian invasion of Hungary – he was hardly courting respectability. (MacDiarmid first joined the Communist Party in 1934 and, because of his Scottish National-ism, was expelled in 1938.) However, in 1962, on the occasion of his seventieth birthday it seemed as if respectability was about to catch up with the poet who wanted his own epitaph to read

'A disgrace to the community'. His *Collected Poems* (1962) appeared, the Foyle Poetry Prize was awarded, and there was much celebration, with eulogies in the international press and appreciations on radio and television. Two years later, he stood as a Communist candidate against the then Prime Minister, Sir Alec Douglas-Home, in the 1964 General Election. Once again he was an irritant to the establishment and the central figure in controversies. And so he remains, the Grand Old Rogue of Scottish letters, relishing the notion that, after producing a great popular poet in Burns, Scotland had enough talent left over to produce a great unpopular poet.

FURTHER READING

MacDiarmid, Hugh. *Lucky Poet*. Methuen, 1943. Jonathan Cape, 1972.
Buthlay, Kenneth. *Hugh MacDiarmid*. 'Writers and Critics' Series, Oliver and Boyd, 1964.
Glen, Duncan. *Hugh MacDiarmid and the Scottish Renaissance*. Chambers, 1964.

The Glen of Silence

By this cold shuddering fit of fear
My heart divines a presence here,
Goddess or ghost yclept;
Wrecker of homes . . .

Where have I heard a silence before
Like this that only a lone bird's cries
And the sound of a brawling burn to-day
Serve in this wide empty glen but to emphasize?

Every doctor knows it – the stillness of foetal death,   5
The indescribable silence over the abdomen then!
A silence literally 'heard' because of the way
It stands out in the auscultation of the abdomen.

Here is an identical silence, picked out
By a bickering burn and a lone bird's wheeple   10
– The foetal death in this great 'cleared' glen
Where the *fear-tholladh nan tighem* has done his foul work
– The tragedy of an unevolved people.

Third Hymn to Lenin

for Muriel Rukeyser

> *None can usurp this height (returned that shade)*
> *But those to whom the miseries of the world*
> *Are miseries, and will not let them rest.*
>   KEATS *Hyperion*

These that have turned the world upside down are come hither also.
                                                    Acts *xvii*,6

The night is far spent, the day is at hand, let us therefore cast off the works of
darkness, and let us put on the armour of light.   Romans *xiii*,12

Glasgow is a city of the sea, but what avails
In this great human Sargasso even that flair,
That resolution to understand all bearings
That is the essence of a seaman's character,
The fruit of first-hand education in the way of ships,   5
The ways of man, and the ways of women even more,
Since these resemble sea and weather most
And are the deepest source of all appropriate lore.

A cloud no bigger than a man's hand, a new
Note in the wind, an allusion over the salt-junk,   10
And seamen are aware of 'a number of things',
That sense of concealed but powerful meanings sunk
In hints that almost pass too quick to seize,
Which must be won out of the abysses
Above and below, is second nature to them   15
But not enough in such a sink as this is.

What seaman in the history of the world before
On such an ocean as you sailed could say
This wave will recede, this advance, knew every wave
By name, and foresaw its inevitable way   20
And the final disposition of the whirling whole;
So identified at every point with the historic flow
That, even as you pronounced, so it occurred?
You turned a whole world right side up, and did so
With no dramatic gesture, no memorable word.   25
Now measure Glasgow for a like laconic overthrow!

On days of revolutionary turning points you literally flourished,
Became clairvoyant, foresaw the movement of classes,
And the probable zig-zags of the revolution
As if on your palm;   30
Not only an analytical mind but also
A great constructive, synthesising mind
Able to build up in thought the new reality
As it must actually come
By force of definite laws eventually,   35
Taking into consideration, of course,
Conscious interference, the bitter struggle
For the tasks still before the Party, and the class it leads
As well as possible diversions and inevitable actions
Of all other classes. – Such clairvoyance is the result   40
Of a profound and all-sided knowledge of life
With all its richness of colour, connexions and relations.
Hence the logic of your speeches – 'like some all-powerful
        feelers
Economic, political, ideological, and so forth.
Which grasp, once for all, all sides as in a vise,   45
And one has no strength left to tear away from their embrace;
Either one yields or decides upon complete failure.'

As some great seaman or some poet grasps
The practical meaning, ideal beauty, traditional fascination,
Intellectual importance and emotional chances combined   50
In any instant in his particular situation,
So here there is a like accumulation of effects,
On countless planes of significance at once,
And all we see is set in riddling terms,
Making aught but myriad-mindedness a dunce.   55

How can the points be taken quickly enough,
Meaning behind meaning, dense forests of cross-reference;
How can the wood be seen for such a chaos of trees;
How from the hydra's mouths glean any sense?
The logic and transitions of the moment taken,   60
On the spur of the moment all the sheer surface
And rapid narrative 'the public wants' secured,
How grasp the 'darker purposes' and win controlling place?

We are but fools who live by headlines else,
Surfriders merely of the day's sensations,   65
Living in the flicker like a cinema fan,
Nor much dedoped, defooled, by any patience.
Mere Study's fingers cannot grasp the roots of power.
Be with me, Lenin, reincarnate in me here,
Fathom and solve as you did Russia erst   70
This lesser maze, you greatest proletarian seer!

Hard test, my master, for another reason.
The whole of Russia had no Hell like this.
There is no place in all the white man's world
So sunk in the unspeakable abyss.   75
Only a country whose chief glory is the Kirk,
A country with our fetish of efficiency and thrift,
With endless loving sentiment to mask the facts,
Has such an infernal masterpiece in its gift.

A horror that might sicken your stomach even,   80
The peak of the capitalist system and the trough of Hell,
Fit testimonial to our ultra-pious race,
A people greedy, lying, and unconscionable
Beyond compare. – Seize on this link, spirit of Lenin, then
And you must needs haul upwards to the light   85
The whole base chain of the phenomena that hold
Europe so far below levels worthy of its might!

Do you know the haunting slum smell? Do you remember
Proust's account of a urinal's dark-green and yellow scent,
Or Gillies' remark when Abelard complained   90
Of Guibert's horrible cooking, worse than excrement,
Yet he had watched them scour the crocks himself:
'He never washes the cloth he scrubs them with.
That gives the taste, the odour; the world's worst yet.'
But no! We've progressed. Words fail for this all-pervasive   95
Slum stench. A corpse beside it is a violet.

'Door after door as we knocked was opened by a shirted man, suddenly and
softly as if impelled forward by the overpowering smell behind him. It is this
smell which is the most oppressive symbol of such lives; choking, nauseat-
ing; the smell of corrupt sweat and unnamed filthiness of body. That smell!
Sometimes it crept out at us past the legs of the householder, insinuatingly,

as if ashamed; sometimes it brazened out foul and pestiferous. Once in a
woman's shilling boarding-house it leapt out and took us by the throat like
an evil beast. The smell of the slums, the unforgettable, the abominable
smell!' – BOLITHO: The Cancer of Empire, describing the slums of Glasgow

Ah, lizard eyes, how I would love to see
You reincarnate here and taking issue
With the piffling spirits of our public men,
Going through them like a machine-gun through crinkled
     tissue,   100
But first of all – in Cranston's tea-rooms say –
With some of our leading wart-hogs calmly sat
Watching the creatures' sardonically toothsome faces
Die out in horror like Alice's Cheshire cat.

We, who have seen the daemons one by one   105
Emerging in the modern world and know full well
Our rapport with the physical world is safe
So long as we avoid all else and dwell,
Heedless of the multiplicity of correspondences
Behind them, on the simple data our normal senses give,   110
Know what vast liberating powers these dark powers disengage,
But leave the task to others and in craven safety live.

Normal, thanks to the determined blindness we possess
To all that might upset our little apple-carts,
Too cautious to do anything about it,   115
Knowing our days are brief, though these slum parts
Harbour hosts of larves, legions of octopuses,
Pulsing in the dark air, with the wills and powers
To rise in scaly depravity to unthinkable heights
And annihilate forever all that is ours.   120

And only here and there a freak like me
Looking at himself, all of him, with intensest scrutiny,
See how he runs round like a dog, every particle
Concentrated on getting in safe somewhere, while he
With equal determination must push himself out,   125
Feel more at all costs, experience more, be shattered more,
Driven towards an unqualifiable upward and onward
That is – all morons feel – suicidally over the score.

Our frantic efforts go all ways and go none;
Incontinent with vain hopes, tireless Micawbers,   130
Banking on what Gladstone said in 1890
Or Christ a few centuries earlier, – there's
No lack of counsellors, of *die List der Vernunft*.
The way to Hell is paved with plenty of talk,
But nothing ever happens – nothing ever will;   135
The future's always rosy, the present no less black.

Clever – and yet we cannot solve this problem even;
Civilised – and flaunting such a monstrous sore;
Christian – in flat defiance of all Christ taught;
Proud of our country with this open sewer at our door,   140
Come, let us shed all this transparent bluff,
Acknowledge our impotence, the prize eunuchs of Europe,
Battening on our shame, and with voices weak as bats'
Proclaiming in ghoulish kirks our base immortal hope.

And what is this impossible problem then?,   145
Only to give a few thousand people enough to eat,
Decent houses and a fair income every week.
What? For nothing? Yes! Scotland can well afford it.

It cannot be done. The poor are always with us,
The Bible says. Would other countries agree?   150
Clearly we couldn't unless they did it too.
All the old arguments against ending Slavery!

Ah, no! These bourgeois hopes are not our aim.

Lenin, lover of music, who dare not listen to it,
Teach us to eschew all the siren voices too   155
And get due *Diesseitigkeit*. Countless petty indulgences
– We give them fine names, like Culture, it is true –
Lure us up this enchanting side-line and up that
When we should stay in stinking vennel and wynd,
Not masturbating our immortal souls,   160
But simply doing some honest service to mankind.

Great forces dedicated to the foulest ends
Are reaping a rich victory in Glasgow here

In life stunted and denied and endless misery,
Preventible disease and 'crime' and death; and standing
    sheer   165
Behind these crowded throughfares with armaments concealed
Ready at any vital move to massacre
These mindless mobs, the gangsters lurk, the officer class,
    ruthless
Watching Glasgow's every step and lusting to attack her.

And freedom's opposing forces are hidden too,   170
But Fascism has its secret agents everywhere
In every coward's castle, shop, bank, manse and school
While few serve Freedom's counter-service there,
Nor can they serve – for all but all men's ears
Are deaf to aught it says, stuffed with the wax   175
Of ignorant prejudice and subsidised inanity
Till Freedom to their minds all access lacks.

And most insidious and stultifying of all
The anti-human forces have instilled the thought
That knowledge has outrun the individual brain   180
Till trifling details only can be brought
Within the scope of any man; and so have turned
Humanity's vast achievements against the human mind
Until a sense of general impotence compels
Most men in petty groves to stay confined.   185

This is the lie of lies – the High Treason to mankind.
No one but fritters half his time away.
It is the human instinct – the will to use it – that's destroyed
Till only one or two in every million men today
Know that thought is reality – and thought alone! –   190
And must absorb all the material – their goal
The mastery by the spirit of all the facts that can be known.

Instead of that we have a Jeans accommodating the stars
To traditional superstitions, and a Barnes who thrids
Divers geometries – Euclidean, Lobatchewskyan,
    Riemannian –   195
And Cepheid variables, white dwarfs, yet stubbornly heads
(Though he admits his futile journey fails to reach

Any solution of the problem of 'God's' relation to Time)
Back to his starting place – to a like betrayal
Of the scientific spirit to a dud Sublime.   200

And in Scotland a Haldane even, rendering great service to
    biological theory
In persistently calling attention to the special form of
    organization
Existing in living things – yet failing greatly
Through his defeatist wish to accept
This principle of organization as axiomatic   205
Instead of tracing its relation to the lower principle of
    organization
Seen in paracrystals, colloids, and so forth.
Threading with great skill the intricate shuttling path
From 'spontaneity' to preoccupation with design,
From the realistic 'moment' to the abstraction of essential
    form   210
And ending with a fusion of all their elements,
At once realistic and abstract.

'Daring and unblushing atheism is creeping abroad and saturating the
working population, which are the proper persons to be saturated with it. I
look to no others. It has been said to me by more than one person, "Let us
write in the style of Hume and Gibbon and seek readers among the higher
classes." I answer "No"; I know nothing of the so-called higher classes but
that they are robbers; I will work towards the raising of the working population above them.' – RICHARD CARLILE

Or like Michael Roberts whose *New Country*
Is the same old country, and mediaeval enough his
    'modern mind'
Confessing that after all he cannot see   215
How civilization can be saved unless confined
Under the authority of a Church which in the West
Can only be the so-called Christian Church.
Perish the thought! Let us take our stand
Not on this infernal old parrot's perch   220
But squarely with Richard Carlile: 'The enemy with whom
    we have to grapple
Is one with whom no peace can be made. Idolatry will not
    parley,

Superstition will not treat or covenant. They must be
    uprooted
Completely for public and individual safety.'

Michael Roberts and All Angels! Auden, Spender, those
    bhoyos,   225
All yellow twicers: not one of them
With a tithe of Carlile's courage and integrity.
Unlike these pseudos I am *of* – not *for* – the working class
And like Carlile know nothing of the so-called higher classes
Save only that they are cheats and murderers,   230
Battening like vampires on the masses.

The illiteracy of the literate! But Glasgow's hordes
Are not even literate save a man or two;
All bogged in words that communicate no thought,
Only mumbo-jumbo, fraudulent clap-trap, ballyhoo.   235
The idiom of which constructive thought avails itself
Is unintelligible save to a small minority
And all the rest wallow in exploded fallacies
And cherish for immortal souls their gross stupidity,
While in the deeper layers of their ignorance who delves   240
Finds in this order – Scotland, other men, themselves.
We do not play or keep any mere game's conventions.
Our concern is human wholeness – the child-like spirit
Newborn every day – not, indeed, as careless of tradition
Nor of the lessons of the past: these it must needs inherit.   245

But as capable of such complete assimilation and surrender,
So all-inclusive, unfenced-off, uncategoried, sensitive and
    tender.
That growth is unconditioned and unwarped – Ah, Lenin,
Life and that more abundantly, thou Fire of Freedom,
Fire-like in your purity and heaven-seeking vehemence,   250
Yet the adjective must not suggest merely meteoric,
Spectacular – not the flying sparks but the intense
Glowing core of your character, your large and splendid
    stability
Made you the man you were – the live heart of all humanity!

Spirit of Lenin, light on this city now!   255

Light up this city now!

Ballad of Aun, King of Sweden

Surely Hell burns a deeper blue
With each noble boast of men like you.

With each noble boast of men like you
– Such men as all but all men it's true.

See what I'm doing for England, you cry,   5
Or for Christendom, civilisation, or some other lie.

And no one remembers the story of Aun,
The Swedish king, who sent son after son

To death, buying with each another span
Of life for himself, the identical plan   10

All governments, all patriots, self-righteously pursue.
How many sons have *you* given, and *you*, and you?

Nine sons in succession was the grim
Record of Aun, till the people rose and slew *him*.

But when will the people rise and slay   15
The ubiquitous Aun of State Murder to-day?

Realising murder is foulest murder no matter
What individual or body for what end does the slaughter!

Scotland Small?

Scotland small? Our multiform, our infinite Scotland *small*?
Only as a patch of hillside may be a cliché corner
To a fool who cries 'Nothing but heather!' Where in
        September another
Sitting there and resting and gazing round
Sees not only heather but blaeberries   5
With bright green leaves and leaves already turned scarlet,
Hiding ripe blue berries; and amongst the sage-green leaves

Of the bog-myrtle the golden flowers of the tormentil shining;
And on the small bare places, where the little Blackface sheep
Found grazing, milkworts blue as summer skies;   10
And down in neglected peat-hags, not worked
In living memory, sphagnum moss in pastel shades
Of yellow, green, and pink; sundew and butterwort
And nodding harebells vying in their colour
With the blue butterflies that poise themselves delicately
    upon them,   15
And stunted rowans with harsh dry leaves of glorious colour
'Nothing but heather!' – How marvellously descriptive!
    And incomplete!

The Glass of Pure Water

'In the de-oxidisation and re-oxidisation of hydrogen in a single drop of
water we have before us, truly, so far as force is concerned, an epitome of the
whole life . . . The burning of coal to move an iron wheel differs only in
detail, and not in essence, from the decomposition of a muscle to effect its
own concentration.'

                                        JAMES HINTON

'We must remember that his analysis was done not intellectually, but by an
immediate process of intuition; that he was able, as it were, to taste the
hydrogen and oxygen in his glass of water.'

                ALDOUS HUXLEY (of D. H. Lawrence)

'Praise of pure water is common in Gaelic poetry.'

                W. J. WATSON, 'Bardachd Ghaidlig'.

Hold a glass of pure water to the eye of the sun!
It is difficult to tell the one from the other
Save by the tiny hardly visible trembling of the water.
This is the nearest analogy to the essence of human life
Which is even more difficult to see.   5
Dismiss anything you can see more easily;
There is a minute indescribable difference
Between one glass of water and another
With slightly different chemical constituents.
The difference between one human life and another   10
Is no greater; colour does not colour the water;
You cannot tell a white man's life from a black man's.
But the lives of these particular slum people

I am chiefly concerned with, like the lives of all
The world's poorest, remind me less   15
Of a glass of water held between my eyes and the sun
– They remind me of the feeling they had
Who saw Sacco and Vanzetti in the death cell
On the eve of their execution.
– One is talking to God.   20

I dreamt last night that I saw one of His angels
Making his centennial report to the Recording Angel
On the condition of human life.
Look at the ridge of skin between your thumb and forefinger.
Look at the delicate lines on it and how they change   25
– How many different things they can express –
As you move out or close in your forefinger and thumb.
And look at the changing shapes – the countless
Little gestures, little miracles of line –
Of your forefinger and thumb as you move them.   30
And remember how much a hand can express,
How a single movement of it can say more
Than millions of words – dropped hand, clenched fist,
Snapping fingers, thumb up, thumb down.
Raised in blessing, clenched in passion, begging,   35
Welcome, dismissal, prayer, applause,
And a million other signs, too slight, too subtle,
Too packed with meaning for words to describe,
A universal language understood by all,
And the angel's report on human life   40
Was the subtlest movement – just like that – and no more;
A hundred years of life on the Earth
Summed up, not a detail missed or wrongly assessed,
In that little inconceivably intricate movement.

The only communication between man and man   45
That says anything worth hearing
– The hidden well-water; the finger of destiny –
Moves as that water, that angel, moved.
Truth is the rarest thing and life
The gentlest, most unobtrusive movement in the world.   50
I cannot speak to you of the poor people of all the world
But among the people in these nearest slums I know

This infinitesimal twinkling, this delicate play
Of tiny signs that not only say more
Than all speech, but all there is to say, 55
All there is to say and to know and to be.
There alone I seldom find anything else,
Each in himself or herself a dramatic whole,
An 'agon' whose validity is timeless.

Our duty is to free that water, to make these gestures, 60
To help humanity to shed all else,
All that stands between any life and the sun,
The quintessence of any life and the sun;
To still all sound save that talking to God;
To end all movements save movements like these. 65
India had that great opportunity centuries ago
And India lost it – and became a vast morass,
Where no water wins free; a monstrous jungle
Of useless movement; a babel
Of stupid voices, drowning the still small voice. 70
It is our turn now; the call is to the Celt.
This little country can overcome the whole world of wrong
As the Lacedaemonians the armies of Persia.
Cornwall – Gaeldom – must stand for the ending
Of the essential immorality of any man controlling 75
Any other – for the ending of all Government
Since all Government is a monopoly of violence;
For the striking of this water out of the rock of Capitalism;
For the complete emergence from the pollution and fog
With which the hellish interests of private property 80
In land, machinery, and credit
Have corrupted and concealed from the sun,
From the gestures of truth, from the voice of God,
Hundreds upon hundreds of millions of men,
Denied the life and liberty to which they were born 85
And fobbed off with a horrible travesty instead
– Self-righteous, sunk in the belief that they are human,
When not a tenth of one per cent show a single gleam
Of the life that is in them under their accretions of filth.

And until that day comes every true poet's place 90
Is to reject all else and be with the lowest,

The poorest – in the bottom of that deepest of wells
In which alone is truth; in which
Is truth only – truth that should shine like the sun,
With a monopoly of movement, and a sound like talking to
     God . . .   95

Facing the Chair

    Here under the radiant rays of the sun
    Where everything grows so vividly
    In the human mind and in the heart,
    Love, life, and all else so beautifully,
    I think again of men as innocent as I am   5
    Pent in a cold unjust walk between steel bars,
    Their trousers slit for the electrodes
    And their hair cut for the cap

    Because of the unconcern of men and women,
    Respectable and respected and professedly Christian,   10
    Idle-busy among the flowers of their gardens here
    Under the gay-tipped rays of the sun,
    And I am suddenly completely bereft
    Of *la grande amitié des choses crées*,
    The unity of life which can only be forged by love.   15

Bracken Hills in Autumn

These beds of bracken, climax of the summer's growth,
Are elemental as the sky or sea.
In still and sunny weather they give back
The sun's glare with a fixed intensity
    As of steel or glass   5
    No other foliage has.

There is a menace in their indifference to man
As in tropical abundance. On gloomy days
They redouble the sombre heaviness of the sky
And nurse the thunder. Their dense growth shuts the
      narrow ways   10
    Between the hills and draws
    Closer the wide valleys' jaws.

This flinty verdure's vast effusion is the more
Remarkable for the shortness of its stay.
From November to May a brown stain on the slopes   15
Downbeaten by frost and rain, then in quick array
    The silvery crooks appear
    And the whole host is here.

Useless they may seem to men and go unused, but cast
Cartloads of them into a pool where the trout are few   20
And soon the swarming animalculae upon them
Will proportionately increase the fishes too.
    Miracles are never far away
    Save bringing new thought to play.

In summer islanded in these grey-green seas where the
    wind plucks   25
The pale underside of the fronds on gusty days
As a land breeze stirs the white caps in a roadstead
Glimpses of shy bog gardens surprise the gaze
    Or rough stuff keeping a ring
    Round a struggling water-spring.   30

Look closely. Even now bog asphodel spikes, still alight at
    the tips,
Sundew lifting white buds like those of the whitlow grass
On walls in spring over its little round leaves
Sparkling with gummy red hairs, and many a soft mass
    Of the curious moss that can clean   35
    A wound or poison a river, are seen.

Ah! well I know my tumultuous days now at their prime
Will be brief as the bracken too in their stay
Yet in them as the flowers of the hills 'mid the bracken
All that I treasure is needs hidden away   40
    And will also be dead
    When its rude cover is shed.

from 'In Memoriam James Joyce'

Let the only consistency
In the course of my poetry
Be like that of the hawthorn tree
Which in early Spring breaks
Fresh emerald, then by nature's law   5
Darkens and deepens and takes
Tints of purple-maroon, rose-madder and straw.

Sometimes these hues are found
Together, in pleasing harmony bound.
Sometimes they succeed each other. But through   10
All the changes in which the hawthorn is dight,
No matter in what order, one thing is sure
– The haws shine ever the more ruddily bright!

And when the leaves have passed
Or only in a few tatters remain   15
The tree to the winter condemned
          Stands forth at last
       Not bare and drab and pitiful,
But a candelabrum of oxidised silver gemmed
By innumerable points of ruby   20
Which dominate the whole and are visible
Even at considerable distance
As flame-points of living fire.
That so it may be
With my poems too at last glance   25
Is my only desire.

All else must be sacrificed to this great cause.
I fear no hardships. I have counted the cost.
I with my heart's blood as the hawthorn with its haws
Which are sweetened and polished by the frost!   30

See how these haws burn, there down the drive,
In this autumn air that feels like cotton wool,
When the earth has the gelatinous limpness of a body dead
          as a whole
While its tissues are still alive!

ROBERT GRAVES

Robert Graves was born 24 July 1895 in Wimbledon, the son of the Irish poet Alfred Perceval Graves, author of the perennially popular song 'Father O'Flynn'. Poetry apart, Alfred Perceval had made a financially and socially rewarding career as inspector of schools for the Southwark district of London and a good second marriage to Amalia von Ranke.

From his father Graves learned the importance of impeccably correct syntax and from his mother a sense of order and self-discipline, characteristics that have manifested themselves throughout his poetic career. Graves had what is conventionally called a privileged upbringing: at a time of great poverty, he was secure and comfortable and accustomed to servants in the home. After attending a series of schools he won a scholarship to Charterhouse.

From Charterhouse Graves planned to go up to Oxford but when England declared war on Germany he immediately decided to enlist, being 'outraged to read of the Germans' cynical violation of Belgian neutrality'. As he was in Wales at the time he took a commission with 'the nearest regimental depot – the Royal Welsh Fusiliers'.

In 1916, at the Somme, Graves was wounded when 'an eight-inch shell burst three paces behind me. I heard the explosion, and felt as though I had been punched rather hard between the shoulder-blades, but without any pain.' So severe was the injury that Graves was given no chance of recovery and his mother was informed of his death. He recovered, and returned to France before eventually being invalided home for the last eighteen months of the war.

The war-shocked Graves needed warmth and companionship and in January 1918 he married Nancy Nicholson, an eighteen-year-old feminist who refused to use her married name. Graves himself recovered enough to begin his studies at St John's College, Oxford. Because of domestic, commercial and medical distractions he failed to take his B.A. but was allowed to submit a recently published critical work, *Poetic Unreason and Other Studies*, as a B.Litt. thesis, and he graduated in 1925. The following year Graves, Nancy, the four children, and their new

friend, the newly divorced American poet Laura Riding, sailed
for Egypt where Graves was Professor of English Literature at
the University of Cairo for a year. When they returned to Islip
Graves and Laura Riding learned the technique of handprinting
and founded the Seizin Press.

Back in England, as Graves said, 'Health and money im-
proved, marriage wore thin . . . Nancy and I said unforgivable
things to each other.' In 1929, after a serious accident to Laura
Riding (she almost died after falling from a fourth-storey
window) Graves and Nancy parted. Nancy took the children
and Graves took Laura Riding to Deya, a fishing and olive-
producing village on the northwest coast of Majorca. Graves had
finished with England as he made clear by calling his autobiography *Goodbye to All That* (1929), a title that has since
passed into the currency of common English phrases.

Like Nancy, Laura Riding was a militant feminist. She and
Graves collaborated on *A Survey of Modernist Poetry* (1927) and
A Pamphlet Against Anthologies (1928) and Graves's poetry
began to assert the feminine principle as the ultimate creative
source, an assertion later elevated to a thematic theology in *The
White Goddess* (1948). In 1936, on the outbreak of the Spanish
Civil War, Graves and Laura Riding left Majorca, 'wandered
around Europe and the United States for three years', and then
parted. Graves spent the Second World War in England 'because
three of my children had joined the Armed Forces'.

After the war Graves returned to Majorca. A second marriage
to Beryl, daughter of Sir Harry Pritchard, resulted in four more
children and with *Poems 1939–1945* (1946) Graves began to
strike the major note in his poetry and to establish himself as the
one outstanding modern poet willing to concentrate almost
entirely on love-poetry. His output has been prodigious; he has
written more than a hundred books of fiction, mythology,
criticism, religion and anything else he discerns under the moon.
His astringent style, his tenacious insistence on Muse-worship,
his aristocratic bearing and his polemical utterances have made
him a well-known and colourful figure throughout the world of
letters. In 1954–5 he delivered the Clark Lectures at Cambridge,
in 1961 he succeeded Auden as Professor of Poetry at Oxford,
and in 1968 he was awarded the Queen's Gold Medal for Poetry.
These honours rest lightly on the man who wrote to me (12
October 1972) in response to some editorial queries, 'All I

am interested in is whether the poems I write are acceptable to the woman for whom I wrote them, and who vets my selection.'

FURTHER READING

Graves, Robert. *Goodbye to All That.* Jonathan Cape, 1929. Revised edition Cassell, 1957.

Graves, Robert. *The White Goddess.* Faber and Faber, 1948. Amended and enlarged edition Faber and Faber, 1952.

Cohen, J. M. *Robert Graves.* 'Writers and Critics' Series, Oliver and Boyd, 1960.

Day, Douglas. *Swifter Than Reason.* University of North Carolina Press, 1963.

Kirkham, Michael. *The Poetry of Robert Graves.* University of London, The Athlone Press, 1969.

Mid-Winter Waking

Stirring suddenly from long hibernation,
I knew myself once more a poet
Guarded by timeless principalities
Against the worm of death, this hillside haunting;
And presently dared open both my eyes.   5

O gracious, lofty, shone against from under,
Back-of-the-mind-far-clouds like towers;
And you, sudden warm airs that blow
Before the expected season of new blossom,
While sheep still gnaw at roots and lambless go –   10

Be witness that on waking, this mid-winter,
I found her hand in mine laid closely
Who shall watch out the Spring with me.
We stared in silence all around us
But found no winter anywhere to see.   15

The Glutton

Beyond the Atlas roams a love-beast;
The aborigines harry it with darts;
Its flesh is esteemed, though of a fishy tang

Tainting the eater's mouth and lips.
Ourselves once, wandering in mid-wilderness   5
And by despair drawn to this diet,
Before the meal was over sat apart
Loathing each other's carrion company.

The Door   *Love poem*

When she came suddenly in
It seemed the door could never close again,
Nor even did she close it – she, she –
The room lay open to a visiting sea
Which no door could restrain.   5

Yet when at last she smiled, tilting her head
To take her leave of me,
Where she had smiled, instead
There was a dark door closing endlessly,
The waves receded.   10

Through Nightmare

Never be disenchanted of
That place you sometimes dream yourself into,
Lying at large remove beyond all dream,
Or those you find there, though but seldom
In their company seated –   5

The untameable, the live, the gentle,
Have you not known them? Whom? They carry
Time looped so river-wise about their house
There's no way in by history's road
To name or number them.   10

In your sleepy eyes I read the journey
Of which disjointedly you tell; which stirs
My loving admiration, that you should travel
Through nightmare to a lost and moated land,
Who are timorous by nature.   15

She Tells Her Love While Half Asleep

She tells her love while half asleep,
   In the dark hours,
      With half-words whispered low:
As Earth stirs in her winter sleep
   And puts out grass and flowers   5
      Despite the snow,
      Despite the falling snow.

To Juan at the Winter Solstice

There is one story and one story only
That will prove worth your telling,
Whether as learned bard or gifted child;
To it all lines or lesser gauds belong
That startle with their shining   5
Such common stories as they stray into.

Is it of trees you tell, their months and virtues,
Or strange beasts that beset you,
Of birds that croak at you the Triple will?
Or of the Zodiac and how slow it turns   10
Below the Boreal Crown,
Prison of all true kings that ever reigned?

Water to water, ark again to ark,
From woman back to woman:
So each new victim treads unfalteringly   15
The never altered circuit of his fate,
Bringing twelve peers as witness
Both to his starry rise and starry fall.

Or is it of the Virgin's silver beauty,
All fish below the thighs?   20
She in her left hand bears a leafy quince;
When, with her right she crooks a finger, smiling,
How may the King hold back?
Royally then he barters life for love.

Or of the undying snake from chaos hatched,   25
Whose coils contain the ocean,
Into whose chops with naked sword he springs,
Then in black water, tangled by the reeds,
Battles three days and nights,
To be spewed up beside her scalloped shore?   30

Much snow is falling, winds roar hollowly,
The owl hoots from the elder,
Fear in your heart cries to the loving-cup:
Sorrow to sorrow as the sparks fly upward.
The log groans and confesses: 35
There is one story and one story only.

Dwell on her graciousness, dwell on her smiling,
Do not forget what flowers
The great boar trampled down in ivy time.
Her brow was creamy as the crested wave,   40
Her sea-blue eyes were wild
But nothing promised that is not performed.

The Survivor

To die with a forlorn hope, but soon to be raised
By hags, the spoilers of the field, to elude their claws
And stand once more on a well-swept parade-ground,
Scarred and bemedalled, sword upright in fist
At head of a new undaunted company: 5

Is this joy? to be doubtless alive again,
And the others dead? Will your nostrils gladly savour
The fragrance, always new, of a first hedge-rose?
Will your ears be charmed by the thrush's melody
Sung as though he had himself devised it?   10

And is this joy: after the double suicide
(Heart against heart) to be restored entire,
To smooth your hair and wash away the life-blood,
And presently seek a young and innocent bride,
Whispering in the dark: 'for ever and ever'?   15

Counting the Beats

You, love, and I,
(He whispers) you and I,
And if no more than only you and I
What care you or I?

Counting the beats, 5
Counting the slow heart beats,
The bleeding to death of time in slow heart beats,
Wakeful they lie.

Cloudless day,
Night, and a cloudless day; 10
Yet the huge storm will burst upon their heads one day
From a bitter sky.

Where shall we be,
(She whispers) where shall we be,
When death strikes home, O where then shall we be 15
Who were you and I?

Not there but here,
(He whispers) only here,
As we are, here, together, now and here,
Always you and I. 20

Counting the beats,
Counting the slow heart beats,
The bleeding to death of time in slow heart beats,
Wakeful they lie.

Questions in a Wood

The parson to his pallid spouse,
    The hangman to his whore,
Do both not mumble the same vows,
    Both knock at the same door?

And when the fury of their knocks   5
   Has waned, and that was that,
What answer comes, unless the pox
   Or one more parson's brat?

Tell me, my love, my flower of flowers,
   True woman to this man,   10
What have their deeds to do with ours
   Or any we might plan?

Your startled gaze, your restless hand,
   Your hair like Thames in flood,
And choked voice, battling to command   15
   The insurgence of your blood:

How can they spell the dark word said
   Ten thousand times a night
By women as corrupt and dead
   As you are proud and bright?   20

And how can I, in the same breath,
   Though warned against the cheat,
Vilely deliver love to death
   Wrapped in a rumpled sheet?

Yet, if from delicacy of pride   25
   We choose to hold apart,
Will no blue hag appear, to ride
   Hell's wager in each heart?

Dialogue on the Headland

SHE: You'll not forget these rocks and what I told you?
HE: How could I? Never: whatever happens.
SHE: What do you think might happen?
   Might you fall out of love? – did you mean that?
HE: Never, never! 'Whatever' was a sop   5
   For jealous listeners in the shadows.
SHE: You haven't answered me. I asked:
   'What do you think might happen?'

HE: Whatever happens: though the skies should fall
    Raining their larks and vultures in our laps –   10
SHE: 'Though the seas turn to slime' – say that –
    'Though water-snakes be hatched with six heads.'
HE: Though the seas turn to slime, or tower
    In an arching wave above us, three miles high –
SHE: 'Though she should break with you' – dare you say
       that? –   15
    'Though she deny her words on oath.'
HE: I had that in mind to say, or nearly;
    It hurt so much I choked it back.
SHE: How many other days can't you forget?
    How many other loves and landscapes?   20
HE: You are jealous?
SHE: Damnably.
HE: The past is past.
SHE: And this?
HE: Whatever happens, this goes on.   25
SHE: Without a future? Sweetheart, tell me now:
    What do you want of me? I must know that.
HE: Nothing that isn't freely mine already.
SHE: Say what is freely yours and you shall have it.
HE: Nothing that, loving you, I could dare take.   30
SHE: O, for an answer with no 'nothing' in it!
HE: Then give me everything that's left.
SHE: Left after what?
HE: After whatever happens:
    Skies have already fallen, seas are slime,   35
    Watersnakes poke and peer six-headedly –
SHE: And I lie snugly in the Devil's arms.
HE: I said: 'Whatever happens.' Are you crying?
SHE: You'll not forget me – ever, ever, ever?

Spoils

When all is over and you march for home,
The spoils of war are easily disposed of:
Standards, weapons of combat, helmets, drums
May decorate a staircase or a study,

While lesser gleanings of the battlefield –   5
Coins, watches, wedding-rings, gold teeth and such –
Are sold anonymously for solid cash.

The spoils of love present a different case,
When all is over and you march for home:
That lock of hair, these letters and the portrait   10
May not be publicly displayed; nor sold;
Nor burned; nor returned (the heart being obstinate) –
Yet never dare entrust them to a safe
For fear they burn a hole through two-foot steel.

Call It a Good Marriage

Call it a good marriage –
For no one ever questioned
Her warmth, his masculinity,
Their interlocking views;
Except one stray graphologist   5
Who frowned in speculation
At her h's and her s's,
His p's and w's.

Though few would still subscribe
To the monogamic axiom   10
That strife below the hip-bones
Need not estrange the heart,
Call it a good marriage:
More drew those two together,
Despite a lack of children,   15
Than pulled them apart.

Call it a good marriage:
They never fought in public,
They acted circumspectly
And faced the world with pride;   20
Thus the hazards of their love-bed
Were none of our damned business –
Till as jurymen we sat on
Two deaths by suicide.

The Face in the Mirror

Grey haunted eyes, absent-mindedly glaring
From wide, uneven orbits; one brow drooping
Somewhat over the eye
Because of a missile fragment still inhering,
Skin deep, as a foolish record of old-world fighting.   5

Crookedly broken nose – low tackling caused it;
Cheeks furrowed; coarse grey hair, flying frenetic;
Forehead, wrinkled and high;
Jowls, prominent; ears, large; jaw, pugilistic;
Teeth, few; lips, full and ruddy; mouth, ascetic.   10

I pause with razor poised, scowling derision
At the mirrored man whose beard needs my attention,
And once more ask him why
He still stands ready, with a boy's presumption,
To court the queen in her high silk pavilion.   15

The Visitation

Drowsing in my chair of disbelief
I watch the door as it slowly opens –
A trick of the night wind?

Your slender body seems a shaft of moonlight
Against the door as it gently closes.   5
Do you cast no shadow?

Your whisper is too soft for credence,
Your tread like blossom drifting from a bough,
Your touch even softer.

You wear that sorrowful and tender mask   10
Which on high mountain tops in heather-flow
Entrances lonely shepherds;

And though a single word scatters all doubts
I quake for wonder at your choice of me:
Why, why and why?   15

Hedges Freaked with Snow

No argument, no anger, no remorse,
  No dividing of blame.
There was poison in the cup – why should we ask
  From whose hand it came?

No grief for our dead love, no howling gales   5
  That through darkness blow,
But the smile of sorrow, a wan winter landscape,
  Hedges freaked with snow.

Song: Dew-Drop and Diamond

The difference between you and her
(Whom I to you did once prefer)
Is clear enough to settle:
She like a diamond shone, but you
Shine like an early drop of dew   5
Poised on a red rose-petal.

The dew-drop carries in its eye
Mountain and forest, sea and sky,
With every change of weather;
Contrariwise, a diamond splits   10
The prospect into idle bits
That none can piece together.

Fact of the Act

On the other side of the world's narrow lane
You lie in bed, your young breasts tingling
With imagined kisses, your lips puckered,
Your fists tight.

Dreaming yourself naked in my arms,   5
Free from discovery, under some holm oak;
The high sun peering through thick branches,
All winds mute.

Endlessly you prolong the moment
Of your delirium: a first engagement,   10
Silent, inevitable, fearful,
Honey-sweet.

Will it be so in fact? Will fact mirror
Your virginal ecstasies:
True love, uncircumstantial,   15
No blame, no shame?

It is for you, now, to say 'come';
It is for you, now, to prepare the bed;
It is for you as the sole hostess
Of your white dreams –   20

It is for you to open the locked gate,
It is for you to shake red apples down,
It is for you to halve them with your hands
That both may eat.

Yet expectation lies as far from fact   25
As fact's own after-glow in memory;
Fact is a dark return to man's beginnings,
Test of our hardihood, test of a wilful
And blind acceptance of each other
As also flesh.   30

Within Reason

You have wandered widely through your own mind
And your own perfect body;
Thus learning, within reason, gentle one,
Everything that can prove worth the knowing.

A concise wisdom never attained by those   5
Bodiless nobodies
Who travel pen in hand through other's minds,
But without reason,
Feeding on manifold contradiction.

To stand perplexed by love's inconsequences 10
Like fire-flies in your hair
Or distant flashes of a summer storm:
Such are the stabs of joy you deal me
Who also wander widely through my mind
And still imperfect body. 15

WILLIAM EMPSON

William Empson was born 27 September 1906 the son of A. R. Empson of Yokefleet Hall, Howden, East Yorkshire. He was educated at Winchester College and at Cambridge where he took a B.A. in mathematics before studying English under I. A. Richards. Empson was an egregiously brilliant undergraduate, producing startling Metaphysical poems and penetrating criticism, and helping to found and edit the magazine *Experiment*. Under the influence of Richards he published his first critical book, the celebrated *Seven Types of Ambiguity* (1930), at the age of twenty-four. Two years later he was endorsed by F. R. Leavis in *New Bearings in English Poetry* as a 'very original' poet whose 'verse always has a rich and strongly characteristic life, for he is as intensely interested in his technique as in his ideas'.

In 1931 Empson began four years teaching English at Tokyo National University at the time, he noted in *Milton's God* (1961), when 'Japan had just begun her swing towards Manchuria and Pearl Harbour.' In 1935 his *Poems* and *Some Versions of Pastoral* appeared and in 1937 he joined the English faculty of Peking National University just as the Sino–Japanese war broke out. For the next two years he followed the combined North-East China Universities into exile from Peking to Yunnan Province.

On the outbreak of the Second World War Empson returned to London to work in the monitoring department of the BBC and then to become Chinese Editor of the BBC's Far Eastern Section. In 1940 his prophetically titled collection, *The Gathering Storm*, was published and in 1941 he married Hester Henrietta Crouse, a South African broadcasting in Afrikaans. Of his propaganda work he remembered he 'once had the honour of being named in rebuttal by Fritzsche himself and called a curly-headed Jew'.

After the war he taught at Peking National University again and, though a British Council sponsored poet, seemed to have renounced poetry to concentrate on criticism. His book *The Structure of Complex Words* was published in 1951 and Empson spent the summers of 1948, 1950 and 1954 teaching at Kenyon College, Ohio. In 1953 he was appointed Professor of English

Literature at Sheffield University and remained there until 1971.

G. S. Fraser, who knows Empson, described him thus in *Vision and Rhetoric* (1959): 'Mr Empson is a poet who has a religious temperament, a scientific world view, the attitude to politics of a traditional English liberal of the best kind, a con-stitutional melancholy and a robust good-humour, a sardonic wit, a gift for expressing the diffidence and passion of romantic personal attachments, a belief in pleasure, a scepticism about abstract systems, and a sharply practical impatience with any-thing he considers cant.'

FURTHER READING

Hamilton, Ian (ed.). *the Review*, 'Special Number: William Empson', Nos 6 and 7, June 1963.

Willis, J. H. *William Empson*, 'Columbia Essays on Modern Writers' Series. Columbia University Press, 1969.

Roma Gill (ed.). *William Empson: The Man and His Work*. Routledge and Kegan Paul, 1974.

To an Old Lady

Ripeness is all; her in her cooling planet
Revere; do not presume to think her wasted.
Project her no projectile, plan nor man it;
Gods cool in turn, by the sun long outlasted.

Our earth alone given no name of god   5
Gives, too, no hold for such a leap to aid her;
Landing, you break some palace and seem odd;
Bees sting their need, the keeper's queen invader.

No, to your telescope; spy out the land;
Watch while her ritual is still to see,   10
Still stand her temples emptying in the sand
Whose waves o'erthrew their crumbled tracery;

Still stand uncalled-on her soul's appanage;
Much social detail whose successor fades,
Wit used to run a house and to play Bridge,   15
And tragic fervour, to dismiss her maids.

Years her precession do not throw from gear.
She reads a compass certain of her pole;
Confident, finds no confines on her sphere,
Whose failing crops are in her sole control.   20

Stars how much further from me fill my night,
Strange that she too should be inaccessible,
Who shares my sun. He curtains her from sight,
And but in darkness is she visible.

Camping Out

And now she cleans her teeth into the lake:
Gives it (God's grace) for her own bounty's sake
What morning's pale and the crisp mist debars:
Its glass of the divine (that Will could break)
Restores, beyond Nature: or lets Heaven take   5
(Itself being dimmed) her pattern, who half awake
Milks between rocks a straddled sky of stars.

Soap tension the star pattern magnifies.
Smoothly Madonna through-assumes the skies
Whose vaults are opened to achieve the Lord.   10
No, it is we soaring explore galaxies,
Our bullet boat light's speed by thousands flies.
Who moves so among stars their frame unties;
See where they blur, and die, and are outsoared.

Arachne

Twixt devil and deep sea, man hacks his caves;
Birth, death; one, many; what is true, and seems;
Earth's vast hot iron, cold space's empty waves:

King spider, walks the velvet roof of streams:
Must bird and fish, must god and beast avoid: 5
Dance, like nine angels, on pin-point extremes.

His gleaming bubble between void and void,
Tribe-membrane, that by mutual tension stands,
Earth's surface film, is at a breath destroyed.

Bubbles gleam brightest with least depth of lands   10
But two is least can with full tension strain,
Two molecules; one, and the film disbands.

We two suffice. But oh beware, whose vain
Hydroptic soap my meagre water saves.
Male spiders must not be too early slain.   15

Letter 1

You were amused to find you too could fear
'The eternal silence of the infinite spaces',
That net-work without fish, that mere
Extended idleness, those pointless places
Who, being possiblized to bear faces,   5
Yours and the light from it, up-buoyed,
Even of the galaxies are void.

I approve, myself, dark spaces between stars;
All privacy's their gift; they carry glances
Through gulfs; and as for messages (thus Mars'   10
Reknown for wisdom their wise tact enhances,
Hanged on the thread of radio advances)
For messages, they are a wise go-between,
And say what they think common-sense has seen.

Only, have we space, common-sense in common,   15
A tribe whose life-blood is our sacrament,
Physics or metaphysics for your showman,
For my physician in this banishment?
Too non-Euclidean predicament.
Where is that darkness that gives light its place?   20
Or where such darkness as would hide your face?

Our jovial sun, if he avoids exploding
(These times are critical), will cease to grin,

Will lose your circumambient foreboding;
Loose the full radiance his mass can win 25
While packed with mass holds all that radiance in;
Flame far too hot not to seem utter cold
And hide a tumult never to be told.

Legal Fiction

Law makes long spokes of the short stakes of men.
Your well fenced out real estate of mind
No high flat of the nomad citizen
Looks over, or train leaves behind.

Your rights extend under and above your claim 5
Without bound; you own land in Heaven and Hell;
Your part of earth's surface and mass the same,
Of all cosmos' volume, and all stars as well.

Your rights reach down where all owners meet, in Hell's
Pointed exclusive conclave, at earth's centre 10
(Your spun farm's root still on that axis dwells);
And up, through galaxies, a growing sector.

You are nomad yet; the lighthouse beam you own
Flashes, like Lucifer, through the firmament.
Earth's axis varies; your dark central cone 15
Wavers, a candle's shadow, at the end.

This Last Pain

This last pain for the damned the Fathers found:
'They knew the bliss with which they were not crowned.'
    Such, but on earth, let me foretell,
    Is all, of heaven or of hell.

Man, as the prying housemaid of the soul, 5
May know her happiness by eye to hole:
    He's safe; the key is lost; he knows
    Door will not open, nor hole close.

3   B C B

'What is conceivable can happen too,'
Said Wittgenstein, who had not dreamt of you;   10
    But wisely; if we worked it long
    We should forget where it was wrong.

Those thorns are crowns which, woven into knots,
Crackle under and soon boil fool's pots;
    And no man's watching, wise and long,   15
    Would ever stare them into song.

Thorns burn to a consistent ash, like man;
A splendid cleanser for the frying-pan:
    And those who leap from pan to fire
    Should this brave opposite admire.   20

All those large dreams by which men long live well
Are magic-lanterned on the smoke of hell;
    This then is real, I have implied,
    A painted, small, transparent slide.

These the inventive can hand-paint at leisure,   25
Or most emporia would stock our measure;
    And feasting in their dappled shade
    We should forget how they were made.

Feign then what's by a decent tact believed
And act that state is only so conceived,   30
    And build an edifice of form
    For house where phantoms may keep warm.

Imagine, then, by miracle, with me,
(Ambiguous gifts, as what gods give must be)
    What could not possibly be there,   35
    And learn a style from a despair.

Homage to the British Museum

There is a Supreme God in the ethnological section;
A hollow toad shape, faced with a blank shield.
He needs his belly to include the Pantheon,

Which is inserted through a hole behind.
At the navel, at the points formally stressed, at the organs of
    sense,   5
Lice glue themselves, dolls, local deities,
His smooth wood creeps with all the creeds of the world.

Attending there let us absorb the cultures of nations
And dissolve into our judgement all their codes.
Then, being clogged with a natural hesitation   10
(People are continually asking one the way out),
Let us stand here and admit that we have no road.
Being everything, let us admit that is to be something,
Or give ourselves the benefit of the doubt;
Let us offer our pinch of dust all to this God,   15
And grant his reign over the entire building.

Aubade

Hours before dawn we were woken by the quake.
My house was on a cliff. The thing could take
Bookloads off shelves, break bottles in a row.
Then the long pause and then the bigger shake.
It seemed the best thing to be up and go.   5

And far too large for my feet to step by.
I hoped that various buildings were brought low.
The heart of standing is you cannot fly.

It seemed quite safe till she got up and dressed.
The guarded tourist makes the guide the rest.   10
Then I said The Garden? Laughing she said No.
Taxi for her and for me healthy rest.
It seemed the best thing to be up and go.

The language problem but you have to try.
Some solid ground for lying could she show?   15
The heart of standing is you cannot fly.

None of these deaths were her point at all.
The thing was that being woken he would bawl

And finding her not in earshot he would know.
I tried saying Half an Hour to pay this call.   20
It seemed the best thing to be up and go.

I slept, and blank as that I would yet lie.
Till you have seen what a threat holds below,
The heart of standing is you cannot fly.

Tell me again about Europe and her pains,   25
Who's tortured by the drought, who by the rains.
Glut me with floods where only the swine can row
Who cuts his throat and let him count his gains.
It seemed the best thing to be up and go.

A bedshift flight to a Far Eastern sky.   30
Only the same war on a stronger toe.
The heart of standing is you cannot fly.

Tell me more quickly what I lost by this,
Or tell me with less drama what they miss
Who call no die a god for a good throw,   35
Who say after two aliens had one kiss
It seemed the best thing to be up and go.

But as to risings, I can tell you why.
It is on contradiction that they grow.
It seemed the best thing to be up and go.   40
Up was the heartening and the strong reply.
The heart of standing is we cannot fly.

Ignorance of Death

Then there is this civilising love of death, by which
Even music and painting tell you what else to love.
Buddhists and Christians contrive to agree about death

Making death their ideal basis for different ideals.
The Communists however disapprove of death   5
Except when practical. The people who dig up

Corpses and rape them are I understand not reported.
The Freudians regard the death-wish as fundamental,
Though 'the clamour of life' proceeds from its rival 'Eros'.

Whether you are to admire a given case for making less
    clamour   10
Is not their story. Liberal hopefulness
Regards death as a mere border to an improving picture.

Because we have neither hereditary nor direct knowledge of
    death
It is the trigger of the literary man's biggest gun
And we are happy to equate it to any conceived calm.   15

Heaven me, when a man is ready to die about something
Other than himself, and is in fact ready because of that,
Not because of himself, that is something clear about himself.

Otherwise I feel very blank upon this topic,
And think that though important, and proper for anyone to
    bring up,   20
It is one that most people should be prepared to be blank
    upon.

Missing Dates

    Slowly the poison the whole blood stream fills.
    It is not the effort nor the failure tires.
    The waste remains, the waste remains and kills.

    It is not your system or clear sight that mills
    Down small to the consequence a life requires;   5
    Slowly the poison the whole blood stream fills.

    They bled an old dog dry yet the exchange rills
    Of young dog blood gave but a month's desires
    The waste remains, the waste remains and kills.

    It is the Chinese tombs and the slag hills   10
    Usurp the soil, and not the soil retires.
    Slowly the poison the whole blood stream fills.

Not to have fire is to be a skin that shrills.
The complete fire is death. From partial fires
The waste remains, the waste remains and kills.   15

It is the poems you have lost, the ills
From missing dates, at which the heart expires.
Slowly the poison the whole blood stream fills.
The waste remains, the waste remains and kills.

Just a Smack at Auden

Waiting for the end, boys, waiting for the end.
What is there to be or do?
What's become of me or you?
Are we kind or are we true?
Sitting two and two, boys, waiting for the end.   5

Shall I build a tower, boys, knowing it will rend
Crack upon the hour, boys, waiting for the end?
Shall I pluck a flower, boys, shall I save or spend?
All turns sour, boys, waiting for the end.

Shall I send a wire, boys? Where is there to send?   10
All are under fire, boys, waiting for the end.
Shall I turn a sire, boys? Shall I choose a friend?
The fat is in the pyre, boys, waiting for the end.

Shall I make it clear, boys, for all to apprehend,
Those that will not hear, boys, waiting for the end,   15
Knowing it is near, boys, trying to pretend,
Sitting in cold fear, boys, waiting for the end?

Shall we send a cable, boys, accurately penned,
Knowing we are able, boys, waiting for the end,
Via the Tower of Babel, boys? Christ will not ascend.   20
He's hiding in his stable, boys, waiting for the end.

Shall we blow a bubble, boys, glittering to distend,
Hiding from our trouble, boys, waiting for the end?

When you build on rubble, boys, Nature will append
Double and re-double, boys, waiting for the end.   25

Shall we make a tale, boys, that things are sure to mend,
Playing bluff and hale, boys, waiting for the end?
It will be born stale, boys, stinking to offend,
Dying ere it fail, boys, waiting for the end.

Shall we go all wild, boys, waste and make them lend,   30
Playing at the child, boys, waiting for the end?
It has all been filed, boys, history has a trend,
Each of us enisled, boys, waiting for the end.

What was said by Marx, boys, what did he perpend?
No good being sparks, boys, waiting for the end.   35
Treason of the clerks, boys, curtains that descend,
Lights becoming darks, boys, waiting for the end.

Waiting for the end, boys, waiting for the end.
Not a chance of blend, boys, things have got to tend.
Think of those who vend, boys, think of how we wend,   40
Waiting for the end, boys, waiting for the end.

Let it go

It is this deep blankness is the real thing strange.
   The more things happen to you the more you can't
      Tell or remember even what they were.

The contradictions cover such a range.
   The talk would talk and go so far aslant.   5
      You don't want madhouse and the whole thing there.

DYLAN THOMAS

Dylan Marlais Thomas was born 27 October 1914 at 5 Cwm-donkin Drive in the 'splendidly ugly sea town' of Swansea, where his father D. J. Thomas taught English at the Grammar School. D. J. gave his son the literary names Dylan (the 'sea son' of the *Mabinogion*) and Marlais (after a nineteenth-century relative who combined radical politics with preaching and Welsh poetry), and encouraged him to read and read aloud. Dylan stayed in his father's house until he was nineteen and liked to call himself 'the Rimbaud of Cwmdonkin Drive'.

Near his house was Cwmdonkin Park which to the poet was 'a world within the world of the sea town' and which contained such unforgettable figures as 'The Hunchback in the Park'. There were also summer holidays at his Aunt Ann Jones's dairy farm, Fern Hill, in North Carmarthenshire; he always remembered that 'the country is holy' ('In country sleep') and relished those days on Fern Hill farm when he was 'young and easy under the apple boughs'.

In 1931 Dylan left school. Apart from acting with the Swansea Little Theatre, reporting for fifteen months for the *South Wales Daily Post*, and lounging about bars and cafés, he devoted himself to writing poetry until he was ready for London. The three years between leaving school and leaving Swansea in 1934 were to be the most prolific creative period of his life. He produced more than 200 poems, including all the *18 Poems*, most of the *Twenty-five Poems*, early versions of many later poems, and ideas that would later be realised in works like *Under Milk Wood*. (By contrast, in the last seven years of his life he wrote only eight poems.)

The publication of 'Light breaks where no sun shines' in *The Listener* of 14 March 1934 provoked angry letters from readers quick to spot obscenity, yet it also drew the admiration of Geoffrey Grigson, Stephen Spender and T. S. Eliot. The *Sunday Referee* awarded him a prize that involved the publication of *18 Poems* by David Archer's Parton Bookshop in 1934.

18 Poems was well received, Edwin Muir in *The Listener*, for example, praising its 'purely poetic force'. By 1936 Edith Sitwell was calling Thomas 'a young man who has every likelihood of becoming a great poet, if only he will work hard enough at subduing his obscurity'. The same year he published *Twenty-five Poems* to a crescendo of critical applause, and met Caitlin Macnamara, a twenty-two-year-old dancer who had been dismissed from the chorus line of the London Palladium for unpunctuality. The two spent a holiday together in the Welsh fishing village of Laugharne – a place that was to remain dear to them – and on 12 July 1937 they were married in Cornwall.

In 1938 the couple moved to Laugharne and watched while his reputation grew.

Despite the critical success of his poetry and his income from wartime films and postwar books and broadcasting, Thomas had great difficulty in regulating his domestic affairs. His drinking was reaching epic proportions and Caitlin Thomas felt that 'the valuable quality of moderation was totally lacking in both of us; in one it was bad enough, but in both it was fatal'. They were, therefore, lucky to have a generous friend in Margaret Taylor, wife of the historian A. J. P. Taylor. In 1947 Mrs Taylor bought an Oxfordshire house for the Thomases, and in 1949 she bought them the Boat House on the estuary of the river Taf in their beloved Laugharne. For the remaining four years of his life the Boat House was home for Dylan and Caitlin and the three children. The house was built on a cliffside with a magnificent view of the bay and in his garden shed, which he called 'the shack', Dylan composed poems like 'Over Sir John's hill', 'Author's Prologue' and 'Poem on his birthday'. He did his best work in the afternoons after the pubs had closed, and would write and revise (sometimes doing up to 200 worksheets for one poem) before going out again in the evenings.

When his *Collected Poems* were published in 1952 Philip Toynbee was not alone in feeling 'that Thomas is the greatest living poet in the English language'. On his third alcoholically punitive trip to America he gave a solo performance of *Under Milk Wood* in Cambridge, Mass., followed a week later by a full-cast performance in New York. The play was a huge success and its author was invited by Stravinsky to write the libretto for a new opera. It seemed he could do nothing wrong as a poet, whereas as a man he could do nothing right.

Back in Laugharne Thomas, now suffering from frequent black-outs, was advised to abstain from alcohol or he might not live long. In October 1953, he went to America for the fourth, and final, time to direct an expanded *Under Milk Wood* in New York. By now his health had deteriorated and his drinking bouts anaesthetised his mind and ravaged his body. On 4 November he was taken to St Vincent's Hospital, New York, in a coma and when Caitlin flew there to be with him she found him

basely humiliated with the disgusting things he dreaded most; not one organ in his body working in its own right, without mechanical assistance; intra-venal feeding, tubes attached blatantly to each vulnerable shy orifice; the head encased in a transparent tent, pumping oxygen into him; the eyes turned up, bulging, unseeing; the breath roaring like a winded horse pound-ing up a slope.

He never regained consciousness and died on 9 November 1953. His body was brought back to Wales and he is buried in St Martin's Churchyard, Laugharne.

FURTHER READING

Brinnin, J. M. *Dylan Thomas in America*. Dent, 1956.
Thomas, Caitlin. *Leftover Life to Kill*. Putnam, 1957.
Davies, Aneirin Talfan. *Dylan: Druid of the Broken Body*. Dent, 1964.
Read, Bill. *The Days of Dylan Thomas*. Weidenfeld and Nicolson, 1964.
Ackerman, John. *Dylan Thomas: His Life and Work*. Oxford University Press, 1964.
Fitzgibbon, Constantine. *The Life of Dylan Thomas*. Dent, 1965.

After the funeral

(*In memory of Ann Jones*)

After the funeral, mule praises, brays,
Windshake of sailshaped ears, muffle-toed tap
Tap happily of one peg in the thick
Grave's foot, blinds down the lids, the teeth in black,
The spittled eyes, the salt ponds in the sleeves,   5
Morning smack of the spade that wakes up sleep,
Shakes a desolate boy who slits his throat
In the dark of the coffin and sheds dry leaves,
That breaks one bone to light with a judgment clout,
After the feast of tear-stuffed time and thistles   10
In a room with a stuffed fox and a stale fern,
I stand, for this memorial's sake, alone
In the snivelling hours with dead, humped Ann

Whose hooded, fountain heart once fell in puddles
Round the parched worlds of Wales and drowned each sun 15
(Though this for her is a monstrous image blindly
Magnified out of praise; her death was a still drop;
She would not have me sinking in the holy
Flood of her heart's fame; she would lie dumb and deep
And need no druid of her broken body). 20
But I, Ann's bard on a raised hearth, call all
The seas to service that her wood-tongued virtue
Babble like a bellbuoy over the hymning heads,
Bow down the walls of the ferned and foxy woods
That her love sing and swing through a brown chapel, 25
Bless her bent spirit with four, crossing birds.
Her flesh was meek as milk, but this skyward statue
With the wild breast and blessed and giant skull
Is carved from her in a room with a wet window
In a fiercely mourning house in a crooked year. 30
I know her scrubbed and sour humble hands
Lie with religion in their cramp, her threadbare
Whisper in a damp word, her wits drilled hollow,
Her fist of a face died clenched on a round pain;
And sculptured Ann is seventy years of stone. 35
These cloud-sopped, marble hands, this monumental
Argument of the hewn voice, gesture and psalm,
Storm me forever over her grave until
The stuffed lung of the fox twitch and cry Love
And the strutting fern lay seeds on the black sill. 40

A Refusal to Mourn the Death, by Fire, of a Child in London

Never until the mankind making
Bird beast and flower
Fathering and all humbling darkness
Tells with silence the last light breaking
And the still hour 5
Is come of the sea tumbling in harness

And I must enter again the round
Zion of the water bead

And the synagogue of the ear of corn
Shall I let pray the shadow of a sound   10
Or sow my salt seed
In the least valley of sackcloth to mourn

The majesty and burning of the child's death.
I shall not murder
The mankind of her going with a grave truth   15
Nor blaspheme down the stations of the breath
With any further
Elegy of innocence and youth.

Deep with the first dead lies London's daughter,
Robed in the long friends,   20
The grains beyond age, the dark veins of her mother,
Secret by the unmourning water
Of the riding Thames.
After the first death, there is no other.

Poem in October

It was my thirtieth year to heaven
Woke to my hearing from harbour and neighbour wood
    And the mussel pooled and the heron
            Priested shore
        The morning beckon   5
With water praying and call of seagull and rook
And the knock of sailing boats on the net webbed wall
        Myself to set foot
            That second
        In the still sleeping town and set forth.   10

    My birthday began with the water-
Birds and the birds of the winged trees flying my name
    Above the farms and the white horses
            And I rose
        In rainy autumn   15
And walked abroad in a shower of all my days.

High tide and the heron dived when I took the road
    Over the border
      And the gates
Of the town closed as the town awoke.   20

  A springful of larks in a rolling
Cloud and the roadside bushes brimming with whistling
    Blackbirds and the sun of October
        Summery
      On the hill's shoulder,   25
Here were fond climates and sweet singers suddenly
Come in the morning where I wandered and listened
    To the rain wringing
      Wind blow cold
In the wood faraway under me.   30

  Pale rain over the dwindling harbour
And over the sea wet church the size of a snail
    With its horns through mist and the castle
      Brown as owls
      But all the gardens   35
Of spring and summer were blooming in the tall tales
Beyond the border and under the lark full cloud.
    There could I marvel
      My birthday
Away but the weather turned around.   40

  It turned away from the blithe country
And down the other air and the blue altered sky
    Streamed again a wonder of summer
      With apples
      Pears and red currants   45
And I saw in the turning so clearly a child's
Forgotten mornings when he walked with his mother
    Through the parables
      Of sun light
And the legends of the green chapels   50

  And the twice told fields of infancy
That his tears burned my cheeks and his heart moved in
      mine.

These were the woods the river and sea
    Where a boy
    In the listening   55
Summertime of the dead whispered the truth of his joy
To the trees and the stones and the fish in the tide.
    And the mystery
      Sang alive
Still in the water and singingbirds.   60

And there could I marvel my birthday
Away but the weather turned around. And the true
    Joy of the long dead child sang burning
      In the sun.
    It was my thirtieth   65
Year to heaven stood there then in the summer noon
Though the town below lay leaved with October blood.
    O may my heart's truth
      Still be sung
On this high hill in a year's turning.   70

The Hunchback in the Park

    The hunchback in the park
    A solitary mister
    Propped between trees and water
    From the opening of the garden lock
    That lets the trees and water enter   5
    Until the Sunday sombre bell at dark

    Eating bread from a newspaper
    Drinking water from the chained cup
    That the children filled with gravel
    In the fountain basin where I sailed my ship   10
    Slept at night in a dog kennel
    But nobody chained him up.

    Like the park birds he came early
    Like the water he sat down
    And Mister they called Hey mister   15
    The truant boys from the town

Running when he had heard them clearly
On out of sound

Past lake and rockery
Laughing when he shook his paper   20
Hunchbacked in mockery
Through the loud zoo of the willow groves
Dodging the park keeper
With his stick that picked up leaves.

And the old dog sleeper   25
Alone between nurses and swans
While the boys among willows
Made the tigers jump out of their eyes
To roar on the rockery stones
And the groves were blue with sailors   30

Made all day until bell time
A woman figure without fault
Straight as a young elm
Straight and tall from his crooked bones
That she might stand in the night   35
After the locks and chains

All night in the unmade park
After the railings and shrubberies
The birds the grass the trees the lake
And the wild boys innocent as strawberries   40
Had followed the hunchback
To his kennel in the dark.

Do not go gentle into that good night

Do not go gentle into that good night,
Old age should burn and rave at close of day;
Rage, rage against the dying of the light.

Though wise men at their end know dark is right,
Because their words had forked no lightning they   5
Do not go gentle into that good night.

Good men, the last wave by, crying how bright
Their frail deeds might have danced in a green bay,
Rage, rage against the dying of the light.

Wild men who caught and sang the sun in flight,   10
And learn, too late, they grieved it on its way,
Do not go gentle into that good night.

Grave men, near death, who see with blinding sight
Blind eyes could blaze like meteors and be gay,
Rage, rage against the dying of the light.   15

And you, my father, there on the sad height,
Curse, bless, me now with your fierce tears, I pray.
Do not go gentle into that good night.
Rage, rage against the dying of the light.

Fern Hill

Now as I was young and easy under the apple boughs
About the lilting house and happy as the grass was green,
   The night above the dingle starry,
    Time let me hail and climb
   Golden in the heydays of his eyes,   5
And honoured among wagons I was prince of the apple towns
And once below a time I lordly had the trees and leaves
    Trail with daisies and barley
   Down the rivers of the windfall light.

And as I was green and carefree, famous among the barns   10
About the happy yard and singing as the farm was home,
   In the sun that is young once only,
    Time let me play and be
   Golden in the mercy of his means,
And green and golden I was huntsman and herdsman, the
       calves   15
Sang to my horn, the foxes on the hills barked clear and cold,
    And the sabbath rang slowly
   In the pebbles of the holy streams.

All the sun long it was running, it was lovely, the hay
Fields high as the house, the tunes from the chimneys,
      it was air   20
  And playing, lovely and watery
    And fire green as grass.
  And nightly under the simple stars
As I rode to sleep the owls were bearing the farm away,
All the moon long I heard, blessed among stables, the
      nightjars   25
  Flying with the ricks, and the horses
    Flashing into the dark.

And then to awake, and the farm, like a wanderer white
With the dew, come back, the cock on his shoulder: it was all
  Shining, it was Adam and maiden,   30
    The sky gathered again
  And the sun grew round that very day.
So it must have been after the birth of the simple light
In the first, spinning place, the spellbound horses walking
      warm
  Out of the whinnying green stable   35
    On to the fields of praise.

And honoured among foxes and pheasants by the gay
      house
Under the new made clouds and happy as the heart was long,
  In the sun born over and over,
    I ran my heedless ways,   40
  My wishes raced through the house high hay
And nothing I cared, at my sky blue trades, that time allows
In all his tuneful turning so few and such morning songs
  Before the children green and golden
    Follow him out of grace,   45

Nothing I cared, in the lamb white days, that time would
      take me
Up to the swallow thronged loft by the shadow of my hand,
  In the moon that is always rising,
    Nor that riding to sleep
  I should hear him fly with the high fields   50
And wake to the farm forever fled from the childless land.

Oh as I was young and easy in the mercy of his means,
　　Time held me green and dying
　　Though I sang in my chains like the sea.

In country sleep

I

Never and never, my girl riding far and near
In the land of the hearthstone tales, and spelled asleep,
Fear or believe that the wolf in a sheepwhite hood
Loping and bleating roughly and blithely shall leap,
　　　　　　　　　　　My dear, my dear,　5
Out of a lair in the flocked leaves in the dew dipped year
To eat your heart in the house of the rosy wood.

Sleep, good, for ever, slow and deep, spelled rare and wise,
My girl ranging the night in the rose and shire
Of the hobnail tales: no gooseherd or swine will turn　10
Into a homestall king or hamlet of fire
　　　　　　　　　And prince of ice
To court the honeyed heart from your side before sunrise
In a spinney of ringed boys and ganders, spike and burn,

Nor the innocent lie in the rooting dingle wooed　15
And staved, and riven among plumes my rider weep.
From the broomed witch's spume you are shielded by fern
And flower of country sleep and the greenwood keep.
　　　　　　　　　Lie fast and soothed,
Safe be and smooth from the bellows of the rushy brood.　20
Never, my girl, until tolled to sleep by the stern

Bell believe or fear that the rustic shade or spell
Shall harrow and snow the blood while you ride wide and
　　near,
For who unmanningly haunts the mountain ravened eaves
Or skulks in the dell moon but moonshine echoing clear　25
　　　　　　　　　From the starred well?
A hill touches an angel. Out of a saint's cell
The nightbird lauds through nunneries and domes of leaves

Her robin breasted tree, three Marys in the rays.
Sanctum sanctorum the animal eye of the wood   30
In the rain telling its beads, and the gravest ghost
The owl at its knelling. Fox and holt kneel before blood.
                                        Now the tales praise
The star rise at pasture and nightlong the fables graze
On the lord's-table of the bowing grass. Fear most   35

For ever of all not the wolf in his baaing hood
Nor the tusked prince, in the ruttish farm, at the rind
And more of love, but the Thief as meek as the dew.
The country is holy: O bide in that country kind,
                                        Know the green good,   40
Under the prayer wheeling moon in the rosy wood
Be shielded by chant and flower and gay may you

Lie in grace. Sleep spelled at rest in the lowly house
In the squirrel nimble grove, under linen and thatch
And star: held and blessed, though you scour the high four   45
Winds, from the dousing shade and the roarer at the latch,
                                        Cool in your vows.
Yet out of the beaked, web dark and the pouncing boughs
Be you sure the Thief will seek a way sly and sure

And sly as snow and meek as dew blown to the thorn,   50
This night and each vast night until the stern bell talks
In the tower and tolls to sleep over the stalls
Of the hearthstone tales my own, lost love; and the soul walks
                                        The waters shorn.
This night and each night since the falling star you were
   born,   55
Ever and ever he finds a way, as the snow falls,

As the rain falls, hail on the fleece, as the vale mist rides
Through the haygold stalls, as the dew falls on the wind-
Milled dust of the apple tree and the pounded islands
Of the morning leaves, as the star falls, as the winged   60
                                        Apple seed glides,
And falls, and flowers in the yawning wound at our sides,
As the world falls, silent as the cyclone of silence.

II

Night and the reindeer on the clouds above the haycocks
And the wings of the great roc ribboned for the fair!   65
The leaping saga or prayer! And high, there, on the hare-
                                        Heeled winds the rooks
Cawing from their black bethels soaring, the holy books
Of birds! Among the cocks like fire the red fox

Burning! Night and the vein of birds in the winged, sloe
    wrist   70
Of the wood! Pastoral beat of blood through the laced leaves!
The stream from the priest black wristed spinney and sleeves
                                        Of thistling frost
Of the nightingale's din and tale! The upgiven ghost
Of the dingle torn to singing and the surpliced   75

Hill of cypresses! The din and tale in the skimmed
Yard of the buttermilk rain on the pail! The sermon
Of blood! The bird loud vein! The saga from mermen
                                        To seraphim
Leaping! The gospel rooks! All tell, this night, of him   80
Who comes as red as the fox and sly as the heeled wind.

Illumination of music! the lulled black-backed
Gull, on the wave with sand in its eyes! And the foal moves
Through the shapen greensward lake, silent, on moonshod
    hooves,
                                        In the winds' wakes.   85
Music of elements, that a miracle makes!
Earth, air, water, fire, singing into the white act,

The haygold haired, my love asleep, and the rift blue
Eyed, in the haloed house, in her rareness and hilly
High riding, held and blessed and true, and so stilly   90
                                        Lying the sky
Might cross its planets, the bell weep, night gather her eyes,
The Thief fall on the dead like the willy nilly dew,

Only for the turning of the earth in her holy
Heart! Slyly, slowly, hearing the wound in her side go   95
Round the sun, he comes to my love like the designed snow,
                                        And truly he

Flows to the strand of flowers like the dew's ruly sea,
And surely he sails like the ship shape clouds. Oh he

Comes designed to my love to steal not her tide raking   100
Wound, nor her riding high, nor her eyes, nor kindled hair,
But her faith that each vast night and the saga of prayer
                                                He comes to take
Her faith that this last night for his unsacred sake
He comes to leave her in the lawless sun awaking   105

Naked and forsaken to grieve he will not come.
Ever and ever by all your vows believe and fear
My dear this night he comes and night without end my dear
                                                Since you were born:
And you shall wake, from country sleep, this dawn and each
    first dawn,   110
Your faith as deathless as the outcry of the ruled sun.

Over Sir John's hill

Over Sir John's hill,
The hawk on fire hangs still;
In a hoisted cloud, at drop of dusk, he pulls to his claws
And gallows, up the rays of his eyes the small birds of the bay
And the shrill child's play   5
Wars
Of the sparrows and such who swansing, dusk, in wrangling
    hedges.
And blithely they squawk
To fiery tyburn over the wrestle of elms until
The flash the noosed hawk   10
Crashes, and slowly the fishing holy stalking heron
In the river Towy below bows his tilted headstone.

Flash, and the plumes crack,
And a black cap of jack-
Daws Sir John's just hill dons, and again the gulled birds
    hare   15
To the hawk on fire, the halter height, over Towy's fins,
In a whack of wind.

There
Where the elegiac fisherbird stabs and paddles
In the pebbly dab-filled   20
Shallow and sedge, and 'dilly dilly,' calls the loft hawk,
'Come and be killed,'
I open the leaves of the water at a passage
Of psalms and shadows among the pincered sandcrabs
      prancing

And read, in a shell,   25
Death clear as a buoy's bell:
All praise of the hawk on fire in hawk-eyed dusk be sung,
When his viperish fuse hangs looped with flames under the
      brand
Wing, and blest shall
Young   30
Green chickens of the bay and bushes cluck, 'dilly dilly,
Come let us die.'
We grieve as the blithe birds, never again, leave shingle and
      elm,
The heron and I,
I young Aesop fabling to the near night by the dingle   35
Of eels, saint heron hymning in the shell-hung distant

Crystal harbour vale
Where the sea cobbles sail,
And wharves of water where the walls dance and the white
      cranes stilt.
It is the heron and I, under judging Sir John's elmed   40
Hill, tell-tale the knelled
Guilt
Of the led-astray birds whom God, for their breast of whistles,
Have mercy on,
God in his whirlwind silence save, who marks the sparrows
      hail,   45
For their soul's song.
Now the heron grieves in the weeded verge. Through windows
Of dusk and water I see the tilting whispering

Heron, mirrored, go,   50
As the snapt feathers snow,

Fishing in the tear of the Towy. Only a hoot owl
Hollows, a grassblade blown in cupped hands, in the looted
    elms
And no green cocks or hens
Shout
Now on Sir John's hill. The heron, ankling the scaly   55
Lowlands of the waves,
Makes all the music; and I who hear the tune of the slow,
Wear-willow river, grave,
Before the lunge of the night, the notes on this time-shaken
Stone for the sake of the souls of the slain birds sailing.   60

In the white giant's thigh

Through throats where many rivers meet, the curlews cry,
Under the conceiving moon, on the high chalk hill,
And there this night I walk in the white giant's thigh
Where barren as boulders women lie longing still

To labour and love though they lay down long ago.   5

Through throats where many rivers meet, the women pray,
Pleading in the waded bay for the seed to flow
Though the names on their weed grown stones are rained
    away,

And alone in the night's eternal, curving act
They yearn with tongues of curlews for the unconceived   10
And immemorial sons of the cudgelling, hacked

Hill. Who once in gooseskin winter loved all ice leaved
In the courters' lanes, or twined in the ox roasting sun
In the wains tonned so high that the wisps of the hay
Clung to the pitching clouds, or gay with any one   15
Young as they in the after milking moonlight lay

Under the lighted shapes of faith and their moonshade
Petticoats galed high, or shy with the rough riding boys,
Now clasp me to their grains in the gigantic glade,

Who once, green countries since, were a hedgerow of joys.   20

Time by, their dust was flesh the swineherd rooted sly,
Flared in the reek of the wiving sty with the rush
Light of his thighs, spreadeagle to the dunghill sky,
Or with their orchard man in the core of the sun's bush
Rough as cows' tongues and thrashed with brambles their
        buttermilk   25
Manes, under his quenchless summer barbed gold to the bone,

Or rippling soft in the spinney moon as the silk
And ducked and draked white lake that harps to a hail stone.

Who once were a bloom of wayside brides in the hawed house
And heard the lewd, wooed field flow to the coming frost,   30
The scurrying, furred small friars squeal, in the dowse
Of day, in the thistle aisles, till the white owl crossed
Their breast, the vaulting does roister, the horned bucks
        climb
Quick in the wood at love, where a torch of foxes foams,
All birds and beasts of the linked night uproar and chime   35

And the mole snout blunt under his pilgrimage of domes,
Or butter fat goosegirls, bounced in a gambo bed,
Their breasts full of honey, under their gander king
Trounced by his wings in the hissing shippen, long dead
And gone that barley dark where their clogs danced in the
        spring,   40
And their firefly hairpins flew, and the ricks ran round –

(But nothing bore, no mouthing babe to the veined hives
Hugged, and barren and bare on Mother Goose's ground
They with the simple Jacks were a boulder of wives) –

Now curlew cry me down to kiss the mouths of their dust.   45

The dust of their kettles and clocks swings to and fro
Where the hay rides now or the bracken kitchens rust
As the arc of the billhooks that flashed the hedges low
And cut the birds' boughs that the minstrel sap ran red.
They from houses where the harvest kneels, hold me hard,   50

Who heard the tall bell sail down the Sundays of the dead
And the rain wring out its tongues on the faded yard,
Teach me the love that is evergreen after the fall leaved
Grave, after Beloved on the grass gulfed cross is scrubbed
Off by the sun and Daughters no longer grieved   55
Save by their long desires in the fox cubbed
Streets or hungering in the crumbled wood: to these
Hale dead and deathless do the women of the hill
Love for ever meridian through the courters' trees

And the daughters of darkness flame like Fawkes fires still.   60

Lament

When I was a windy boy and a bit
And the black spit of the chapel fold,
(Sighed the old ram rod, dying of women),
I tiptoed shy in the gooseberry wood,
The rude owl cried like a telltale tit,   5
I skipped in a blush as the big girls rolled
Ninepin down on the donkeys' common,
And on seesaw sunday nights I wooed
Whoever I would with my wicked eyes,
The whole of the moon I could love and leave   10
All the green leaved little weddings' wives
In the coal black bush and let them grieve.

When I was a gusty man and a half
And the black beast of the beetles' pews,
(Sighed the old ram rod, dying of bitches),   15
Not a boy and a bit in the wick-
Dipping moon and drunk as a new dropped calf,
I whistled all night in the twisted flues,
Midwives grew in the midnight ditches,
And the sizzling beds of the town cried, Quick! –   20
Whenever I dove in a breast high shoal,
Wherever I ramped in the clover quilts,
Whatsoever I did in the coal-
Black night, I left my quivering prints.

When I was a man you could call a man   25
And the black cross of the holy house,
(Sighed the old ram rod, dying of welcome),
Brandy and ripe in my bright, bass prime,
No springtailed tom in the red hot town
With every simmering woman his mouse   30
But a hillocky bull in the swelter
Of summer come in his great good time
To the sultry, biding herds, I said,
Oh, time enough when the blood creeps cold,
And I lie down but to sleep in bed,   35
For my sulking, skulking, coal black soul!

When I was a half of the man I was
And serve me right as the preachers warn,
(Sighed the old ram rod, dying of downfall),
No flailing calf or cat in a flame   40
Or hickory bull in milky grass
But a black sheep with a crumpled horn,
At last the soul from its foul mousehole
Slunk pouting out when the limp time came;
And I gave my soul a blind, slashed eye,   45
Gristle and rind, and a roarers' life,
And I shoved it into the coal black sky
To find a woman's soul for a wife.

Now I am a man no more no more
And a black reward for a roaring life,   50
(Sighed the old ram rod, dying of strangers),
Tidy and cursed in my dove cooed room
I lie down thin and hear the good bells jaw –
For, oh, my soul found a Sunday wife
In the coal black sky and she bore angels!   55
Harpies around me out of her womb!
Chastity prays for me, piety sings,
Innocence sweetens my last black breath,
Modesty hides my thighs in her wings,
And all the deadly virtues plague my death!   60

In my Craft or Sullen Art

In my craft or sullen art
Exercised in the still night
Where only the moon rages
And the lovers lie abed
With all their griefs in their arms,   5
I labour by singing light
Not for ambition or bread
Or the strut and trade of charms
On the ivory stages
But for the common wages   10
Of their most secret heart.

Not for the proud man apart
From the raging moon, I write
On these spindrift pages
Not for the towering dead   15
With their nightingales and psalms
But for the lovers, their arms
Round the griefs of the ages,
Who pay no praise or wages
Nor heed my craft or art.   20

PHILIP LARKIN

Philip Larkin was born 9 August 1922 in Coventry where his father was City Treasurer for over twenty years. He was educated at King Henry VIII School, Coventry, and recalls a 'comfortable and secure' upbringing. When he went to read English at St John's College in wartime Oxford he remembers (in the introduction to the 1964 edition of his novel *Jill*) the 'almost-complete suspension of concern for the future' and the lack of careerism.

At Oxford Larkin was impressed and influenced by Kingsley Amis with whom he shared a passion for traditional jazz (characteristically Larkin dislikes modern jazz because it has none of the nostalgic elegance of traditional jazz, and he links Charlie Parker, the *avant garde* saxophonist, with Pound and Picasso as the three alliterative villains of modernism). Larkin's own poetic *persona* has many affinities with the unromantic, empirically-minded, sceptical antihero who has appeared, in various forms, in Amis's novels. While at Oxford Larkin heard a talk at the English Club by Vernon Watkins (in 1943) which made him such an enthusiastic disciple of Yeats that he published his own Yeatsian collection, *The North Ship*, in 1945. He soon, however, switched his allegiance to Thomas Hardy.

Larkin has always worked as a librarian (in Leicester, in Belfast, and currently at the University of Hull) and has refused either to seek or to accept publicity. As one of the poets in Robert Conquest's *New Lines* anthology of 1956 he was classified as a 'Movement' poet and his poem 'Church Going' (included in *New Lines* and in Larkin's own 1955 collection *The Less Deceived*) became probably the most discussed poem of the 1950s. Those sympathetic to the Movement praised it for its reflective grace and quiet dignity. Those against found it negative and undramatic.

Larkin is unmarried, undemonstrative, unwilling to be a public figure. Indeed, in a radio tribute broadcast on his fiftieth birthday, he summed up his work and achievement simply and typically: 'I seem to have spent my life waiting for poems to turn up.'

FURTHER READING
Timms, David. *Philip Larkin*. 'Modern Writers' Series, Oliver and Boyd, 1973.

Church Going

Once I am sure there's nothing going on
I step inside, letting the door thud shut.
Another church: matting, seats, and stone,
And little books; sprawlings of flowers, cut
For Sunday, brownish now; some brass and stuff   5
Up at the holy end; the small neat organ;
And a tense, musty, unignorable silence,
Brewed God knows how long. Hatless, I take off
My cycle-clips in awkward reverence,

Move forward, run my hand around the font.   10
From where I stand, the roof looks almost new –
Cleaned, or restored? Someone would know: I don't.
Mounting the lectern, I peruse a few
Hectoring large-scale verses, and pronounce
'Here endeth' much more loudly than I'd meant.   15
The echoes snigger briefly. Back at the door
I sign the book, donate an Irish sixpence,
Reflect the place was not worth stopping for.

Yet stop I did: in fact I often do,
And always end much at a loss like this,   20
Wondering what to look for; wondering, too,
When churches fall completely out of use
What we shall turn them into, if we shall keep
A few cathedrals chronically on show,
Their parchment, plate and pyx in locked cases,   25
And let the rest rent-free to rain and sheep.
Shall we avoid them as unlucky places?

Or, after dark, will dubious women come
To make their children touch a particular stone;
Pick simples for a cancer; or on some   30
Advised night see walking a dead one?

Power of some sort or other will go on
In games, in riddles, seemingly at random;
But superstition, like belief, must die,
And what remains when disbelief has gone?   35
Grass, weedy pavement, brambles, buttress, sky,

A shape less recognizable each week,
A purpose more obscure. I wonder who
Will be the last, the very last, to seek
This place for what it was; one of the crew   40
That tap and jot and know what rood-lofts were?
Some ruin-bibber, randy for antique,
Or Christmas-addict, counting on a whiff
Of gown-and-bands and organ-pipes and myrrh?
Or will he be my representative,   45

Bored, uninformed, knowing the ghostly silt
Dispersed, yet tending to this cross of ground
Through suburb scrub because it held unspilt
So long and equably what since is found
Only in separation – marriage, and birth,   50
And death, and thoughts of these – for which was built
This special shell? For, though I've no idea
What this accoutred frowsty barn is worth,
It pleases me to stand in silence here;

A serious house on serious earth it is,   55
In whose blent air all our compulsions meet,
Are recognized, and robed as destinies.
And that much never can be obsolete,
Since someone will forever be surprising
A hunger in himself to be more serious,   60
And gravitating with it to this ground,
Which, he once heard, was proper to grow wise in,
If only that so many dead lie round.

Lines on a Young Lady's Photograph Album

At last you yielded up the album, which,
Once open, sent me distracted. All your ages
Matt and glossy on the thick black pages!
Too much confectionary, too rich:
I choke on such nutritious images.   5

My swivel eye hungers from pose to pose –
In pigtails, clutching a reluctant cat;
Or furred yourself, a sweet girl-graduate;
Or lifting a heavy-headed rose
Beneath a trellis, or in a trilby hat   10

(Faintly disturbing, that, in several ways) –
From every side you strike at my control,
Not least through these disquieting chaps who loll
At ease about your earlier days:
Not quite your class, I'd say, dear, on the whole.   15

But o, photography! as no art is,
Faithful and disappointing! that records
Dull days as dull, and hold-it smiles as frauds,
And will not censor blemishes
Like washing-lines, and Hall's Distemper boards,   20

But shows the cat as disinclined, and shades
A chin as doubled when it is, what grace
Your candour thus confers upon her face!
How overwhelmingly persuades
That this is a real girl in a real place,   25

In every sense empirically true!
Or is it just *the past*? Those flowers, that gate,
These misty parks and motors, lacerate
Simply by being over; you
Contract my heart by looking out of date.   30

Yes, true; but in the end, surely, we cry
Not only at exclusion, but because

It leaves us free to cry. We know *what was*
Won't call on us to justify
Our grief, however hard we yowl across   35

The gap from eye to page. So I am left
To mourn (without a chance of consequence)
You, balanced on a bike against a fence;
To wonder if you'd spot the theft
Of this one of you bathing; to condense,   40

In short, a past that no one now can share,
No matter whose your future; calm and dry,
It holds you like a heaven, and you lie
Unvariably lovely there,
Smaller and clearer as the years go by.   45

Toads

Why should I let the toad *work*
    Squat on my life?
Can't I use my wit as a pitchfork
    And drive the brute off?

Six days of the week it soils   5
    With its sickening poison –
Just for paying a few bills!
    That's out of proportion.

Lots of folk live on their wits:
    Lecturers, lispers,   10
Losels, loblolly-men, louts –
    They don't end as paupers;

Lots of folk live up lanes
    With fires in a bucket,
Eat windfalls and tinned sardines –   15
    They seem to like it.

Their nippers have got bare feet,
    Their unspeakable wives

Are skinny as whippets – and yet
  No one actually *starves*.   20

Ah, were I courageous enough
  To shout *Stuff your pension!*
But I know, all too well, that's the stuff
  That dreams are made on:

For something sufficiently toad-like   25
  Squats in me, too;
Its hunkers are heavy as hard luck,
  And cold as snow,

And will never allow me to blarney
  My way to getting   30
The fame and the girl and the money
  All at one sitting.

I don't say, one bodies the other
  One's spiritual truth;
But I do say it's hard to lose either,   35
  When you have both.

Toads Revisited

Walking around in the park
Should feel better than work:
The lake, the sunshine,
The grass to lie on,

Blurred playground noises   5
Beyond black-stockinged nurses –
Not a bad place to be.
Yet it doesn't suit me,

Being one of the men
You meet of an afternoon: 10
Palsied old step-takers,
Hare-eyed clerks with the jitters,

Waxed-fleshed out-patients
Still vague from accidents,
And characters in long coats   15
Deep in the litter-baskets –

All dodging the toad work
By being stupid or weak.
Think of being them!
Hearing the hours chime,   20

Watching the bread delivered,
The sun by clouds covered,
The children going home;
Think of being them,

Turning over their failures   25
By some bed of lobelias,
Nowhere to go but indoors,
No friends but empty chairs –

No, give me my in-tray,
My loaf-haired secretary,   30
My shall-I-keep-the-call-in-Sir:
What else can I answer,

When the lights come on at four
At the end of another year?
Give me your arm, old toad;   35
Help me down Cemetery Road.

Mr Bleaney

'This was Mr Bleaney's room. He stayed
The whole time he was at the Bodies, till
They moved him.' Flowered curtains, thin and frayed,
Fall to within five inches of the sill,

Whose window shows a strip of building land,   5
Tussocky, littered. 'Mr Bleaney took

My bit of garden properly in hand.'
Bed, upright chair, sixty-watt bulb, no hook

Behind the door, no room for books or bags –
'I'll take it.' So it happens that I lie   10
Where Mr Bleaney lay, and stub my fags
On the same saucer-souvenir, and try

Stuffing my ears with cotton-wool, to drown
The jabbering set he egged her on to buy.
I know his habits – what time he came down,   15
His preference for sauce to gravy, why

He kept on plugging at the four aways –
Likewise their yearly frame: the Frinton folk
Who put him up for summer holidays,
And Christmas at his sister's house in Stoke.   20

But if he stood and watched the frigid wind
Tousling the clouds, lay on the fusty bed
Telling himself that this was home, and grinned,
And shivered, without shaking off the dread

That how we live measures our own nature,   25
And at his age having no more to show
Than one hired box should make him pretty sure
He warranted no better, I don't know.

Love Songs in Age

She kept her songs, they took so little space
    The covers pleased her:
One bleached from lying in a sunny place,
One marked in circles by a vase of water,
One mended, when a tidy fit had seized her,   5
    And coloured, by her daughter –
So they had waited, till in widowhood
She found them, looking for something else, and stood

4-2

Relearning how each frank submissive chord
  Had ushered in   10
Word after sprawling hyphenated word,
And the unfailing sense of being young
Spread out like a spring-woken tree, wherein
  That hidden freshness, sung,
That certainty of time laid up in store   15
As when she played them first. But, even more,

The glare of that much-mentioned brilliance, love,
  Broke out, to show
Its bright incipience sailing above,
Still promising to solve, and satisfy,   20
And set unchangeably in order. So
  To pile them back, to cry,
Was hard, without lamely admitting how
It had not done so then, and could not now.

The Whitsun Weddings

That Whitsun, I was late getting away:
  Not till about
One-twenty on the sunlit Saturday
Did my three-quarters-empty train pull out,
All windows down, all cushions hot, all sense   5
Of being in a hurry gone. We ran
Behind the backs of houses, crossed a street
Of blinding windscreens, smelt the fish-dock; thence
The river's level drifting breadth began,
Where sky and Lincolnshire and water meet.   10

All afternoon, through the tall heat that slept
  For miles inland,
A slow and stopping curve southwards we kept.
Wide farms went by, short-shadowed cattle, and
Canals with floatings of industrial froth;   15
A hothouse flashed uniquely: hedges dipped
And rose: and now and then a smell of grass
Displaced the reek of buttoned carriage-cloth

Until the next town, new and nondescript,
Approached with acres of dismantled cars.   20

At first, I didn't notice what a noise
   The weddings made
Each station that we stopped at: sun destroys
The interest of what's happening in the shade,
And down the long cool platforms whoops and skirls   25
I took for porters larking with the mails,
And went on reading. Once we started, though,
We passed them, grinning and pomaded, girls
In parodies of fashion, heels and veils,
All posed irresolutely, watching us go,   30

As if out on the end of an event
   Waving goodbye
To something that survived it. Struck, I leant
More promptly out next time, more curiously,
And saw it all again in different terms: 35
The fathers with broad belts under their suits
And seamy foreheads; mothers loud and fat;
An uncle shouting smut; and then the perms,
The nylon gloves and jewellery-substitutes,
The lemons, mauves, and olive-ochres that   40

Marked off the girls unreally from the rest.
   Yes, from cafés
And banquet-halls up yards, and bunting-dressed
Coach-party annexes, the wedding-days
Were coming to an end. All down the line   45
Fresh couples climbed aboard: the rest stood round;
The last confetti and advice were thrown,
And, as we moved, each face seemed to define
Just what it saw departing: children frowned
At something dull; fathers had never known   50

Success so huge and wholly farcical;
   The women shared
The secret like a happy funeral;
While girls, gripping their handbags tighter, stared
At a religious wounding. Free at last,   55

And loaded with the sum of all they saw,
We hurried towards London, shuffling gouts of steam.
Now fields were building-plots, and poplars cast
Long shadows over major roads, and for
Some fifty minutes, that in time would seem   60

Just long enough to settle hats and say
    I nearly died,
A dozen marriages got under way.
They watched the landscape, sitting side by side
– An Odeon went past, a cooling tower,   65
And someone running up to bowl – and none
Thought of the others they would never meet
Or how their lives would all contain this hour.
I thought of London spread out in the sun,
Its postal districts packed like squares of wheat: 70

There we were aimed. And as we raced across
    Bright knots of rail
Past standing Pullmans, walls of blackened moss
Came close, and it was nearly done, this frail
Travelling coincidence; and what it held   75
Stood ready to be loosed with all the power
That being changed can give. We slowed again,
And as the tightening brakes took hold, there swelled
A sense of falling, like an arrow-shower
Sent out of sight, somewhere becoming rain.   80

Ambulances

Closed like confessionals, they thread
Loud noons of cities, giving back
None of the glances they absorb.
Light glossy grey, arms on a plaque,
They come to rest at any kerb: 5
All streets in time are visited.

Then children strewn on steps or road,
Or women coming from the shops
Past smells of different dinners, see

A wild white face that overtops   10
Red stretcher-blankets momently
As it is carried in and stowed,

And sense the solving emptiness
That lies just under all we do,
And for a second get it whole,   15
So permanent and blank and true.
The fastened doors recede. *Poor soul*,
They whisper at their own distress;

For borne away in deadened air
May go the sudden shut of loss   20
Round something nearly at an end,
And what cohered in it across
The years, the unique random blend
Of families and fashions, there

At last begin to loosen. Far   25
From the exchange of love to lie
Unreachable inside a room
That traffic parts to let go by
Brings closer what is left to come,
And dulls to distance all we are.   30

Reference Back

That was a pretty one, I heard you call
From the unsatisfactory hall
To the unsatisfactory room where I
Played record after record, idly,
Wasting my time at home, that you   5
Looked so much forward to.

Oliver's *Riverside Blues*, it was. And now
I shall, I suppose, always remember how
The flock of notes those antique negroes blew
Out of Chicago air into   10
A huge remembering pre-electric horn
The year after I was born

Three decades later made this sudden bridge
From your unsatisfactory age
To my unsatisfactory prime.   15

Truly, though our element is time,
We are not suited to the long perspectives
Open at each instant of our lives.
They link us to our losses: worse,
They show us what we have as it once was,   20
Blindingly undiminished, just as though
By acting differently we could have kept it so.

Afternoons

Summer is fading:
The leaves fall in ones and twos
From trees bordering
The new recreation ground.
In the hollows of afternoons   5
Young mothers assemble
At swing and sandpit
Setting free their children.

Behind them, at intervals,
Stand husbands in skilled trades,   10
An estateful of washing,
And the albums, lettered
Our Wedding, lying
Near the television:
Before them, the wind   15
Is ruining their courting-places

That are still courting-places
(But the lovers are all in school),
And their children, so intent on
Finding more unripe acorns,   20
Expect to be taken home.
Their beauty has thickened.
Something is pushing them
To the side of their own lives.

Vers de Société

My wife and I have asked a crowd of craps
To come and waste their time and ours: perhaps
You'd care to join us? In a pig's arse, friend.
Day comes to an end.
The gas fire breathes, the trees are darkly swayed.   5
And so *Dear Warlock-Williams: I'm afraid* –

Funny how hard it is to be alone.
I could spend half my evenings, if I wanted,
Holding a glass of washing sherry, canted
Over to catch the drivel of some bitch   10
Who's read nothing but *Which*;
Just think of all the spare time that has flown

Straight into nothingness by being filled
With forks and faces, rather than repaid
Under a lamp, hearing the noise of wind,   15
And looking out to see the moon thinned
To an air-sharpened blade.
A life, and yet how sternly it's instilled

All solitude is selfish. No one now
Believes the hermit with his gown and dish   20
Talking to God (who's gone too); the big wish
Is to have people nice to you, which means
Doing it back somehow.
Virtue is social. Are, then, these routines

Playing at goodness, like going to church?   25
Something that bores us, something we don't do well
(Asking that ass about his fool research)
But try to feel, because, however crudely,
It shows us what should be?
Too subtle, that. Too decent, too. Oh hell,   30

Only the young can be alone freely.
The time is shorter now for company,
And sitting by a lamp more often brings

Not peace, but other things.
Beyond the light stand failure and remorse   35
Whispering *Dear Warlock-Williams: Why, of course* –

The Explosion

On the day of the explosion
Shadows pointed towards the pithead:
In the sun the slagheap slept.

Down the lane came men in pitboots
Coughing oath-edged talk and pipe-smoke,   5
Shouldering off the freshened silence.

One chased after rabbits: lost them;
Came back with a nest of lark's eggs;
Showed them; lodged them in the grasses.

So they passed in beards and moleskins,   10
Fathers, brothers, nicknames, laughter,
Through the tall gates standing open.

At noon, there came a tremor; cows
Stopped chewing for a second; sun,
Scarfed as in a heat-haze, dimmed.   15

The dead go on before us, they
Are sitting in God's house in comfort,
We shall see them face to face –

Plain as lettering in the chapels
It was said, and for a second   20
Wives saw men of the explosion

Clearer than in life they managed –
Gold as on a coin, or walking
Somehow from the sun towards them,

One showing the eggs unbroken.   25

The Building

Higher than the handsomest hotel
The lucent comb shows up for miles, but see,
All round it close-ribbed streets rise and fall
Like a great sigh out of the last century.
The porters are scruffy; what keep drawing up 5
At the entrance are not taxis; and in the hall
As well as creepers hangs a frightening smell.

There are paperbacks, and tea at so much a cup,
Like an airport lounge, but those who tamely sit
On rows of steel chairs turning the ripped mags 10
Haven't come far. More like a local bus.
These outdoor clothes and half-filled shopping-bags
And faces restless and resigned, although
Every few minutes comes a kind of nurse

To fetch someone away: the rest refit 15
Cups back to saucers, cough, or glance below
Seats for dropped gloves or cards. Humans, caught
On ground curiously neutral, homes and names
Suddenly in abeyance; some are young,
Some old, but most at that vague age that claims 20
The end of choice, the last of hope; and all

Here to confess that something has gone wrong.
It must be error of a serious sort,
For see how many floors it needs, how tall
It's grown by now, and how much money goes 25
In trying to correct it. See the time,
Half-past eleven on a working day,
And these picked out of it; see, as they climb

To their appointed levels, how their eyes
Go to each other, guessing; on the way 30
Someone's wheeled past, in washed-to-rags ward
    clothes:
They see him, too. They're quiet. To realise
This new thing held in common makes them quiet,

For past these doors are rooms, and rooms past those,
And more rooms yet, each one further off   35

And harder to return from; and who knows
Which he will see, and when? For the moment, wait,
Look down at the yard. Outside seems old enough:
Red brick, lagged pipes, and someone walking by it
Out to the car park, free. Then, past the gate,   40
Traffic; a locked church; short terraced streets
Where kids chalk games, and girls with hair-dos fetch

Their separates from the cleaners – O world,
Your loves, your chances, are beyond the stretch
Of any hand from here! And so, unreal   45
A touching dream to which we all are lulled
But wake from separately. In it, conceits
And self-protecting ignorance congeal
To carry life, collapsing only when

Called to these corridors (for now once more   50
The nurse beckons –). Each gets up and goes
At last. Some will be out by lunch, or four;
Others, not knowing it, have come to join
The unseen congregations whose white rows
Lie set apart above – women, men;   55
Old, young; crude facets of the only coin

This place accepts. All know they are going to die.
Not yet, perhaps not here, but in the end,
And somewhere like this. That is what it means,
This clean-sliced cliff; a struggle to transcend   60
The thought of dying, for unless its powers
Outbuild cathedrals nothing contravenes
The coming dark, though crowds each evening try

With wasteful, weak, propitiatory flowers.

CHARLES TOMLINSON

Charles Tomlinson was born 8 January 1927 in Stoke-on-Trent, the son of a clerk in an estate agent's office. Tomlinson's father could quote bits of 'Gunga Din' and his grandmother the whole of Hood's 'The Song of the Shirt' but, otherwise, literature was not something the young Tomlinson was familiar with. He remembers Stoke-on-Trent as

a long settlement stretching out across splendid country. So that I went in and out from the black to the green frequently, fished a lot at weekends (the fishing clubs there keep people sane) and by sitting and watching the water learned close observation and love of water perhaps.

(Unless otherwise identified, all quotations from Tomlinson are taken from correspondence with the poet.)

At Longton High School two teachers, Cecil Scrimgeour and the German refugee Gerhard Kuttner, introduced Tomlinson to French and German poetry, and also encouraged an interest in politics, history, psychology and European music. When an Arts Council exhibition of Paul Klee's work came to Hanley, Tomlinson became fascinated by modern painting and still says 'Cézanne is my god'.

At Cambridge, where he read English at Queens' College on a scholarship, Tomlinson developed an ambition to be a film director but, after many rejected scripts, he became in 1948 an elementary schoolteacher. In 1948, too, he married Brenda Raybould, who had read history at Bedford College, London (they have two daughters), and spent most of his spare time in London painting. In 1951 he spent nine months as private secretary to Percy Lubbock in Italy – where he wrote the poems for his first collection *The Necklace* (1955) – before returning to London. Then, in 1956, he became lecturer and finally Reader in English poetry at Bristol University.

His first major poetic success was the publication, in 1958, of *Seeing is Believing* in the USA – two years before it appeared in the UK. Tomlinson had studied the work of Wallace Stevens, Marianne Moore and William Carlos Williams and his affinities with these Americans facilitated the appreciation of his work in the USA. In an essay in *The Modern Age* (edited by Boris Ford, 1961) Tomlinson was contemptuous of postwar English poetry where 'one has a provincial laziness of mind adopted as a public attitude and as the framework for an equally provincial verse' and he has consistently identified himself with international attitudes and idioms.

Tomlinson's position in modern English poetry, then, is an unusual one. Instead of drawing on the English tradition he has been demonstratively exotic, reflecting the influence of French symbolists and American modernists and working within an aesthetic ambiance that openly accommodates philosophical discussion of music and painting and political theory. Yet for all the intellectual equipment and perceptual apparatus his work has consistently drawn attention to particulars and he is now able to write 'about Stoke where I was born: I had first to escape its constrictions, find a cleansing and cleansed language before I could go back to confront it all again'. He also says that his poetry 'now develops between periods of painting' and it is this combination of visual intensity and intellectual curiosity that gives his poetry lucid depths as well as a brilliant surface.

FURTHER READING

Bedient, Calvin. 'On Charles Tomlinson' in *British Poetry Since 1960* ed. Michael Schmidt and Grevel Lindop. Carcanet Press, 1973.

The Crane

That insect, without antennae, over its
Cotton-spool lip, letting
An almost invisible tenuity
Of steel cable, drop
Some seventy feet, with the   5
Grappling hook hidden also
Behind a dense foreground
Among which it is fumbling, and
Over which, mantis-like
It is begging or threatening, gracile   10
From a clear sky – that paternal
Constructive insect, without antennae,
Would seem to assure us that
'The future is safe, because
It is in my hands.' And we do not   15

Doubt this veracity, we can only
Fear it – as many of us
As pause here to remark
Such silent solicitude
For lifting intangible weights   20
Into real walls.

Steel: the night shift

Slung from the gantries cranes
patrol in air and parry
lights the furnaces fling up at them.
Clamour is deepest in the den beneath,
fire fiercest at the frontier where   5
an arm of water doubles
and disjoints it. There is a principle, a pulse
in all these molten and metallic contraries,
this sweat unseen. For men
facelessly habituated to the glare   10
outstare it, guide the girders
from their high and iron balconies
and keep the simmering slag-trucks
feeding heap on heap
in regular, successive, sea-on-shore   15
concussive bursts of dry
and falling sound. And time
is all this measured voice would seem
to ask, until it uncreate
the height and fabric of the light-   20
lunged, restive, flame-eroded night.

The Gossamers

Autumn. A haze is gold
By definition. This one lit
The thread of gossamers
That webbed across it
Out of shadow and again   5
Through rocking spaces which the sun

Claimed in the leafage. Now
I saw for what they were
These glitterings in grass, on air,
Of certainties that ride and plot   10
The currents in their tenuous stride
And, as they flow, must touch
Each blade and, touching, know
Its green resistance. Undefined
The haze of autumn in the mind   15
Is gold, is glaze.

The Weathercocks

Bitten and burned into mirrors of thin gold,
the weathercocks, blind from the weather,
have their days of seeing as they
grind round on their swivels.

A consciousness of pure metal   5
begins to melt when (say)
that light 'which never was'
begins to be

And catches the snow's accents
in each dip and lap, and the wide   10
stains on the thawed ploughland are like continents
across the rumpled map.

Their gold eyes hurt
at the corduroy lines come clear whose grain
feels its way over the shapes of the rises   15
joining one brown accord of stain and stain.

And the patterning stretches, flown
out on a wing of afternoon cloud that the sun
is changing to sea-wet sandflats,
hummocked in tiny dunes like the snow half-gone –   20

As if the sole wish of the light
were to harrow with mind matter, to shock
wide the glance of the tree-knots and the stone-eyes
the sun is bathing, to waken the weathercocks.

Swimming Chenango Lake

Winter will bar the swimmer soon.
  He reads the water's autumnal hesitations
A wealth of ways: it is jarred,
  It is astir already despite its steadiness,
Where the first leaves at the first   5
  Tremor of the morning air have dropped
Anticipating him, launching their imprints
  Outwards in eccentric, overlapping circles.
There is a geometry of water, for this
  Squares off the cloud's redundances   10
And sets them floating in a nether atmosphere
  All angles and elongations: every tree
Appears a cypress as it stretches there
  And every bush that shows the season,
A shaft of fire. It is a geometry and not   15
  A fantasia of distorting forms, but each
Liquid variation answerable to the theme
  It makes away from, plays before:
It is a consistency, the grain of the pulsating flow.
  But he has looked long enough, and now   20
Body must recall the eye to its dependence
  As he scissors the waterscape apart
And sways it to tatters. Its coldness
  Holding him to itself, he grants the grasp,
For to swim is also to take hold   25
  On water's meaning, to move in its embrace
And to be, between grasp and grasping free.
  He reaches in-and-through to that space
The body is heir to, making a where
  In water, a possession to be relinquished   30
Willingly at each stroke. The image he has torn
  Flows-to behind him, healing itself,
Lifting and lengthening, splayed like the feathers
  Down an immense wing whose darkening spread
Shadows his solitariness: alone, he is unnamed   35
  By this baptism, where only Chenango bears a name
In a lost language he begins to construe –
  A speech of destinies and derisions, of half-

Replies to the questions his body must frame
   Frogwise across the all but penetrable element.   40
Human, he fronts it and, human, he draws back
   From the interior cold, the mercilessness
That yet shows a kind of mercy sustaining him.
   The last sun of the year is drying his skin
Above a surface a mere mosaic of tiny shatterings,   45
   Where a wind is unscaping all images in the flowing obsidian,
The going-elsewhere of ripples incessantly shaping.

Prometheus

Summer thunder darkens, and its climbing
   Cumulae, disowning our scale in the zenith,
Electrify this music: the evening is falling apart.
   Castles-in-air; on earth: green, livid fire.
The radio simmers with static to the strains   5
   Of this mock last-day of nature and of art.

We have lived through apocalypse too long:
   Scriabin's dinosaurs! Trombones for the transformation
That arrived by train at the Finland Station,
   To bury its hatchet after thirty years in the brain   10
Of Trotsky. Alexander Nikolayevitch, the events
   Were less merciful than your mob of instruments.

Too many drowning voices cram this waveband.
   I set Lenin's face by yours –
Yours, the fanatic ego of eccentricity against   15
   The systematic son of a school inspector
Tyutchev on desk – for the strong man reads
   Poems as the antisemite pleads: 'A Jew was my friend.'

Cymballed firesweeps. Prometheus came down
   In more than orchestral flame and Kerensky fled   20
Before it. The babel of continents gnaws now
   And tears at the silk of those harmonies that seemed
So dangerous once. You dreamed an end
   Where the rose of the world would go out like a close in
     music.

Population drags the partitions down 25
 And we are a single town of warring suburbs:
I cannot hear such music for its consequence:
 Each sense was to have been reborn
Out of a storm of perfumes and light
 To a white world, an in-the-beginning. 30

In the beginning, the strong man reigns:
 Trotsky, was it not then you brought yourself
To judgement and to execution, when you forgot
 Where terror rules, justice turns arbitrary?
Chromatic Prometheus, myth of fire, 35
 It is history topples you in the zenith.

Blok, too, wrote The Scythians
 Who should have known: he who howls
With the whirlwind, with the whirlwind goes down.
 In this, was Lenin guiltier than you 40
When, out of a merciless patience grew
 The daily prose such poetry prepares for?

Scriabin, Blok, men of extremes,
 History treads out the music of your dreams
Through blood, and cannot close like this 45
 In the perfection of anabasis. It stops. The trees
Continue raining though the rain has ceased
 In a cooled world of incessant codas:

Hard edges of the houses press
 On the after-music senses, and refuse to burn, 50
Where an ice-cream van circulates the estate
 Playing Greensleeves, and at the city's
Stale new frontier even ugliness
 Rules with the cruel mercy of solidities.

Assassin

> The rattle in Trotsky's throat and his wild boar's moans
> *Piedra de Sol*

Blood I foresaw. I had put by
 The distractions of the retina, the eye

That like a child must be fed and comforted
　　With patterns, recognitions. The room
Had shrunk to a paperweight of glass and he   5
　　To the centre and prisoner of its transparency.

He rasped pages. I knew too well
　　The details of that head. I wiped
Clean the glance and saw
　　Only his vulnerableness. Under my quivering   10
There was an ease, save for that starched insistence
　　While paper snapped and crackled as in October air.

Sound drove out sight. We inhabited together
　　One placeless cell. I must put down
This rage of the ear for discrimination, its absurd   15
　　Dwelling on ripples, liquidities, fact
Fastening on the nerve gigantic paper burrs.
　　The gate of history is straiter than eye's or ear's.

In imagination, I had driven the spike
　　Down and through. The skull had sagged in its blood.   20
The grip, the glance – stained but firm –
　　Held all at its proper distance and now hold
This autumnal hallucination of white leaves
　　From burying purpose in a storm of sibilance.

I strike. I am the future and my blow   25
　　Will have it now. If lightning froze
It would hover as here, the room
　　Riding in the crest of the moment's wave,
In the deed's time, the deed's transfiguration
　　And as if that wave would never again recede.   30

The blood wells. Prepared for this
　　This I can bear. But papers
Snow to the ground with a whispered roar:
　　The voice, cleaving their crescendo, is his
Voice, and his the animal cry   35
　　That has me then by the roots of the hair.

Fleshed in that sound, objects betray me,
　　Objects are my judge: the table and its shadow,

Desk and chair, the ground a pressure
    Telling me where it is that I stand   40
Before wall and window-light:
    Mesh of the curtain, wood, metal, flesh:

A dying body that refuses death,
    He lurches against me in his warmth and weight,
As if my arm's length blow   45
    Had transmitted and spent its strength
Through blood and bone; and I, spectred,
    The body that rose against me were my own.

Woven from the hair of that bent head,
    The thread that I had grasped unlabyrinthed all –   50
Tightrope of history and necessity –
    But the weight of a world unsteadies my feet
And I fall into the lime and contaminations
    Of contingency; into hands, looks, time.

Against Extremity

Let there be treaties, bridges,
    Chords under the hands, to be spanned
Sustained: extremity hates a given good
    Or a good gained. That girl who took
Her life almost, then wrote a book   5
    To exorcise and to exhibit the sin,
Praises a friend there for the end she made
    And each of them becomes a heroine.
The time is in love with endings. The time's
    Spoiled children threaten what they will do,   10
And those they cannot shake by petulance
    They'll bribe out of their wits by show.
Against extremity, let there be
    Such treaties as only time itself
Can ratify, a bond and test   15
    Of sequential days, and like the full
Moon slowly given to the night,
    A possession that is not to be possessed.

The Fox Gallery

A long house –
the fox gallery you called
its upper storey, because
you could look down to see
(and did) the way a fox would   5
cross the field beyond
and you could follow out, window
to window, the fox's way
the whole length of the meadow
parallel with the restraining line   10
of wall and pane, or as far
as that could follow the sense of all
those windings. Do you remember
the morning I woke you with the cry
Fox fox and the animal   15
came on – not from side
to side, but straight
at the house and we craned
to see more and more, the most
we could of it and then   20
watched it sheer off deterred
by habitation, and saw
how utterly the two worlds were
disparate, as that perfect
ideogram for agility   25
and liquefaction flowed
away from us rhythmical
and flickering and
that flare was final.

On Water

'Furrow' is inexact:
no ship could be
converted to a plough
travelling this vitreous ebony:

seal it in sea-caves and   5
you cannot still it:
image on image bends
where half-lights fill it

with illegible depths
and lucid passages,   10
bestiary of stones,
book without pages:

and yet it confers
as much as it denies:
we are orphaned and fathered   15
by such solid vacancies:

Mackinnon's Boat

Faced to the island, Mackinnon's boat
  Arcs out: the floats of his creels
Cling to the shelter half a mile away
  Of Tarner's cliff. Black, today
The waters will have nothing to do with the shaping   5
  Or unshaping of human things. No image
Twists beside the riding launch, there to repeat
  Its white and blue, its unrigged mast
Slanting from the prow in which a dog
  Now lies stretched out – asleep   10
It seems, but holds in steady view
  Through all-but-closed eyes the grey-black
Water travelling towards it. The surface,
  Opaque as cliffstone, moves scarred
By a breeze that strikes against its grain   15
  In ruffled hatchings. Distance has disappeared,
Washed out by mist, but a cold light
  Keeps here and there re-touching it,
Promising transparencies of green and blue
  Only to deny them. The visible sea   20
Remains a sullen frontier to
  Its unimaginable fathoms. The dog eyes

Its gliding shapes, but the signs he can recognize
    Are land signs: he is here
Because men are here, unmindful   25
    Of this underworld of Mackinnon's daily dealings.
As the creels come in, he'll lie
    Still watching the waters, nostrils
Working on seasmells, but indifferent
    To the emerging haul, clawed and crawling.   30
The cliff lifts near, and a guttural cry
    Of cormorants raises his glance: he stays
Curled round on himself: his world
    Ignores this waste of the in-between,
Air and rock, stained, crag-sheer   35
    Where cormorants fret and flock
Strutting the ledges. The two men
    Have sited their destination. Mackinnon
Steering, cuts back the engine and Macaskill
    Has the light floats firm and then   40
The weight of the freighted creels is on his rope –
    A dozen of them – the coil spitting
Water as it slaps and turns on the windlass
    Burning Macaskill's palms paying it in.
As the cold, wet line is hauled, the creels   45
    Begin to arrive. And, inside, the flailing
Seashapes pincered to the baits, drop
    Slithering and shaken off like thieves
Surprised, their breath all at once grown rare
    In an atmosphere they had not known existed.   50
Hands that have much to do yet, dealing
    With creel on creel, drag out the catch
And feeling the cage-nets, re-thread each fault.
    Crabs, urchins, dogfish, and star,
All are unwanted and all are   55
    Snatched, slaughtered, or flung to their freedom –
Some, shattering on the cordage
    They too eagerly clung to. Hands must be cruel
To keep the pace spry to undo and then
    To re-tie, return the new-baited traps   60
To water, but an ease makes one
    The disparate links of the concerted action

Between the first drawing in
    And the let down crash of stone-weighted baskets.
There is more to be done still. The trough of the gunwhale   65
    Is filled with the scrabbling armour of defeat;
Claw against claw, not knowing
    What it is they fight, they swivel
And bite on air until they feel
    The palpable hard fingers of their real   70
Adversary close on them; and held
    In a knee-grip, must yield to him.
The beaked claws are shut and bound
    By Mackinnon. Leaning against the tiller,
He impounds each one alive   75
    In the crawling hatch. And so the boat
Thrusts on, to go through a hundred and more creels
    Before the return. Macaskill throws
To Mackinnon a cigarette down the length
    Of half the craft. Cupping   80
They light up. Their anonymity, for a spell,
    Is at an end, and each one
Free to be himself once more
    Sharing the rest that comes of labour.
But labour must come of rest: and already   85
    They are set towards it, and soon the floats
Of the next creel-drift will rise
    Low in the water. An evasive light
Brightens like mist rolling along the sea,
    And the blue it beckoned – blue   90
Such as catches and dies in an eye-glance –
    Glints out its seconds. Making a time
Where no day has a name, the smells
    Of diesel, salt, and tobacco mingle:
They linger down a wake whose further lines   95
    Are beginning to slacken and fall back to where
Salt at last must outsavour name and time
    In the alternation of the forgetful waters.

The Compact: At Volterra

The crack in the stone, the black filament
  Reaching into the rockface unmasks
More history than Etruria or Rome
  Bequeathed this place. The ramparted town
Has long outlived all that; for what   5
  Are Caesar or Scipio beside
The incursion of the slow abyss, the daily
  Tribute the dry fields provide

Trickling down? There is a compact
  To undo the spot, between the unhurried sun   10
Edging beyond this scene, and the moon,
  Risen already, that has stained
Through with its pallor the remaining light:
  Unreal, that clarity of lips and wrinkles
Where shadow investigates each fold,   15
  Scaling the cliff to the silhouetted stronghold.

Civic and close-packed, the streets
  Cannot ignore this tale of unshorable earth
At the town brink; furrow, gully,
  And sandslide guide down   20
Each seeping rivulet only to deepen
  The cavities of thirst, dry out
The cenozoic skeleton, appearing, powdering away,
  Uncovering the chapped clay beneath it.

There is a compact between the cooling earth   25
  And every labyrinthine fault that mines it –
The thousand mouths whose language
  Is siftings, whisperings, rumours of downfall
That might, in a momentary unison,
  Silence all, tearing the roots of sound out   30
With a single roar; but the cicadas
  Chafe on, grapevine entwines the pergola

Gripping beyond itself. A sole farm
  Eyes space emptily. Those

Who abandoned it still wire   35
   Their vines between lopped willows:
Their terraces, fondling the soil together,
   Till up to the drop that which they stand to lose:
Refusing to give ground before they must,
   They pit their patience against the dust's vacuity.   40

The crack in the stone, the black filament
   Rooting itself in dreams, all live
At a truce, refuted, terracing; as if
   Unreasoned care were its own and our
Sufficient reason, to repair the night's derisions,   45
   Repay the day's delight, here where the pebbles
Of half-ripe grapes abide their season,
   Their fostering leaves outlined by unminding sky.

Over Elizabeth Bridge: a circumvention
to a friend in Budapest

. . . my heart which owes this past a calm future.
                         ATTILA JÓZSEF, *By the Danube*

Three years, now, the curve of Elizabeth Bridge
Has caught at some half-answering turn of mind –
Not recollection, but uncertainty
Why memory should need so long to find
A place and peace for it: that uncertainty   5
And restless counterpointing of a verse
'So wary of its I', Iván, is me:

Why should I hesitate to fix a meaning?
The facts were plain. A church, a riverside,
And, launched at the further bank, a parapet   10
Which, at its setting-out, must swerve or ride
Sheer down the bulk of the defenceless nave,
But with a curious sort of courteousness,
Bends by and on again. That movement gave

A pause to thoughts, which overeagerly   15
Had fed on fresh experience and the sense

That too much happened in too short a time
In this one city: self-enravelled, dense
With its own past, even its silence was
Rife with explanations, drummed insistent   20
As traffic at this church's window-glass.

How does the volley sound in that man's ears
Whom history did not swerve from, but elected
To face the squad? Was it indifference,
Fear, or sudden, helpless peace reflected   25
In the flash, for Imre Nagy? – another kind
Of silence, merely, that let in the dark
Which closed on Rajk's already silenced mind?

Here, past is half a ruin, half a dream –
Islanded patience, work of quiet hands,   30
Repainting spandrels that out-arched the Turk
In this interior. These are the lands
Europe and Asia, challenging to yield
A crop, or having raised one, harvest it,
Used for a highroad and a battlefield.   35

The bridge has paid the past its compliment:
The far bank's statuary stand beckoning
Where it flows, in one undeviating span,
Across the frozen river. That reckoning
Which József owed was cancelled in his blood,   40
And yet his promise veered beyond the act,
His verse grown calm with all it had withstood.

During Rain

Between
slats of the garden
bench, and strung
to their undersides
ride clinging
rain-drops, white   5
with transmitted
light as the bench

with paint: ranged
irregularly   10
seven staves of them
shine out
against the space
behind: untroubled
by the least breeze they   15
seem not to move
but one
by one as if
suddenly ripening
tug themselves free   20
and splash
down to be
replaced by an identical
and instant twin:
the longer you   25
look at it
the stillness proves
one flow unbroken
of new, false pearls,
dropped seeds of now   30
becoming then.

The Way In

The needle-point's swaying reminder
   Teeters at thirty, and the flexed foot
Keeps it there. Kerb-side signs
   For demolitions and new detours,
A propped pub, a corner lopped, all   5
   Bridle the pressures that guide the needle.

I thought I knew this place, this face
   A little worn, a little homely.
But the look that shadows softened
   And the light could grace, keeps flowing away from me   10
In daily change; its features, rendered down,
   Collapse expressionless, and the entire town

Sways in the fume of the pyre. Even the new
  And mannerless high risers tilt and wobble
Behind the deformations of acrid heat –   15
  A century's lath and rafters. Bulldozers
Gobble a street up, but already a future seethes
  As if it had waited in the crevices:

A race in transit, a nomad hierarchy:
  Cargoes of debris out of these ruins fill   20
Their buckled prams; their trucks and hand-carts wait
  To claim the dismantlings of a neighbourhood –
All that grimy care from wastage gleans,
  From scrap-iron down to heaps of magazines.

Slowing, I see the faces of a pair   25
  Behind their load: he shoves and she
Trails after him, a sextagenarian Eve,
  Their punishment to number every hair
Of what remains. Their clothes come of their trade –
  They wear the cast-offs of a lost decade.   30

The place had failed them anyhow, and their pale
  Absorption staring past this time
And dusty space we occupy together,
  Gazes the new blocks down – not built for them;
But what they are looking at they do not see.   35
  No Eve, but mindless Mnemosyne,

She is our lady of the nameless metals, of things
  No hand has made, and no machine
Has cut to a nicety that takes the mark
  Of clean intention – at best, the guardian   40
Of all that our daily contact stales and fades,
  Rusty cages and lampless lampshades.

Perhaps those who have climbed into their towers
  Will eye it all differently, the city spread
In unforeseen configurations, and living with this,   45
  Will find that civility I can only miss – and yet
It will need more than talk and trees
  To coax a style from these disparities.

The needle-point's swaying reminder
  Teeters: I go with uncongealing traffic now
Out onto the cantilevered road, window on window
  Sucked backwards at the level of my wheels.
Is it patience or anger most renders the will keen?
  This is a daily discontent. This is the way in.

THOM GUNN

Thom Gunn was born 29 August 1929 in Gravesend, the son of a journalist whose work made it necessary for the family to change town every so often until 1937 when they settled in Hampstead where Gunn attended University College School. Gunn had a happy, uncomplicated childhood and remembers reading Beatrix Potter and E. Nesbit and playing with friends on Hampstead Heath. 'I was quite a self-enclosed middle-class boy', he wrote to me, 'till the death of my mother when I was fourteen; after which I spent about half the year in Hampstead and the other half with aunts in Snodland, Kent, where I worked on their milk round quite often.'

Before going up to Trinity College, Cambridge, Gunn did two years national service in the army. Apart from the exhilaration of basic training he felt 'the rest of my time in the army was the most boring two years of my life' – only justified by the time it gave him for reading. After the army he worked in Paris for six months attempting, in the evenings, to write a Proustian novel. Then, weary of the weight of the narrative, he returned to poetry, an earlier interest. While he was still a Cambridge undergraduate his first book, *Fighting Terms* (1954), was published.

After spending some time in Rome on a studentship he got a fellowship at Stanford University and since moving to North California in 1954 he has spent most of his time there. He worked under Yvor Winters at Stanford and was fascinated by his concept of the 'will' (which he linked with Sartre's use of the word). He also discovered American poetry, particularly Wallace Stevens, William Carlos Williams and Hart Crane. The impact of Winters, American poetry in general, existential theory and the Californian landscape all combined to make *The Sense of Movement* (1957) a powerful book. Indeed to some it seemed like an assault on sensitivity.

After spells at Stanford and at San Antonio, Texas, Gunn spent eight years as a lecturer at the University of California, Berkeley. The publication of *My Sad Captains* in 1961 showed him experimenting with syllabic verse though, as subsequent collections show, he has not abandoned metre. Since 1966 he has lived as a free-lance writer in San Francisco where, he feels, he is likely to remain.

FURTHER READING

Dodsworth, Martin (ed.). *The Survival of Poetry*. Faber and Faber, 1970. Contains Dodsworth's own essay 'Thom Gunn: Poetry as Action and Submission'.

Bold, Alan. *Thom Gunn and Ted Hughes*. 'Modern Writers' Series, Oliver and Boyd, 1976.

The Wound

The huge wound in my head began to heal
About the beginning of the seventh week.
Its valleys darkened, its villages became still:
For joy I did not move and dared not speak;
Nor doctors would cure it, but time, its patient skill.   5

And constantly my mind returned to Troy.
After I sailed the seas I fought in turn
On both sides, sharing even Helen's joy
Of place, and growing up – to see Troy burn –
As Neoptolemus, that stubborn boy.   10

I lay and rested as prescription said.
Manoeuvred with the Greeks, or sallied out
Each day with Hector. Finally my bed
Became Achilles' tent, to which the lout
Thersites came reporting numbers dead.   15

I was myself: subject to no man's breath:
My own commander was my enemy.
And while my belt hung up, sword in the sheath,
Thersites shambled in and breathlessly
Cackled about my friend Patroclus' death.   20

I called for armour, rose, and did not reel.
But, when I thought, rage at his noble pain
Flew to my head, and turning I could feel
My wound break open wide. Over again
I had to let those storm-lit valleys heal.   25

5

On the Move

' Man, you gotta Go '

The blue jay scuffling in the bushes follows
Some hidden purpose, and the gust of birds
That spurts across the field, the wheeling swallows,
Have nested in the trees and undergrowth.
Seeking their instinct, or their poise, or both,   5
One moves with an uncertain violence
Under the dust thrown by a baffled sense
Or the dull thunder of approximate words.

On motorcycles, up the road, they come:
Small, black, as flies hanging in heat, the Boys,   10
Until the distance throws them forth, their hum
Bulges to thunder held by calf and thigh.
In goggles, donned impersonality,
In gleaming jackets trophied with the dust,
They strap in doubt – by hiding it, robust –   15
And almost hear a meaning in their noise.

Exact conclusion of their hardiness
Has no shape yet, but from known whereabouts
They ride, direction where the tires press.
They scare a flight of birds across the field: 20
Much that is natural, to the will must yield.
Men manufacture both machine and soul,
And use what they imperfectly control
To dare a future from the taken routes.

It is a part solution, after all.   25
One is not necessarily discord
On earth; or damned because, half animal,
One lacks direct instinct, because one wakes
Afloat on movement that divides and breaks.
One joins the movement in a valueless world,   30
Choosing it, till, both hurler and the hurled,
One moves as well, always toward, toward.

A minute holds them, who have come to go:
The self-defined, astride the created will
They burst away; the towns they travel through   35
Are home for neither bird nor holiness,
For birds and saints complete their purposes.
At worst, one is in motion; and at best,
Reaching no absolute, in which to rest,
One is always nearer by not keeping still.   40

Vox Humana

Being without quality
I appear to you at first
as an unkempt smudge, a blur,
an indefinite haze, mere-
ly pricking the eyes, almost   5
nothing. Yet you perceive me.

I have been always most close
when you had least resistance,
falling asleep, or in bars;
during the unscheduled hours,   10
though strangely without substance,
I hang, there and ominous.

Aha, sooner or later
you will have to name me, and,
as you name, I shall focus,   15
I shall become more precise.
O Master (for you command
in naming me, you prefer)!

I was, for Alexander,
the certain victory; I   20
was hemlock for Socrates;
and, in the dry night, Brutus
waking before Philippi
stopped me, crying out 'Caesar!'

Or if you call me the blur   25
that in fact I am, you shall
yourself remain blurred, hanging
like smoke indoors. For you bring,
to what you define now, all
there is, ever, of future.   30

In Santa Maria Del Popolo

Waiting for when the sun an hour or less
Conveniently oblique makes visible
The painting on one wall of this recess
By Caravaggio, of the Roman School,
I see how shadow in the painting brims   5
With a real shadow, drowning all shapes out
But a dim horse's haunch and various limbs,
Until the very subject is in doubt.

But evening gives the act, beneath the horse
And one indifferent groom, I see him sprawl,   10
Foreshortened from the head, with hidden face,
Where he has fallen, Saul becoming Paul.
O wily painter, limiting the scene
From a cacophony of dusty forms
To the one convulsion, what is it you mean   15
In that wide gesture of the lifting arms?

No Ananias croons a mystery yet,
Casting the pain out under name of sin.
The painter saw what was, an alternate
Candour and secrecy inside the skin.   20
He painted, elsewhere, that firm insolent
Young whore in Venus' clothes, those pudgy cheats,
Those sharpers; and was strangled, as things went,
For money, by one such picked off the streets.

I turn, hardly enlightened, from the chapel   25
To the dim interior of the church instead,
In which there kneel already several people,
Mostly old women: each head closeted

In tiny fists holds comfort as it can.
Their poor arms are too tired for more than this   30
– For the large gesture of solitary man,
Resisting, by embracing, nothingness.

The Byrnies

The heroes paused upon the plain.
When one of them but swayed, ring mashed on ring:
    Sound of the byrnie's knitted chain,
Vague evocations of the constant Thing.

They viewed beyond a salty hill   5
Barbaric forest, mesh of branch and root
    – A huge obstruction growing still,
Darkening the land, in quietness absolute.

That dark was fearful – lack of presence –
Unless some man could chance upon or win   10
    Magical signs to stay the essence
Of the broad light that they adventured in.

Elusive light of light that went
Flashing on water, edging round a mass,
    Inching across fat stems, or spent   15
Lay thin and shrunk among the bristling grass.

Creeping from sense to craftier sense,
Acquisitive, and loss their only fear,
    These men had fashioned a defence
Against the nicker's snap, and hostile spear.   20

Byrnie on byrnie! as they turned
They saw light trapped between the man-made joints,
    Central in every link it burned,
Reduced and steadied to a thousand points.

Thus for each blunt-faced ignorant one   25
The great grey rigid uniform combined

Safety with virtue of the sun.
Thus concepts linked like chainmail in the mind.

Reminded, by the grinding sound,
Of what they sought, and partly understood,   30
    They paused upon that open ground,
A little group above the foreign wood.

My Sad Captains

One by one they appear in
the darkness: a few friends, and
a few with historical
names. How late they start to shine!
but before they fade they stand   5
perfectly embodied, all

the past lapping them like a
cloak of chaos. They were men
who, I thought, lived only to
renew the wasteful force they   10
spent with each hot convulsion.
They remind me, distant now.

True, they are not at rest yet,
but now that they are indeed
apart, winnowed from failures,   15
they withdraw to an orbit
and turn with disinterested
hard energy, like the stars.

The Goddess

When eyeless fish meet her on
her way upward, they gently
turn together in the dark
brooks. But naked and searching
as a wind, she will allow   5
no hindrance, none, and bursts up

through potholes and narrow flues
seeking an outlet. Unslowed
by fire, rock, water or clay,
she after a time reaches   10
the soft abundant soil, which
still does not dissipate her

force – for look! sinewy thyme
reeking in the sunlight; rats
breeding, breeding, in their nests;   15
and the soldier by a park
bench with his greatcoat collar
up, waiting all evening for

a woman, any woman
her dress tight across her ass   20
as bark in moonlight. Goddess,
Proserpina: it is we,
vulnerable, quivering,
who stay you to abundance.

Touch

You are already
asleep. I lower
myself in next to
you, my skin slightly
numb with the restraint   5
of habits, the patina of
self, the black frost
of outsideness, so that even
unclothed it is
a resilient chilly   10
hardness, a superficially
malleable, dead
rubbery texture.

You are a mound
of bedclothes, where the cat   15
in sleep braces

its paws against your
calf through the blankets,
and kneads each paw in turn.

Meanwhile and slowly   20
I feel a is it
my own warmth surfacing or
the ferment of your whole
body that in darkness beneath
the cover is stealing   25
bit by bit to break
down that chill.

                    You turn and
hold me tightly, do
you know who   30
I am or am I
your mother or
the nearest human being to
hold on to in a
dreamed pogrom.   35

What I, now loosened,
sink into is an old
big place, it is
there already, for
you are already   40
there, and the cat
got there before you, yet
it is hard to locate.
What is more, the place is
not found but seeps   45
from our touch in
continuous creation, dark
enclosing cocoon round
ourselves alone, dark
wide realm where we   50
walk with everyone.

Pierce Street

Nobody home. Long threads of sunlight slant
Past curtains, blind, and slat, through the warm room.
The beams are dazzling, but, random and scant,
Pierce where they end
               small areas of the gloom   5
On curve of chairleg or a green stalk's bend.

I start exploring. Beds and canvases
Are shapes in each room off the corridor,
Their colours muted, square thick presences
Rising between
               the ceiling and the floor,   10
A furniture inferred much more than seen.

Here in the seventh room my search is done.
A bluefly circles, irregular and faint.
And round the wall above me friezes run:
Fixed figures drawn
               in charcoal or in paint.   15
Out of night now the flesh-tint starts to dawn.

Some stand there as if muffled from the cold,
Some naked in it, the wind around a roof.   20
But armed, their holsters as if tipped with gold.
And twice life-size –
               in line, in groups, aloof,
They all stare down with large abstracted eyes.

A silent garrison, and always there,   25
They are the soldiers of the imagination
Produced by it to guard it everywhere.
Bodied within
               the limits of their station
As, also, I am bodied in my skin,   30

They vigilantly preserve as they prevent
And are the things they guard, having some time stood
Where the painter reached to make them permanent.

The floorboards creak.
                  The house smells of its wood.   35
Those who are transitory can move and speak.

Rites of Passage

Something is taking place.
Horns bud bright in my hair.
My feet are turning hoof.
And Father, see my face
– Skin that was damp and fair   5
Is barklike and, feel, rough.

See Greytop how I shine.
I rear, break loose, I neigh
Snuffing the air, and harden
Towards a completion, mine.   10
And next I make my way
Adventuring through your garden.

My play is earnest now.
I canter to and fro.
My blood, it is like light.   15
Behind an almond bough,
Horns gaudy with its snow,
I wait live, out of sight.

All planned before my birth
For you, Old Man, no other.   20
Whom your groin's trembling warns.
I stamp upon the earth
A message to my mother.
And then I lower my horns.

The Messenger

Is this man turning angel as he stares
At one red flower whose name he does not know,
   The velvet face, the black-tipped hairs?

His eyes dilated like a cat's at night,
His lips move somewhat but he does not speak   5
   Of what completes him through his sight.

His body makes to imitate the flower,
Kneeling, with splayed toes pushing at the soil,
   The source, crude, granular, and sour.

His stillness answers like a looking glass   10
The flower's, it is repose of unblown flame
   That nests within the glow of grass.

Later the news, to branch from sense and sense,
Bringing their versions of the flower in small
   Outward into intelligence.   15

But meanwhile, quiet and reaching as a flame,
He bends, gazing not at but into it,
   Tough stalk, and face without a name.

Sunlight

Some things, by their affinity light's token,
Are more than shown: steel glitters from a track;
Small glinting scoops, after a wave has broken,
Dimple the water in its draining back;

Water, glass, metal, match light in their raptures,   5
Flashing their many answers to the one.
What captures light belongs to what it captures:
The whole side of a world facing the sun,

Re-turned to woo the original perfection,
Giving itself to what created it,   10
And wearing green in sign of its subjection.
It is as if the sun were infinite.

But angry flaws are swallowed by the distance;
It varies, moves, its concentrated fires
Are slowly dying – the image of persistence   15
Is an image, only, of our own desires:

Desire and knowledge touch without relating.
The system of which sun and we are part
Is both imperfect and deteriorating.
And yet the sun outlasts us at the heart.   20

Great seedbed, yellow centre of the flower,
Flower on its own, without a root or stem,
Giving all colour and all shape their power,
Still recreating in defining them,

Enable us, altering like you, to enter   25
Your passionless love, impartial but intense,
And kindle in acceptance round your centre,
Petals of light lost in your innocence.

TED HUGHES

Ted Hughes was born 17 August 1930 in Mytholmroyd, a small town in the Pennines in West Yorkshire. As a child he spent much time on the moors retrieving the birds and animals that his brother had shot down. This pursuit of animals gave him a thematic base which he has never abandoned, and the speech of his childhood gave him the natural rhythm he has retained in his poetry. As he put it in a *London Magazine* interview with Egbert Faas (January 1971): 'I grew up in West Yorkshire. They have a very distinctive dialect there . . . Without it, I doubt if I would ever have written verse. And in the case of the West Yorkshire dialect, of course, it connects you directly and in your most intimate self to middle English poetry.'

When Hughes was seven the family moved to Mexborough, a coal-mining town in South Yorkshire where his parents took a newsagent's and tobacconist's shop. There, as he wrote in *Poetry in the Making* (1967), he 'soon discovered a farm in the nearby country that supplied all my needs, and soon after, a private estate, with woods and lakes. My friends were town boys, sons of colliers and railwaymen, and with them I led one life, but all the time I was leading this other life on my own in the country.' Again a love of natural solitude went hand in hand with dialect poetry. When he read *King Lear* at school 'I suddenly recognized what Shakespearean language was . . . it was super-crude. It was backyard improvisation. It was dialect taken to the limit. That was it . . . it was inspired dialect.' Shakespeare has remained his favourite writer.

In 1948 Hughes won an Open Exhibition in English to Pembroke College, Cambridge, but before going up he did two years National Service as an RAF ground wireless mechanic in East Yorkshire. It was not a demanding job and he spent most of his time reading Shakespeare. When he got to Cambridge he felt disinclined to stay with the English course and switched to Anthropology and Archaeology.

After graduating in 1954 Hughes worked as a rose gardener, a nightwatchman and a reader for J. Arthur Rank, the film organisation, at Pinewood Studios. In 1956 he married Sylvia Plath and they spent that summer trekking through France and

Spain and spent five weeks writing and relaxing in a Spanish fishing village. Back in Cambridge Hughes worked as a school-teacher and, in 1957, he and his wife went to the USA. That year Hughes's first book, *The Hawk in the Rain*, was well received and he became established as an outstandingly original poet with an uncanny insight into the animal world. The book won the New York Poetry Centre's First Publication Award and in 1959 Hughes received a Guggenheim fellowship and spent the summer travelling across the USA before returning, in December, to England where he and his wife found a small flat in London. When *Lupercal* appeared in 1960 it more than ful-filled the promise of the first book and showed that Hughes was by no means limited to 'animal poems'.

In 1961 Hughes and Sylvia Plath bought an old manor house in Devon. In 1962 the couple separated and Sylvia Plath re-turned to London and her suicide of 1963. The effect of this tragedy is something Hughes has been unwilling to discuss publicly and for the next few years he concentrated on children's books: *The Earth Owl and Other Moon People* (1963), *How the Whale Became* (1963) and *Nessie the Mannerless Monster* (1964). Then in 1967 he published *Wodwo* and it was at once clear that the dark pessimism latent in the early poems had manifested itself in a new and disturbing way. Hughes seemed to be map-ping paths of personal survival in a destructive universe. This was taken even further in *Crow* (1970).

In 1970 Hughes married Carole Orchard and the couple went to Persia for the first performance of *Orghast*, a dramatic event utilising a theatrically effective language especially invented by the poet. It is, however, for his electrifying shock treatment of the English language that he is now internationally known.

FURTHER READING

Bold, Alan. *Thom Gunn and Ted Hughes*. 'Modern Writers' Series, Oliver and Boyd, 1976.

Sagar, Keith. *The Art of Ted Hughes*. Cambridge University Press, 1975.

Roarers in a Ring

Snow fell as for Wenceslas.
  The moor foamed like a white
Running sea. A starved fox
  Stared at the inn light.

In the red gridded glare of peat,   5
 Faces sweating like hams,
Farmers roared their Christmas Eve
 Out of the low beams.

Good company kept a laugh in the air
 As if they tossed a ball   10
To top the skip of a devil that
 Struck at it with his tail,

Or struck at the man who held it long.
 They so tossed laughter up
You would have thought that if they did not   15
 Laugh, they must weep.

Therefore the ale went round and round.
 Their mouths flung wide
The cataract of a laugh, lest
 Silence drink blood.   20

And their eyes were screwed so tight,
 While their grand bellies shook –
O their flesh would drop to dust
 At the first sober look.

The air was new as a razor,   25
 The moor looked like the moon,
When they all went roaring homewards
 An hour before dawn.

Those living images of their deaths
 Better than with skill   30
Blindly and rowdily balanced
 Gently took their fall

While the world under their footsoles
 Went whirling still
Gay and forever, in the bottomless black   35
 Silence through which it fell.

Hawk Roosting

I sit in the top of the wood, my eyes closed.
Inaction, no falsifying dream
Between my hooked head and hooked feet:
Or in sleep rehearse perfect kills and eat.

The convenience of the high trees!   5
The air's buoyancy and the sun's ray
Are of advantage to me;
And the earth's face upward for my inspection.

My feet are locked upon the rough bark.
It took the whole of Creation   10
To produce my foot, my each feather:
Now I hold Creation in my foot

Or fly up, and revolve it all slowly –
I kill where I please because it is all mine.
There is no sophistry in my body: 15
My manners are tearing off heads –

The allotment of death.
For the one path of my flight is direct
Through the bones of the living.
No arguments assert my right: 20

The sun is behind me.
Nothing has changed since I began.
My eye has permitted no change.
I am going to keep things like this.

An Otter

I

Underwater eyes, an eel's
Oil of water body, neither fish nor beast is the otter:
Four-legged yet water-gifted, to outfish fish;
With webbed feet and long ruddering tail
And a round head like an old tomcat.   5

Brings the legend of himself
From before wars or burials, in spite of hounds and
      vermin-poles;
  Does not take root like the badger. Wanders, cries;
    Gallops along land he no longer belongs to;
    Re-enters the water by melting.   10

    Of neither water nor land. Seeking
Some world lost when first he dived, that he cannot come at
      since,
  Takes his changed body into the holes of lakes;
    As if blind, cleaves the stream's push till he licks
    The pebbles of the source; from sea   15

    To sea crosses in three nights
Like a king in hiding. Crying to the old shape of the starlit
      land,
  Over sunken farms where the bats go round,
    Without answer. Till light and birdsong come
    Walloping up roads with the milk wagon.   20

II

The hunt's lost him. Pads on mud,
Among sedges, nostrils a surface bead,
The otter remains, hours. The air,
Circling the globe, tainted and necessary,

Mingling tobacco-smoke, hounds and parsley,   25
Comes carefully to the sunk lungs.
So the self under the eye lies,
Attendant and withdrawn. The otter belongs

In double robbery and concealment –
From water that nourishes and drowns, and from land   30
That gave him his length and the mouth of the hound.
He keeps fat in the limpid integument

Reflections live on. The heart beats thick,
Big trout muscle out of the dead cold;
Blood is the belly of logic; he will lick   35
The fishbone bare. And can take stolen hold

On a bitch otter in a field full
Of nervous horses, but linger nowhere.
Yanked above hounds, reverts to nothing at all,
To this long pelt over the back of a chair.   40

Second Glance at a Jaguar

Skinfull of bowls, he bowls them,
The hip going in and out of joint, dropping the spine
With the urgency of his hurry
Like a cat going along under thrown stones, under cover,
Glancing sideways, running   5
Under his spine. A terrible, stump-legged waddle
Like a thick Aztec disemboweller,
Club-swinging, trying to grind some square
Socket between his hind legs round,
Carrying his head like a brazier of spilling embers,   10
And the black bit of his mouth, he takes it
Between his back teeth, he has to wear his skin out,
He swipes a lap at the water-trough as he turns,
Swivelling the ball of his heel on the polished spot,
Showing his belly like a butterfly,   15
At every stride he has to turn a corner
In himself and correct it. His head
Is like the worn down stump of another whole jaguar,
His body is just the engine shoving it forward,
Lifting the air up and shoving on under,   20
The weight of his fangs hanging the mouth open,
Bottom jaw combing the ground. A gorged look,
Gangster, club-tail lumped along behind gracelessly,
He's wearing himself to heavy ovals,
Muttering some mantrah, some drum-song of murder   25
To keep his rage brightening, making his skin
Intolerable, spurred by the rosettes, the cain-brands,
Wearing the spots off from the inside,
Rounding some revenge. Going like a prayer-wheel,
The head dragging forward, the body keeping up,   30
The hind legs lagging. He coils, he flourishes
The blackjack tail as if looking for a target,
Hurrying through the underworld, soundless.

Gog

I

I woke to a shout: 'I am Alpha and Omega.'
Rocks and a few trees trembled
Deep in their own country,
I ran and an absence bounded beside me.

The dog's god is a scrap dropped from the table.   5
The mouse's saviour is a ripe wheat grain.
Hearing the Messiah cry
My mouth widens in adoration.

How fat are the lichens!
They cushion themselves on the silence.   10
The air wants for nothing.
The dust, too, is replete.

What was my error? My skull has sealed it out.
My great bones are massed in me.
They pound on the earth, my song excites them.   15
I do not look at the rocks and stones, I am frightened of what
     they see.

I listen to the song jarring my mouth
Where the skull-rooted teeth are in possession.
I am massive on earth. My feetbones beat on the earth
Over the sounds of motherly weeping . . .   20

Afterwards I drink at a pool quietly.
The horizon bears the rocks and trees away into twilight.
I lie down. I become darkness.
Darkness that all night sings and circles stamping.

II

The sun erupts. The moon is deader than a skull.   25
The grass-head waves day and night and will never know it
     exists.
The stones are as they were. And the creatures of earth
Are mere rainfall rivulets, in flood or empty paths.

The atoms of saints' brains are swollen with the vast bubble of
    nothing.
Everywhere the dust is in power.					30

Then whose
Are these
Eyes,
    eyes and
Dance of wants,					35
Of offering?

Sun and moon, death and death,
Grass and stones, their quick peoples, and the bright particles
Death and death and death –

Her mirrors.					40

III

Out through the dark archways of earth, under the ancient
    lintel overwritten with roots,
Out between the granite jambs, gallops the hooded horseman
    of iron.
Out of the wound-gash in the earth, the horseman mounts,
    shaking his plumes clear of dark soil.
Out of the blood-dark womb, gallops bowed the horseman of
    iron.
The blood-crossed Knight, the Holy Warrior, hooded with
    iron, the seraph of the bleak edge.					45
Gallops along the world's ridge in moonlight.

Through slits of iron, his eyes have found the helm of the
    enemy, the grail,
The womb-wall of the dream that crouches there, greedier
    than a foetus,
Suckling at the root-blood of the origins, the salt-milk drug of
    the mothers.

Shield him from the dipped glance, flying in half light, that
    tangles the heels,					50
The grooved kiss that swamps the eyes with darkness.
Bring him to the ruled slab, the octaves of order,

The law and mercy of number. Lift him
Out of the octopus maw and the eight lunatic limbs
Of the rocking, sinking cradle.   55

The unborn child beats on the womb-wall.
He will need to be strong
To follow his weapons towards the light.
Unlike Coriolanus, follow the blades right through Rome

And right through the smile   60
That is the judge's fury
That is the wailing child
That is the ribboned gift
That is the starved adder
That is the kiss in the dream   65
That is the nightmare pillow
That is the seal of resemblances
That is illusion
That is illusion

The rider of iron, on the horse shod with vaginas of iron,   70
Gallops over the womb that makes no claim, that is of stone.
His weapons glitter under the lights of heaven.
He follows his compass, the lance-blade, the gunsight, out
Against the fanged grail and tireless mouth
Whose cry breaks his sleep   75
Whose coil is under his ribs
Whose smile is in the belly of woman
Whose satiation is in the grave.

Out under the blood-dark archway, gallops bowed the
    horseman of iron.

Skylarks

I

The lark begins to go up
Like a warning
As if the glove were uneasy –

Barrel-chested for heights,
Like an Indian of the high Andes,   5

A whippet head, barbed like a hunting arrow,

But leaden
With muscle
For the struggle
Against   10
Earth's centre.

And leaden
For ballast
In the rocketing storms of the breath.

Leaden   15
Like a bullet
To supplant
Life from its centre.

II

Crueller than owl or eagle

A towered bird, shot through the crested head   20
With the command, Not die

But climb

Climb

Sing

Obedient as to death a dead thing.   25

III

I suppose you just gape and let your gaspings
Rip in and out through your voicebox
                                        O lark

And sing inwards as well as outwards
Like a breaker of ocean milling the shingle   30
                                        O lark

O song, incomprehensibly both ways –
Joy! Help! Joy! Help!
                    O lark

                    IV

My idleness curdles   35
Seeing the lark labour near its cloud
Scrambling
In a nightmare difficulty
Up through the nothing

Its feathers thrash, its heart must be drumming like a motor, 40
As if it were too late, too late

Dithering in ether
Its song whirls faster and faster
And the sun whirls
The lark is evaporating   45
Till my eye's gossamer snaps
          and my hearing floats back widely to earth

After which the sky lies blank open
Without wings, and the earth is a folded clod.

Only the sun goes silently and endlessly on with the lark's
     song.   50

                    V

All the dreary Sunday morning
Heaven is a madhouse
With the voices and frenzies of the larks,

Squealing and gibbering and cursing

Heads flung back, as I see them,   55
Wings almost torn off backwards – far up

Like sacrifices set floating
The cruel earth's offerings

The mad earth's missionaries.

VI

Like those flailing flames   60
That lift from the fling of a bonfire
Claws dangling full of what they feed on

The larks carry their tongues to the last atom
Battering and battering their last sparks out at the limit –
So it's a relief, a cool breeze   65
When they've had enough, when they're burned out
And the sun's sucked them empty
And the earth gives them the O.K.

And they relax, drifting with changed notes

Dip and float, not quite sure if they may   70
Then they are sure and they stoop

And maybe the whole agony was for this

The plummeting dead drop

With long cutting screams buckling like razors

But just before they plunge into the earth   75

They flare and glide off low over grass, then up
To land on a wall-top, crest up,

Weightless,
Paid-up,
Alert,   80

Conscience perfect.

A Childish Prank

Man's and woman's bodies lay without souls,
Dully gaping, foolishly staring, inert
On the flowers of Eden.
God pondered.

The problem was so great, it dragged him asleep.   5

Crow laughed.
He bit the Worm, God's only son,
Into two writhing halves.

He stuffed into man the tail half
With the wounded end hanging out.   10

He stuffed the head half head first into woman
And it crept in deeper and up
To peer out through her eyes
Calling its tail-half to join up quickly, quickly
Because O it was painful.   15

Man awoke being dragged across the grass.
Woman awoke to see him coming.
Neither knew what had happened.

God went on sleeping.

Crow went on laughing.   20

Song for a Phallus

There was a boy was Oedipus
  Stuck in his Mammy's belly
His Daddy'd walled the exit up
  He was a horrible fella
                Mamma   Mamma   5

You stay in there his Daddy cried
  Because a Dickybird
Has told the world when you get born
  You'll treat me like a turd
                Mamma   Mamma   10

His Mammy swelled and wept and swelled
  With a bang he busted out

His Daddy stropped his hacker
  When he heard that baby shout

                          Mamma   Mamma 15

O do not chop his winkle off
  His Mammy cried with horror
Think of the joy will come of it
  Tomorrer and tomorrer

                          Mamma   Mamma 20

But Daddy had the word from God
  He took that howling brat
He tied its legs in crooked knots
  And threw it to the cat

                          Mamma   Mamma 25

But Oedipus he had the luck
  For when he hit the ground
He bounced up like a jackinabox
  And knocked his Daddy down

                          Mamma   Mamma 30

He hit his Daddy such a whack
  Stone dead his Daddy fell
His cry went straight to God above
  His ghost it went to Hell

                          Mamma   Mamma 35

The Dickybird came to Oedipus
  You murderous little sod
The Sphynx will bite your bollocks off
  This order comes from God

                          Mamma   Mamma 40

The Sphynx she waved her legs at him
  And opened wide her maw
Oedipus stood stiff and wept
  At the dreadful thing he saw

                          Mamma   Mamma 45

He stood there on his crooked leg
  The Sphynx began to bawl

Four legs three legs two legs one leg
  Who goes on them all

                Mamma   Mamma 50

Oedipus took an axe and split
  The Sphynx from top to bottom
The answers aren't in me, he cried
  Maybe your guts have got em

                Mamma   Mamma 55

And out there came ten thousand ghosts
  All in their rotten bodies
Crying, You will never know
  What a cruel bastard God is

                Mamma   Mamma 60

Next came out his Daddy dead
  And shrieked about the place
He stabs his Mammy in the guts
  And smiles into her face

                Mamma   Mamma 65

Then out his Mammy came herself
  The blood poured from her bucket
What you can't understand, she cried
  You sleep on or sing to it

                Mamma   Mamma 70

Oedipus raised his axe again
  The World is dark, he cried
The World is dark one inch ahead
  What's on the other side?

                Mamma   Mamma 75

He split his Mammy like a melon
  He was drenched with gore
He found himself curled up inside
  As if he had never been bore

                Mamma   Mamma 80

Lovesong

He loved her and she loved him
His kisses sucked out her whole past and future or tried to
He had no other appetite
She bit him she gnawed him she sucked
She wanted him complete inside her   5
Safe and sure forever and ever
Their little cries fluttered into the curtains

Her eyes wanted nothing to get away
Her looks nailed down his hands his wrists his elbows
He gripped her hard so that life   10
Should not drag her from that moment
He wanted all future to cease
He wanted to topple with his arms round her
Off that moment's brink and into nothing
Or everlasting or whatever there was   15
Her embrace was an immense press
To print him into her bones
His smiles were spider bites
So he would lie still till she felt hungry
His words were occupying armies   20
Her laughs were an assassin's attempts
His looks were bullets daggers of revenge
Her glances were ghosts in the corner with horrible secrets
His whispers were whips and jackboots
Her kisses were lawyers steadily writing   25
His caresses were the last hooks of a castaway
Her love-tricks were the grinding of locks
And their deep cries crawled over the floors
Like an animal dragging a great trap
His promises were the surgeon's gag   30
Her promises took the top off his skull
She would get a brooch made of it
His vows pulled out all her sinews
He showed her how to make a love-knot
Her vows put his eyes in formalin   35
At the back of her secret drawer
Their screams stuck in the wall

Their heads fell apart into sleep like the two halves
Of a lopped melon, but love is hard to stop
In their entwined sleep they exchanged arms and legs   40
In their dreams their brains took each other hostage

In the morning they wore each other's face

Song of Woe

Once upon a time
There was a person
Wretched in every vein –
His heart pumped woe.
Trying to run it clear   5
His heart pumped only more muddy woe.
He looked at his hands, and they were woe.
His legs there, long, bony and remote
Like the legs of a stag in wet brambles,
They also were woe.   10
His shirt over the chair at night
Was like a curtain over the finale
Of all things.

He walked out onto a field
And the trees were grief –   15
Cemetery non-beings.
The clouds bore their burdens of grief
Into non-being.
The flowers
The birds, the spiders   20
Staring into space like sacrifices
Clung with madman's grip
To the great wheel of woe.

So he flung them out among the stars –
Trees, toppling clouds, birds and insects,   25
He was rid of them.
He flung away the field and its grass,
The whole grievous funeral,
His clothes and their house,
And sat naked on the naked earth   30

And his mouth filled his eyes filled
With the same muddy woe.

So he abandoned himself, his body, his blood –
He left it all lying on the earth
And held himself resolute   35
As the earth rolled slowly away
Smaller and smaller away
Into non-being.

And there at last he had it
As his woe struggled out of him   40
With a terrific cry
Staring after the earth
And stood out there in front of him,
His howling transfigured double.

And he was rid of it.   45
And he wept with relief,
With joy, laughing, he wept –

And at last, tear by tear,
Something came clear.

SYLVIA PLATH

Sylvia Plath was born 27 October 1932 in Boston, Massachu-
setts, the daughter of two German-speaking intellectuals: Otto
Plath, professor of biology at Boston University and author of
Bumblebees and their Ways; and Aurelia Schober, who had met
Otto Plath while studying for a master's degree in German.
Sylvia spent an 'ocean childhood' in the seashore town of
Winthrop, Massachusetts, and felt that 'my vision of the sea is
the clearest thing I own'.

When she was eight her father died and she never completely
recovered from this emotional loss. Mrs Plath took a teaching
job and moved the family inland to Wellesley, Massachusetts.
At one of Mrs Plath's Sunday-school sessions Sylvia heard her
mother read Matthew Arnold's 'The Forsaken Merman' and
'saw the gooseflesh on my skin . . . it was the poetry . . . I had
fallen into a new way of being happy.'

In 1950 she went to Smith College with a scholarship. As well
as poetry prizes she won, first, a national fiction contest, and,
then, a guest editorship with *Mademoiselle* magazine. After four
hectic weeks in New York, she returned home in a deep depression and tried to kill herself. The circumstances of this episode
form the substance of her autobiographical novel, *The Bell Jar*,
published under the pseudonym Victoria Lucas in 1963.

In 1954 she studied German at Harvard, took courses in
creative writing, and worked at her Smith thesis on the double
personality of Dostoevsky's novels. Simultaneously she was
developing a poetic personality (which reflected her interest in
poets like John Crowe Ransom and Theodore Roethke) and
earned $750 from published pieces and prizes in the year
1954–5.

She graduated in 1955 and went to Newnham College, Cambridge, on a Fulbright Fellowship. At Cambridge she met Ted
Hughes and the couple were married on 16 June 1956. They
spent a summer in France and Spain before returning to Cambridge where she continued her studies while her husband
worked as a schoolteacher. In 1957 the Hugheses moved to the
USA where she taught for a while at Smith College. In 1958–9
they lived in Boston where she attended Robert Lowell's poetry

classes at the university. In December 1959 they returned to England.

In a little London flat, on 1 April 1960, Sylvia's first child, Frieda Rebecca, was born and she was radiantly happy at being a mother, telling of her sense of fulfilment in letters to friends. The same year her first book of poems, *The Colossus*, was published, showing her still very much an American poet in manner and motivation. In 1961 the Hugheses moved to an old manor house in a village in Devon. There her second child, Nicholas Farrar Hughes, was born on 17 January 1962.

Later that year Ted Hughes and Sylvia Plath separated and in Christmas 1962 Sylvia and the two children found a flat, near Primrose Hill, where Yeats had lived. It was a dreadful winter for Sylvia as A. Alvarez remembered:

'Meanwhile, a recurrent trouble, her sinuses were bad; the pipes in her newly converted flat froze solid; there was still no telephone and no word from the psychotherapist (to whom she'd written); the weather continued monstrous. Illness, loneliness, depression and cold, combined with the demands of two small children, were too much for her.'

She continued to write emotionally intense and formally brittle poems some of which, like 'Edge', dramatically anticipate her death. This finally came on 11 February 1963 after she had gassed herself. When *Ariel* was published posthumously in 1965 the poetry-reading public were ready to make a martyr of her, the confessional poet who had died in the name of artistic intensity. It would be a mistake to regard her final work only as clinical evidence of suicidal despair. To the end her work displayed universally valid insights with a consummate artistic integrity.

FURTHER READING

Aird, Eileen. *Sylvia Plath*. 'Modern Writers' Series, Oliver and Boyd, 1973·
Newman, Charles (ed.). *The Art of Sylvia Plath*. Faber and Faber, 1970.
Alvarez, A. *The Savage God*. Weidenfeld and Nicolson, 1971.

Tulips

The tulips are too excitable, it is winter here.
Look how white everything is, how quiet, how snowed-in.
am learning peacefulness, lying by myself quietly

As the light lies on these white walls, this bed, these hands.
I am nobody; I have nothing to do with explosions.   5
I have given my name and my day-clothes up to the nurses
And my history to the anaesthetist and my body to surgeons.

They have propped my head between the pillow and the
          sheet-cuff
Like an eye between two white lids that will not shut.
Stupid pupil, it has to take everything in.   10
The nurses pass and pass, they are no trouble,
They pass the way gulls pass inland in their white caps,
Doing things with their hands, one just the same as another,
So it is impossible to tell how many there are.

My body is a pebble to them, they tend it as water   15
Tends to the pebbles it must run over, smoothing them gently.
They bring me numbness in their bright needles, they bring
          me sleep.
Now I have lost myself I am sick of baggage –
My patent leather overnight case like a black pillbox,
My husband and child smiling out of the family photo;   20
Their smiles catch onto my skin, little smiling hooks.

I have let things slip, a thirty-year-old cargo boat
Stubbornly hanging on to my name and address.
They have swabbed me clear of my loving associations.
Scared and bare on the green plastic-pillowed trolley   25
I watched my teaset, my bureaus of linen, my books
Sink out of sight, and the water went over my head.
I am a nun now, I have never been so pure.

I didn't want any flowers, I only wanted
To lie with my hands turned up and be utterly empty.   30
How free it is, you have no idea how free –
The peacefulness is so big it dazes you,
And it asks nothing, a name tag, a few trinkets.
It is what the dead close on, finally; I imagine them
Shutting their mouths on it, like a Communion tablet.   35

The tulips are too red in the first place, they hurt me.
Even through the gift paper I could hear them breathe

6   B C B

Lightly, through their white swaddlings, like an awful baby.
Their redness talks to my wound, it corresponds.
They are subtle: they seem to float, though they weigh me
    down,   40
Upsetting me with their sudden tongues and their colour,
A dozen red lead sinkers round my neck.

Nobody watched me before, now I am watched.
The tulips turn to me, and the window behind me
Where once a day the light slowly widens and slowly thins, 45
And I see myself, flat, ridiculous, a cut-paper shadow
Between the eye of the sun and the eyes of the tulips,
And I have no face, I have wanted to efface myself.
The vivid tulips eat my oxygen.

Before they came the air was calm enough,   50
Coming and going, breath by breath, without any fuss.
Then the tulips filled it up like a loud noise.
Now the air snags and eddies round them the way a river
Snags and eddies round a sunken rust-red engine.
They concentrate my attention, that was happy   55
Playing and resting without committing itself.

The walls, also, seem to be warming themselves.
The tulips should be behind bars like dangerous animals;
They are opening like the mouth of some great African cat,
And I am aware of my heart: it opens and closes   60
Its bowl of red blooms out of sheer love of me.
The water I taste is warm and salt, like the sea,
And comes from a country far away as health.

Berck-Plage

(I)

This is the sea, then, this great abeyance.
How the sun's poultice draws on my inflammation.

Electrifyingly-coloured sherbets, scooped from the freeze
By pale girls, travel the air in scorched hands.

Why is it so quiet, what are they hiding?   5
I have two legs, and I move smilingly.

A sandy damper kills the vibrations;
It stretches for miles, the shrunk voices

Waving and crutchless, half their old size.
The lines of the eye, scalded by these bald surfaces,   10

Boomerang like anchored elastics, hurting the owner.
Is it any wonder he puts on dark glasses?

Is it any wonder he affects a black cassock?
Here he comes now, among the mackerel gatherers

Who wall up their backs against him.   15
They are handling the black and green lozenges like the parts
      of a body.

The sea, that crystallized these,
Creeps away, many-snaked, with a long hiss of distress.

                           (II)
This black boot has no mercy for anybody.
Why should it, it is the hearse of a dead foot,   20

The high, dead, toeless foot of this priest
Who plumbs the well of his book,

The bent print bulging before him like scenery.
Obscene bikinis hide in the dunes,

Breasts and hips a confectioner's sugar   25
Of little crystals, titillating the light,

While a green pool opens its eye,
Sick with what it has swallowed –

Limbs, images, shrieks. Behind the concrete bunkers
Two lovers unstick themselves   30

                                        6-2

O white sea-crockery,
What cupped sighs, what salt in the throat . . .

And the onlooker, trembling,
Drawn like a long material

Through a still virulence,   35
And a weed, hairy as privates.

(III)
On the balconies of the hotel, things are glittering.
Things, things –

Tubular steel wheelchairs, aluminium crutches.
Such salt-sweetness. Why should I walk   40

Behind the breakwater, spotty with barnacles?
I am not a nurse, white and attendant,

I am not a smile.
These children are after something, with hooks and cries,

And my heart too small to bandage their terrible faults.   45
This is the side of a man: his red ribs,

The nerves bursting like trees, and this is the surgeon:
One mirrory eye –

A facet of knowledge.
On a striped mattress in one room   50

An old man is vanishing.
There is no help in his weeping wife.

Where are the eye-stones, yellow and valuable,
And the tongue, sapphire of ash.

(IV)
A wedding-cake face in a paper frill.   55
How superior he is now.

It is like possessing a saint.
The nurses in their wing-caps are no longer so beautiful;

They are browning, like touched gardenias.
The bed is rolled from the wall.   60

This is what it is to be complete. It is horrible.
Is he wearing pajamas or an evening suit

Under the glued sheet from which his powdery beak
Rises so whitely unbuffeted?

They propped his jaw with a book until it stiffened   65
And folded his hands, that were shaking: goodbye, goodbye.

Now the washed sheets fly in the sun,
The pillow cases are sweetening.

It is a blessing, it is a blessing:
The long coffin of soap-coloured oak,   70

The curious bearers and the raw date
Engraving itself in silver with marvellous calm.

(V)
The grey sky lowers, the hills like a green sea
Run fold upon fold far off, concealing their hollows,

The hollows in which rock the thoughts of the wife –   75
Blunt, practical boats

Full of dresses and hats and china and married daughters.
In the parlour of the stone house

One curtain is flickering from the open window,   80
Flickering and pouring, a pitiful candle.

This is the tongue of the dead man: remember, remember.
How far he is now, his actions

Around him like livingroom furniture, like a décor.
As the pallors gather –   85

The pallors of hands and neighbourly faces,
The elate pallors of flying iris.

They are flying off into nothing: remember us.
The empty benches of memory look over stones,

Marble facades with blue veins, and jelly-glassfuls of
    daffodils.   90
It is so beautiful up here: it is a stopping place.

(VI)
The natural fatness of these lime leaves! –
Pollarded green balls, the trees march to church.

The voice of the priest, in thin air,
Meets the corpse at the gate,   95

Addressing it, while the hills roll the notes of the dead bell;
A glitter of wheat and crude earth.

What is the name of that colour? –
Old blood of caked walls the sun heals,

Old blood of limb stumps, burnt hearts.   100
The widow with her black pocketbook and three daughters,

Necessary among the flowers,
Enfolds her face like fine linen,

Not to be spread again.
While a sky, wormy with put-by smiles,   105

Passes cloud after cloud.
And the bride flowers expend a freshness,

And the soul is a bride
In a still place, and the groom is red and forgetful, he is
    featureless.

(VII)

Behind the glass of this car   110
The world purrs, shut-off and gentle.

And I am dark-suited and still, a member of the party,
Gliding up in low gear behind the cart.

And the priest is a vessel,
A tarred fabric, sorry and dull,   115

Following the coffin on its flowery cart like a beautiful woman,
A crest of breasts, eyelids and lips

Storming the hilltop.
Then, from the barred yard, the children

Smell the melt of shoe-blacking,   120
Their faces turning, wordless and slow,

Their eyes opening
On a wonderful thing –

Six round black hats in the grass and a lozenge of wood,
And a naked mouth, red and awkward.   125

For a minute the sky pours into the hole like plasma.
There is no hope, it is given up.

Lesbos

Viciousness in the kitchen!
The potatoes hiss.
It is all Hollywood, windowless,
The fluorescent light wincing on and off like a terrible migraine,
Coy paper strips for doors –   5
Stage curtains, a window's frizz.
And I, love, am a pathological liar,
And my child – look at her, face down on the floor,
Little unstrung puppet, kicking to disappear –

Why she is schizophrenic,   10
Her face red and white, a panic,
You have stuck her kittens outside your window
In a sort of cement well
Where they crap and puke and cry and she can't hear.
You say you can't stand her,   15
The bastard's a girl.
You who have blown your tubes like a bad radio
Clear of voices and history, the staticky
Noise of the new.
You say I should drown the kittens. Their smell!   20
You say I should drown my girl.
She'll cut her throat at ten if she's mad at two.
The baby smiles, fat snail,
From the polished lozenges of orange linoleum.
You could eat him. He's a boy.   25
You say your husband is just no good to you.
His Jew-Mama guards his sweet sex like a pearl.
You have one baby, I have two.
I should sit on a rock off Cornwall and comb my hair.
I should wear tiger pants, I should have an affair.   30
We should meet in another life, we should meet in air,
Me and you.

Meanwhile there's a stink of fat and baby crap.
I'm doped and thick from my last sleeping pill.
The smog of cooking, the smog of hell   35
Floats our heads, two venomous opposites,
Our bones, our hair.
I call you Orphan, orphan. You are ill.
The sun gives you ulcers, the wind gives you T.B.
Once you were beautiful.   40
In New York, in Hollywood, the men said: 'Through?
Gee baby, you are rare.'
You acted, acted, acted for the thrill.
The impotent husband slumps out for a coffee.
I try to keep him in,   45
An old pole for the lightning,
The acid baths, the skyfuls off of you.
He lumps it down the plastic cobbled hill,
Flogged trolley. The sparks are blue.

The blue sparks spill,   50
Splitting like quartz into a million bits.

O jewel! O valuable!
That night the moon
Dragged its blood bag, sick
Animal   55
Up over the harbour lights.
And then grew normal,
Hard and apart and white.
The scale-sheen on the sand scared me to death.
We kept picking up handfuls, loving it,   60
Working it like dough, a mulatto body,
The silk grits.
A dog picks up your doggy husband. He went on.

Now I am silent, hate
Up to my neck,   65
Thick, thick.
I do not speak.
I am packing the hard potatoes like good clothes,
I am packing the babies,
I am packing the sick cats.   70
O vase of acid,
It is love you are full of. You know who you hate.
He is hugging his ball and chain down by the gate
That opens to the sea
Where it drives in, white and black   75
Then spews it back.
Every day you fill him with soul-stuff, like a pitcher.
You are so exhausted.
Your voice my ear-ring,
Flapping and sucking, blood-loving bat.   80
That is that. That is that.
You peer from the door,
Sad hag. 'Every woman's a whore.
I can't communicate.'

I see your cute décor   85
Close on you like the fist of a baby
Or an anemone, that sea

Sweetheart, that kleptomaniac.
I am still raw.
I say I may be back.   90
You know what lies are for.

Even in your Zen heaven we shan't meet.

The Bee Meeting

Who are these people at the bridge to meet me? They are the
        villagers –
The rector, the midwife, the sexton, the agent for bees.
In my sleeveless summery dress I have no protection,
And they are all gloved and covered, why did nobody tell me?
They are smiling and taking out veils tacked to ancient hats. 5

I am nude as a chicken neck, does nobody love me?
Yes, here is the secretary of bees with her white shop smock,
Buttoning the cuffs at my wrists and the slit from my neck to
        my knees.
Now I am milkweed silk, the bees will not notice.
They will not smell my fear, my fear, my fear.   10

Which is the rector now, is it that man in black?
Which is the midwife, is that her blue coat?
Everybody is nodding a square black head, they are knights in
        visors,
Breastplates of cheesecloth knotted under the armpits.
Their smiles and their voices are changing. I am led through
        a beanfield.   15

Strips of tinfoil winking like people.
Feather dusters fanning their hands in a sea of bean flowers,
Creamy bean flowers with black eyes and leaves like bored
        hearts.
Is it blood clots the tendrils are dragging up that string?
No, no, it is scarlet flowers that will one day be edible.   20

Now they are giving me a fashionable white straw Italian hat
And a black veil that moulds to my face, they are making me
    one of them.
They are leading me to the shorn grove, the circle of hives.
Is it the hawthorn that smells so sick?
The barren body of hawthorn, etherizing its children.   25

Is it some operation that is taking place?
It is the surgeon my neighbours are waiting for,
This apparition in a green helmet,
Shining gloves and white suit.
Is it the butcher, the grocer, the postman, someone I know? 30

I cannot run, I am rooted, and the gorse hurts me
With its yellow purses, its spiky armoury.
I could not run without having to run forever.
The white hive is snug as a virgin,
Sealing off her brood cells, her honey, and quietly humming. 35

Smoke rolls and scarves in the grove.
The mind of the hive thinks this is the end of everything.
Here they come, the outriders, on their hysterical elastics.
If I stand very still, they will think I am cow parsley,
A gullible head untouched by their animosity,   40

Not even nodding, a personage in a hedgerow.
The villagers open the chambers, they are hunting the queen.
Is she hiding, is she eating honey? She is very clever.
She is old, old, old, she must live another year, and she
    knows it.
While in their fingerjoint cells the new virgins   45

Dream of a duel they will win inevitably,
A curtain of wax dividing them from the bridge flight,
The upflight of the murderess into a heaven that loves her.
The villagers are moving the virgins, there will be no killing.
The old queen does not show herself, is she so ungrateful? 50

I am exhausted, I am exhausted –
Pillar of white in a blackout of knives.
I am the magician's girl who does not flinch.

The villagers are untying their disguises, they are shaking
    hands.
Whose is that long white box in the grove, what have they
    accomplished, why am I cold.   55

Daddy

You do not do, you do not do
Any more, black shoe
In which I have lived like a foot
For thirty years, poor and white,
Barely daring to breathe or Achoo.   5

Daddy, I have had to kill you.
You died before I had time –
Marble-heavy, a bag full of God,
Ghastly statue with one grey toe
Big as a Frisco seal   10

And a head in the freakish Atlantic
Where it pours bean green over blue
In the waters off beautiful Nauset.
I used to pray to recover you.
Ach, du.   15

In the German tongue, in the Polish town
Scraped flat by the roller
Of wars, wars, wars.
But the name of the town is common.
My Polack friend   20

Says there are a dozen or two.
So I never could tell where you
Put your foot, your root,
I never could talk to you.
The tongue stuck in my jaw.   25

It stuck in a barb wire snare.
Ich, ich, ich, ich,
I could hardly speak.

I thought every German was you.
And the language obscene.   30

An engine, an engine
Chuffing me off like a Jew.
A Jew to Dachau, Auschwitz, Belsen.
I began to talk like a Jew.
I think I may well be a Jew.   35

The snows of the Tyrol, the clear beer of Vienna
Are not very pure or true.
With my gypsy ancestress and my weird luck
And my Taroc pack and my Taroc pack
I may be a bit of a Jew.   40

I have always been scared of *you*,
With your Luftwaffe, your gobbledygoo.
And your neat moustache
And your Aryan eye, bright blue.
Panzer-man, panzer-man, O You –   45

Not God but a swastika
So black no sky could squeak through.
Every woman adores a Fascist,
The boot in the face, the brute
Brute heart of a brute like you.   50

You stand at the blackboard, daddy,
In the picture I have of you,
A cleft in your chin instead of your foot
But no less a devil for that, no not
Any less the black man who   55

Bit my pretty red heart in two.
I was ten when they buried you.
At twenty I tried to die
And get back, back, back to you.
I thought even the bones would do.   60

But they pulled me out of the sack,
And they stuck me together with glue.

And then I knew what to do.
I made a model of you,
A man in black with a Meinkampf look   65

And a love of the rack and the screw.
And I said I do, I do.
So daddy, I'm finally through.
The black telephone's off at the root,
The voices just can't worm through.   70

If I've killed one man, I've killed two –
The vampire who said he was you
And drank my blood for a year,
Seven years, if you want to know.
Daddy, you can lie back now.   75

There's a stake in your fat black heart
And the villagers never liked you.
They are dancing and stamping on you.
They always *knew* it was you.
Daddy, daddy, you bastard, I'm through.   80

Lady Lazarus

I have done it again.
One year in every ten
I manage it –

A sort of walking miracle, my skin
Bright as a Nazi lampshade,   5
My right foot

A paperweight,
My face a featureless, fine
Jew linen.

Peel off the napkin   10
O my enemy.
Do I terrify? –

The nose, the eye pits, the full set of teeth?
The sour breath
Will vanish in a day.   15

Soon, soon the flesh
The grave cave ate will be
At home on me

And I a smiling woman.
I am only thirty.   20
And like the cat I have nine times to die.

This is Number Three.
What a trash
To annihilate each decade.

What a million filaments.   25
The peanut-crunching crowd
Shoves in to see

Them unwrap me hand and foot –
The big strip tease.
Gentlemen, ladies   30

These are my hands
My knees.
I may be skin and bone,

Nevertheless, I am the same, identical woman.
The first time it happened I was ten.   35
It was an accident.

The second time I meant
To last it out and not come back at all.
I rocked shut

As a seashell.   40
They had to call and call
And pick the worms off me like sticky pearls.

Dying
Is an art, like everything else.
I do it exceptionally well.   45

I do it so it feels like hell.
I do it so it feels real.
I guess you could say I've a call.

It's easy enough to do it in a cell.
It's easy enough to do it and stay put.   50
It's the theatrical

Comeback in broad day
To the same place, the same face, the same brute
Amused shout:

'A miracle!'   55
That knocks me out.
There is a charge

For the eyeing of my scars, there is a charge
For the hearing of my heart –
It really goes.   60

And there is a charge, a very large charge
For a word or a touch
Or a bit of blood

Or a piece of my hair or my clothes.
So, so, Herr Doktor.   65
So, Herr Enemy.

I am your opus,
I am your valuable,
The pure gold baby

That melts to a shriek.   70
I turn and burn.
Do not think I underestimate your great concern.

Ash, ash –
You poke and stir.
Flesh, bone, there is nothing there –   75

A cake of soap,
A wedding ring,
A gold filling.

Herr God, Herr Lucifer
Beware   80
Beware

Out of the ash
I rise with my red hair
And I eat men like air.   85

NOTES TO THE POEMS

EDWIN MUIR

Unlike many of his poetic contemporaries Edwin Muir was no technical innovator. Pound wanted to 'make it new', but Muir wanted to make it eternal. Unlike Eliot, whose erudition persuaded his critics to admit the validity of his technical experiments, Muir favoured a traditional approach to poetry. His formal repertoire was not large but, by constant writing and revision, he gained mastery of his medium. Muir came to poetry late and did not have the young man's creative impetuosity. More importantly, his deep seriousness and constant meditation on the fable of life precluded verbal pyrotechnics.

In *An Autobiography* he described his feelings on beginning a poetic career at the age of thirty-five.

'I had no training; I was too old to submit myself to contemporary influences; and I had acquired in Scotland a deference towards ideas which made my entrance into poetry difficult. Though my imagination had begun to work I had no technique by which I could give expression to it. There were the rhythms of English poetry on the one hand, the images in my mind on the other. All I could do at the start was to force the one, creaking and complaining, into the mould of the other . . . I began to write poetry simply because what I wanted to say could not have gone properly into prose. I wanted so much to say it that I had no thought left to study the form in which alone it could be said.'

Perhaps the strongest influence on Muir's poetry was the symbolic discursiveness of Wordsworth. Though Muir modestly felt that 'Wordsworth is not a poet to be imitated', he shares with Wordsworth an intense imaginative engagement that repeatedly elevates an otherwise prosaic style.

In his childhood Muir had heard his mother reciting ballads, and their simple narrative logic influenced his own narrative poems, like 'The Little General' and 'The Combat'. From the ballads too he learned the strength of conventional rhymes. Thus the mechanics of a Muir poem are relatively straightforward. One of his favourite devices is to open with a descriptive passage and then to move on to a philosophical commentary on the earlier observations. A good example of this is 'The Good Town'. Even his epithets seem essential rather than unusual, as in 'warm hearth', 'lonely stream', 'noisy world', 'unequal battle', etc. The use of language is functional, pointing to a meaning and never inviting the reader to admire euphony for its own sake. Muir is a philosophical poet and his thought is, to a large extent, his poetry.

Muir looked back on his life and saw it as a fable. There was his happy rural childhood, then the trauma of life in a big industrial city, then the salvation of his marriage and subsequent serenity. In imagination Muir saw these stages as Eden, the Fall into the labyrinth, and Paradise Regained. He increasingly strove to return to Eden via the imagination and to live there with an informed innocence as a result of experience. Simultaneously he discovered Christianity and introduced Christian symbolism into his poetry: the Transfiguration, the Incarnation, etc.

Muir saw his insular Orkney childhood as a time when he experienced 'the original vision of the world' and felt 'our first childhood is the only time in our lives when we exist within immortality'. So his search was for a second childhood where innocence would be welcomed, not ridiculed. He wanted others to perceive the Fable behind the Story of their lives. Because he felt that the insensitivity of the adult world and the harsh environment of modern city life destroyed the child's glimpse of Eden, his ideal society was rural and compact. There is no insistence, no proselytising, in Muir's poetry. He was sure there was a fabulous dimension to life and his poems were offered as evidence of that dimension.

The Wayside Station

This poem, from *The Narrow Place* (1934), shows Muir moving from appearance to the mythical significance of a scene, its place in the fable of life. The poem describes an actual landscape only to provide a realistic base from which Muir can launch his theme: those aspects of the eternal.

The poem was written in the winter of 1940–1. Muir was living at St Andrews and working in Dundee's Food Office:

'I had to change trains every morning at Leuchars, and in the winter mornings particularly there was generally a long wait in the cold and bleak station. In midwinter the dawn had hardly come as I stamped up and down to keep warm; and over everything hung the thought of war' (BBC broadcast, 'Chapbook', 3 August 1952).

The Little General

This poem, also from *The Narrow Place*, remembers the landlord who drove Muir's father out of the farm on Wyre.

'He came over to Wyre every spring to shoot the wild birds. I remember one soft spring day when the light seemed to be opening up the world after the dark winter . . . The General was walking through the field below our house in his little brown jacket with the brown leather tabs on the shoulders, his neat little knickerbockers and elegant little brown boots; a feather curled on his hat, and his little pointed beard seemed to curl too. Now and then he raised his silver gun, the white smoke curled upward, birds fell, suddenly heavy after seeming so light; our cattle, who were grazing in the field, rushed away in alarm at the noise, then stopped and looked round in wonder at the strange little man. It was a mere picture; I did not feel angry with the General or sorry for the birds; I was entranced with the bright gun, the white smoke, and particularly with the soft brown tabs of leather on the shoulders of his jacket' (*An Autobiography*).

When he came to make a poem of the memory Muir set the General in a mythical island, a bringer of death who is himself destroyed by his obsessive ritual. The General has become an unthinking part of a deterministic world.

2] *sound:* strait.

4–5] By his compulsion to take part in the 'pious ritual' the hunter and the hunted are both caught in 'the boundless trap'.

7] The bird's feather in the General's cap is evidence of his previous involvement in 'the boundless trap' and a reminder of death.

The Transmutation

This poem is from *The Voyage* (1946) a book written mainly in Edinburgh where in 1942 Muir had joined the British Council. In 1939 Muir had rediscovered Christianity and the same year he completed the first version of his autobiography *The Story and the Fable*. As he put it in a letter to a friend, he could 'see life timelessly'. The wanderings in the haunted maze of Glasgow were over and he now believed that life was not meaningless, but eternal. In this poem Muir expressed his belief that human actions are immortal, are continually transformed into significance on a higher plane. We unconsciously act out an eternal drama. It is as if Eternity had determined the pattern of our life and then extracted the significance of each moment. The joy was in perceiving this pattern, and Muir felt he had done so. He sees everything being transformed, 'transmuted', until it will 'stand beyond all change' (line 2). We do not decay in time, but pass through it. In Muir's imaginative world once something had happened it 'can never pass away' (line 14).

3] *the unmoving dream:* the eternal fable.

9] *the child plays still:* cf. 'I was returning from the nursing home [where his wife was recuperating from an illness] one day – it was the last day of February 1939 – when I saw some schoolboys playing at marbles on the pavement; the old game had "come round" again at its own time, known only to children, and it seemed a simple little rehearsal for a resurrection, promising a timeless renewal of life' (*An Autobiography*).

In Love for Long

This, the last poem in *The Voyage*, was one of Muir's own favourites among his own poems.

'I was up at Swanston [a village outside Edinburgh] in the Pentlands one Saturday morning during the war. It was in late summer; a dull, cloudy, windless day, quite warm. I was sitting in the grass, looking at the thatched cottages and the hills, when I realised that I was fond of them, suddenly and without reason, and for themselves, not because the cottages were quaint or the hills romantic. I had an unmistakeable warm feeling for the ground I was sitting on, as if I were in love with the earth itself, and the clouds, and the soft subdued light. I had felt these things before, but that afternoon they seemed to crystallise, and the poem came out of them' (BBC broadcast, 'Chapbook', 3 September 1952).

The poem has a hint of Wordsworthian pantheism in it as will become apparent if its mood is compared with the opening of the 'Ode: Intimations of Immortality from Recollections of Early Childhood'.

The Labyrinth

The poems written in Prague between 1945 and 1948 were collected in *The Labyrinth* (1949), which was a success for Muir.

The title-poem is a meditation on being trapped by circumstances. While it uses the Greek myth of Theseus and the Minotaur there are strong autobiographical elements. In a broadcast (BBC 'Chapbook', 3 September 1952) Muir said that the Theseus myth seemed to him 'an image of human life with its errors and ignorance and endless intricacy'. In the Greek myth Theseus (whose heroic feats included the destruction of Procrustes and the Cretan bull) volunteered to be one of the seven youths who, with seven maidens, were sent annually by Athens to be fed to the Minotaur. In Crete Ariadne gave Theseus a sword to slay the Minotaur and a ball of thread to find his way out of the labyrinth. In Muir's treatment of the myth the labyrinth stands for the restrictive, soul-destroying aspects of human existence. It is clear, too, that he was thinking of his own time in the Glasgow slums.

1] *I:* i.e. Theseus. When Muir uses the first personal pronoun he usually means us to understand the poet is speaking. 'The Labyrinth', however, like 'The Transfiguration', is a dramatic monologue with autobiographical overtones.

1-35] Muir winds the reader into this long labyrinthine sentence to establish the sense of being trapped.

2] *the tall and echoing passages:* In his 'Writers and Critics' book on Muir, P. H. Butter convincingly argues that this phrase refers to the Glasgow slums, as the phrase 'is rather unexpected as applied to the maze, but is appropriate to streets of high tenements'.

6] *the bull:* the Minotaur was half-man, half-bull.

12] *the world:* a world transfigured, intensely appreciated, because denied in the labyrinth. By line 23 it has become 'The lovely world' and by line 65 'the real world'.

24-5] Like Muir, Theseus has a horror of being trapped again.

29-34] This description of the fear of regressing into the labyrinth owes much to the imagery of Kafka. Cf. *The Trial*, Chapter 3, 'The Empty Interrogation Chamber'.

47] *It is a world:* i.e. the endless repetition experienced by those in the labyrinth does exist and for many it is all they know of the world, for they never make the imaginative leap to see the fabulous pattern of their lives.

48] *I saw the gods:* in the broadcast referred to Muir said 'I wanted also to give an image of the life of the gods, to whom all that is confusion down here is clear and harmonious as seen eternally.' This God's-eye view of the world, was a condition Muir aspired to. Illuminated by such a vision, he could eliminate trivia from the pattern of his life and see the significant parts of the eternal whole.

65] *the real world:* Muir suggests that it is the visionary presentation of reality that is true, while the empirical view of the world is fallacious.

70] *my soul has birdwings to fly free:* through the liberating power of the imagination he can raise himself above the everyday world. Possibly a reference to Daedalus, who built the labyrinth, and also made himself wings to escape from Crete.

The Transfiguration

Of the two aspects of Muir's vision, it is the negative fears that haunt 'The Labyrinth'. That poem describes the experience of being trapped and suggests the alternative, imaginative freedom, as a dream. By way of contrast 'The Transfiguration', also from *The Labyrinth*, shows a world transformed by religious ecstasy. Here is the passage from Chapter 17 of St Matthew's Gospel describing the Transfiguration:

'1   And after six days Jesus taketh Peter, James, and John his brother, and bringeth them up into an high mountain apart,

2   And was transfigured before them: and his face did shine as the sun, and his raiment was white as the light.'

In Muir's poem it is the world that is transfigured by this event. In 1940 Muir had written to a friend saying 'I believe in God, in the immortality of the soul, and that Christ is the greatest figure who ever appeared in the history of mankind.' This comes over strongly in the poem, though Muir asks us to share Christ's vision, not for empty homage. In a broadcast (BBC 'Chapbook', 3 September 1952) he said:

'I had always been deeply struck by the story of the Transfiguration in the Gospels, and I had felt that perhaps at the moment of Christ's Transfiguration everything was transfigured, mankind, and the animals, and the simplest natural objects . . . Perhaps in the imagination of mankind the Transfiguration has become a powerful symbol, standing for many things, and among them those transformations of reality which the imagination itself creates.'

1] *we:* the disciples.
5] *source of all our seeing:* imagination. The act of seeing is a visionary experience, not simply a visual one.
7] *the clear unfallen world:* Eden. The poem is Muir's description of Eden.
13] *Was it a vision?:* an earlier version reads 'Was it delusion?' Muir was never dogmatic or facile about a Paradise regained through the imagination.
15] *the everlasting world:* this has an identical cadence to 'the clear unfallen world' (line 7) and is a development of it. Muir's poems often progress in this way, concepts being enriched as the poem develops.
21] *this:* the everyday world. Muir refused to accept that the so-called 'real' world of popular assumption was anything of the kind.
25] *the wild and tame together:* In *An Autobiography*, speaking about his feelings towards the animal world, Muir writes: 'All guilt seeks expiation and the end of guilt, and our blood-guiltiness towards the animals tries to find release in visions of a day when man and the beasts will live in friendship and the lion will lie down with the lamb' (Isaiah 11: 6).
29] *the starting-day:* Eden.
31] 'Unto the pure all things *are* pure', The Epistle of Paul to Titus 1: 15.
32–3] In a dream described in *An Autobiography* Muir remembered a journey with a stranger:

'As we passed the last houses I saw a dark, shabby man with a dagger in his hand; he was wearing rags bound round his feet, so that he walked quite

soundlessly . . . I took him to be a robber or a murderer . . . But as he came
nearer I saw that his eyes . . . were filled with a profound, violent adoration
such as I had never seen in human eyes before.'

Many of Muir's images come from dreams which, he held, gave 'knowledge
of my real self and simultaneously knowledge of immortality'.

36] *the labyrinth:* see the poem 'The Labyrinth'.

45] *that radiant kingdom:* the world transformed by love and imaginative
insight. In poem after poem Muir tells of being in Eden for intense moments,
yet 'the world' – the everyday, empirical world – always intervenes to blur
the vision. Here, 'the world/Rolled back into its place'. In 'The Labyrinth'
he (in the person of Theseus) exists in the empirical world but knows 'there's
another', knows that by imaginative effort he can enter the radiant kingdom.
It is always there 'And blossoms for itself while time runs on' (line 49).

50] *come again:* the second coming of Christ.

62] *Judas:* in a letter quoted in P. H. Butter's *Edwin Muir: Man and Poet*
Muir writes 'The idea of Judas going back into innocence has often been
with me.'

The Combat

Muir felt 'that sleep, in which we pass a third of our existence, is a mode of
experience, and our dreams a part of reality' (*An Autobiography*). Muir's
psychoanalytic treatment involved recording his dreams for interpretive
analysis. Many of Muir's poems are based on dreams, and 'The Combat',
from *The Labyrinth*, is his most celebrated dream-poem. It tells of a setting
in which two unevenly matched animal antagonists fight a perpetual battle.
Like 'Hunter and quarry' in 'The Little General', both victor and van-
quished have become trapped in this irrational ritual. In *An Autobiography*
he describes the dream:

'In the dream I was walking with some people in the country, when I saw
a shining grey bird in the field. I turned and said in an awed voice, "It's a
heron". We went towards it, but as we came nearer it spread its tail like a
peacock, so that we could see nothing else. As the tail grew I saw that it was
not round, but square, an impenetrable grey hedge of feathers; and at once I
knew that its body was not a bird's body now, but an animal's, and that
behind that gleaming hedge it was walking away from us on four feet padded
like a leopard's or a tiger's. Then, confronting it in the field, there appeared
an ancient, dirty-coloured animal with a head like that of an old sheep or a
mangy dog. Its eyes were soft and brown; it was alone against the splendid-
tailed beast; yet it stood its ground and prepared to fight the danger coming
towards it, whether that was death or merely humiliation and pain. From
their look I could see that the two animals knew each other, that they had
fought a countless number of times and after this battle would fight again,
that each meeting would be the first meeting, and that the dark, patient
animal would always be defeated, and the bright, fierce animal would always
win. I did not see the fight, but I knew it would be ruthless and shameful,
with a meaning of some kind perhaps, but no comfort.'

The Good Town

In 1945 Muir went to Czechoslovakia as Director of the British Council Institute in Prague. He had requested this post, partly because of his happy memories of his 1921 visit. When the Communists staged a *coup* in February 1948 Muir was appalled and left the country in July. Such is the background to 'The Good Town', one of the longest poems in *The Labyrinth*. In a broadcast (BBC 'Chapbook', 3 September 1952) Muir said that in Prague he had

'an idea for two poems about towns, one to be called "The Good Town", and the other "The Bad Town"; and I intended the towns to stand as symbols of two ways of life. But as things were then shaping in Prague, I saw that the only way to treat the theme was to describe a good town turning into a bad one. Yet the poem is not really about Prague or any other place, but about something that was happening in Europe. Stories of what was occurring in other countries to whole families, whole communities, became absorbed into the poem, which I tried to make into a symbolic picture of a vast change.'

4] *the doors stood open:* As always when he presents an image of goodness Muir recalls his childhood in Orkney. In *An Autobiography* he wrote of the strangeness of Glasgow: 'At the Bu and Garth [farms in Orkney] we never thought of locking the door at night, and during the day, at least in summer, it always stood open.'

29] *new concrete houses:* Muir had a horror of the impersonality of city life.

One Foot in Eden

In Rome the ubiquitous presence of religious images delighted Muir and gave him a sense of the reality of the Incarnation. When he published, at the age of sixty-nine, a new collection of poems he called it *One Foot in Eden* (1956) because he had attained a personal serenity and a belief in immortality. In *Belonging* Willa Muir said: 'The poems he wrote mostly at Newbattle were published separately in 1956 with the title: *One Foot in Eden*, and that title was a true one. Only one foot in Eden, the other firmly on earth.'

2] *the other land:* the real, the empirical world, as opposed to the visionary one.

3] *growing late:* this invokes both the feeling of apocalypse in a post-atomic world and Muir's sense that his own death was not distant.

4–13] This passage owes much to the parable of the sower and the seed in Matthew 13.

5] *love and hate:* this perpetual coexistence of opposites, in Muir's opinion, offered man a choice. The dichotomy is repeated in 'corn and tares' (line 8), 'Evil and good' (line 11), 'charity and sin' (line 12), 'grief and charity' (line 22).

6] Seemingly arbitrary events take place in eternity, the 'phantom ground' of 'The Transmutation'.

8] *tares:* weeds. Taking his cue from the parable of the sower and the seed, Muir shows how good seems inseparable from evil but when things come to final fruition evil can be cast aside.

14] *the root:* the original impulse of life.

The Horses

This, from *One Foot in Eden*, is Muir's most famous poem. There has been argument whether the horses are symbols or real. I think for Muir they were both, though a person raised in a city might find this attitude eccentric. Muir was brought up among animals and he said in *An Autobiography* of his early work, 'when I wrote about horses they were my father's plough-horses as I saw them when I was four or five'. In 'The Horses' man's fascination with technology has almost totally destroyed him. The hydrogen bomb has destroyed most of the world and in the aftermath of this destruction Muir imagines man regaining Paradise by going back to his roots in nature.

2] *seven days war:* In Genesis God creates the 'heavens and the earth' in seven days. In Muir's poem it takes man exactly the same time to 'put the world to sleep'.

3] *strange horses:* strange in the sense of being unfamiliar. There is no question of post-nuclear mutation.

4] *covenant:* cf. Genesis 9: 12 where God tells Noah of 'the covenant which I make between me and you and every living creature'.

7] *On the second day:* maintains the biblical tone of this new genesis as do 'On the third day' (line 9) and 'On the sixth day' (line 10). This prepares us for the abrupt 'Thereafter/Nothing' (lines 11–12) which utilises the line-break with dramatic effect.

8] *The radios failed:* all man-made instruments are condemned: the warship aimlessly drifts by (line 9), the plane crashes (line 11), the tractors rust (line 24). Man is systematically deprived of the artefacts on which he has become so dependent.

19] *That old bad world:* ironically parodies Shakespeare's 'brave new world,/ That has such people in't!' (*The Tempest*, v.i.183).

29] *gone back:* this is the journey back to Eden.

39] *strange to us:* cf. line 3.

53] *their coming our beginning:* the final line of the poem, like the first line of Genesis, announces a new world.

'I see the image'

From a group of poems found in manuscript after Muir's death. Muir, while personally serene, was pessimistic about the world. At times he abandoned his vision of the Millennium and gave the darker side of man's nature. The poem imagines the past as a time when man was emerging as a distinct species. He imagines the future as uncertain: there is no guarantee of man's survival. This poem shows that at the very end of his life Muir was seeking a new direction. His philosophical, mystical style had been perfected with *One Foot in Eden*. Though old, he was ready to try something else.

HUGH MACDIARMID

Although in this anthology we are concerned with MacDiarmid as a writer of poetry in English (which he has been, almost exclusively, since the 1930s) it is impossible to appreciate his stature without considering his early development. Before he adopted the pseudonym 'Hugh MacDiarmid' C. M. Grieve published, in 1923, *Annals of the Five Senses* and demonstrated a real gift for constructing felicitous and striking English poems:

> The Fool
> 'He said that he was God.
> "We are well met", I cried,
> "I've always hoped I should
> Meet God before I died."
>
> I slew him then and cast
> His corpse into a pool,
> – But how I wish he had
> Indeed been God, the fool.'

This ability to fit a subtle narrative into two strictly rhymed quatrains shows a considerable mastery of English metric.

However, the year that *Annals* appeared Grieve was bringing out *The Scottish Chapbook*, the self-styled organ of a 'great Scottish Literary Renaissance'. To substantiate the editorial aspirations a first poem by 'Hugh MacDiarmid' was published:

> The Watergaw
> 'Ae weet forenicht i' the yow-trummle
> I saw yon antrin thing.
> A watergaw wi' its chitterin' licht
> Ayont the on-ding;
> ·An' I thocht o' the last wild look ye gied
> Afore ye deed!
>
> There was nae reek i' the laverock's hoose
> That nicht – an' nane i' mine;
> But I hae thocht o' that foolish licht
> Ever sin' syne;
> An' I think that mebbe at last I ken
> What your look meant then.'

The language used here does not conform to any one local dialect, nor is it a poetic reconstruction of spoken Scots. Instead MacDiarmid had consulted Jamieson's *Etymological Dictionary of the Scottish Language* and responded emotionally to the words therein.

Rationalising his own poetic practice in *Lucky Poet* MacDiarmid talked about 'the act of poetry being the reverse of what it is usually thought to be; not an idea gradually shaping itself in words, but deriving entirely from words'. This notion of a poetry of linguistic response applied only to the early lyrics. In *A Drunk Man* the intellectual impulse was certainly as important as the linguistic response, for MacDiarmid was gradually developing his poetry into a vehicle for thought on the assumption that poetry could say anything – literally – more memorably than prose.

It was this determination to use poetry as a means of education rather than edification that offended his disciples and frightened off the neophytes. From his Zarathustrian isolation in the Shetlands MacDiarmid became a man with a mission. He had joined the Communist Party in 1934 and, in line with marxist theory, believed that a combination of scientific insight and technological expertise could free mankind from economic restrictions and from obsolete modes of thought. He wanted a poetry packed with information, capable of shocking the reader out of his ignorance and inspiring him with an ambition to extend his own consciousness.

I asked MacDiarmid how he, a confirmed Anglophobe, could justify writing in English especially after he had proven himself a master of vernacular poetry. He replied in a letter (4 October 1972).

'With regard despite my political and cultural propensities to my latterly writing so much in English, this has been due to a shift in my fundamental intellectual interests. More and more I have been concerned with scientific matters, and I found it impossible to express these at any rate with the necessary precision even in my aggrandized Scots – even English does not have anything like an adequate scientific vocabulary – one must use all sorts of *ad hoc* neologisms, and that is one of the reasons why I had to eke out my English with all sorts of words and phrases from other languages – of course that is the very way English itself has been built up.'

The Glen of Silence

This poem comes from the chapter 'On Seeing Scotland Whole' from *Lucky Poet* and emphasises MacDiarmid's belief that the development of Scotland was deliberately arrested. After the defeat of the Clans at Culloden in 1746, the British Government (with the approval of the Scottish Lowland commercial establishment) initiated a quasi-genocidal policy against the Gaelicspeaking Highlands. The Clans were disarmed, known Jacobite families were persecuted, Highland dress was proscribed. Then the Highland people were cleared from their land to make way for, first, sheep and, later, deer. Consequently, Gaelic culture was destroyed and Scotland became increasingly assimilated by England. To a nationalist like MacDiarmid this was interpreted as the destruction of the quintessentially Scottish part of Scotland and the reduction of the country to a region of England. Hence the 'foetal death' of line 5. The penultimate line of the closing stanza extends the *abcb*-quatrain pattern and prolongs the tragic conclusion. The italicised lines that precede the poem are taken from G. M. Cookson's translation of Aeschylus's *The Seven Against Thebes*.

8] *auscultation:* the application of the ear or stethoscope to the body in order to 'hear' its condition.

10] *wheeple:* Scottish word for a long drawn-out cry.

12] *fear-tholladh nan tighem:* Gaelic phrase meaning 'Destroyer of homes'.

Third Hymn to Lenin

Extracts from this poem appeared in *Lucky Poet* and the entire poem was first published in the April 1955 issue of MacDiarmid's own magazine, *The Voice of Scotland*. All *Three Hymns to Lenin* were published in 1957.

The first two hymns are in Scots and powerfully express MacDiarmid's desire for revolutionary social change:

> 'What maitters't wha we kill
> To lessen that foulest murder that deprives
>   Maist men o' real lives!'
>   'First Hymn to Lenin'

> 'Oh, it's nonsense, nonsense, nonsense,
> Nonsense at this time o' day
> That breid-and-butter problems
> S'ud be in ony man's way.'
>   'Second Hymn to Lenin'

When he came to write the 'Third Hymn' MacDiarmid was ready to specify reasons for his hatred of capitalism. In 1941 he had returned to Glasgow to work in a Clydeside factory and here he completed the composition of this poem (which was planned in Shetland). By using the Glasgow slums as a symbol of capitalism – and in the 1930s the conditions in Glasgow had earned the city world infamy – MacDiarmid evoked a contemporary inferno to which people were condemned by accident of birth and poverty of environment, not because they had committed any sin.

In calling on the figure of the dead Lenin to light up Glasgow MacDiarmid is, of course, deliberately drawing a religious parallel with Christ, much as Alexander Blok did in his poem *The Twelve*. Indeed in the 'First Hymn' MacDiarmid had said

> 'Christ's cited no' by chance or juist because
> You mark the greatest turnin'-point since him'

and in many of his poems he invests Marxism with mystical qualities. In a real sense the metaphorical content of Marxism – the dialectical movement of a personified History, the advance of the anonymous masses at the expense of titled individuals, the sudden metamorphosis of society – is used by MacDiarmid in much the same way as Pound uses Greek mythology, or Yeats astrology, or Graves the White Moon Goddess.

Title] In a note to the poem MacDiarmid says: 'An alternative title would be "Glasgow Invokes The Spirit of Lenin" but, with slight alterations of local detail it is, of course, equally applicable to any other big city under the Capitalist system.'

35–40] While Marx laid down 'definite laws' (dialectical materialism) according to which the revolution would inevitably occur, Lenin believed in 'conscious interference' and operated as the leader of a conspiratorial élite – the Bolsheviks.

43–7] MacDiarmid cannot now place this quotation but thinks it 'probably from some scientific book I was reading at the time'.

55] *myriad-mindedness*: a favourite expression of MacDiarmid. In *The Kind of Poetry I Want* he characteristically explains his use of the epithet when he says the poet must

> 'Be μινδεδνεος (a phrase I have borrowed
> From a Greek monk, who applies it
> To a Patriarch of Constantinople)'

73] *like this:* the Glasgow slums.

76] *the Kirk:* cf. 'Calvinism is no worse or better than any other religion; its excesses were due entirely to the fact that from the beginnings its spread was closely connected with English policy and that it became England's ideological damper for suffocating Scottish action' (*Lucky Poet*).

96ff.] The quotation following line 96 is from William Bolitho's *The Cancer of Empire* (1924).

101] *Cranston's tea-rooms:* MacDiarmid's own note identifies this as a 'Well-known Glasgow restaurant, former resort of Glasgow Labour M.P.s and leading supporters'.

133] *die List der Vernunft:* the cunning of reason.

154] *Lenin, lover of music:* cf.:

'Like most Russians, Lenin was sensitive to music; but Gorky tells us that on one occasion, after listening to Beethoven's Appassionata Sonata and exclaiming that he "would like to listen to it every day: it is marvellous superhuman music – I always think with pride . . . what marvellous things human beings can do", he screwed up his eyes and smiled sadly and added: "But I can't listen to music too often. It affects your nerves, makes you want to say stupid, nice things, and stroke the heads of people who could create such beauty while living in this vile hell. And now you mustn't stroke anyone's head – you might get your hand bitten off"' (EDMUND WILSON, *The Triple Thinkers* (1952)).

156] *Diesseitigkeit:* one-sidedness.

193] *a Jeans:* Sir James Jeans (1877–1946) the astronomer and mathematician, wrote popular books like *The Mysterious Universe* (1930).

194] *a Barnes:* Ernest William Barnes (1874–1953), mathematician and churchman who wrote books like *Scientific Theory and Religion* (1933) to try to justify religion in terms of modern scientific discoveries.

195] Nikolai Ivanovich Lobachevski (1793–1856) is the founder of non-Euclidean geometry, and Georg Friedrich Bernhard Riemann (1826–66) developed his own non-Euclidean geometrical system.

196] *Cepheid variables:* pulsating stars whose luminosity varies regularly.

195] *white dwarfs:* relatively small stars that have exhausted their hydrogen and collapsed down to very high densities.

201] *a Haldane:* John Scott Haldane (1860–1936), biologist born in Edinburgh.

207] *colloids:* substances which seem to be dissolved yet cannot pass through a membrane.

212ff.]: The quotation following line 212 introduces us to Richard Carlile (1790–1843) the radical journalist who spent more than nine years in jail for his propagandist work. After being imprisoned for blasphemy he began his periodical *The Republican* from Dorchester jail.

213] *Michael Roberts:* poet and anthologist (1902–48) whose anthology *New Country* appeared in 1933.

225] *Auden, Spender, those bhoyos:* The leading British political poets of the 1930s failed to make any favourable impression on MacDiarmid whose 'First Hymn to Lenin' predated their work (as C. Day Lewis acknowledged in *A Hope for Poetry*). In a poem, 'British Leftish Poetry, 1930–1940' MacDiarmid composed this sardonic epitaph:

> 'Auden, MacNeice, Day Lewis, I have read them all,
> Hoping against hope to hear the authentic call . . .
> And know the explanation I must pass is this
> – You cannot light a match on a crumbling wall.'

Ballad of Aun, King of Sweden

This poem, from *A Kist of Whistles and Other Poems* (1943) tries to undermine the reader's complacency by directly accusing him of complicity in social evil.

Scotland Small?

This poem appeared in the *Collected Poems* along with other extracts from *Impavidi Progrediamur* which itself will ultimately form part – along with *The Kind of Poetry I Want* and *In Memoriam James Joyce* – of a mammoth poetic sequence. 'Scotland Small?' was written in the Shetlands and illustrates MacDiarmid's love-affair with Scotland. Technically the poem proceeds like the refutation of a fallacious proposition: though physically small Scotland can constitute a whole world to those with the vision to perceive it.

The Glass of Pure Water

This appeared with a number of 'Hitherto Uncollected' poems in *Collected Poems*. It was written in the 1930s. As in the 'Third Hymn to Lenin' MacDiarmid identifies himself with 'The world's poorest' (line 15). The poet's own position in the 1930s was financially bad enough to give him sympathy with victims of poverty.

Beginning with an account of a dream in which an angel sums up a century of life with a mere gesture, MacDiarmid goes on to assert that the wordless eloquence of poor people is evidence of a huge untapped source of latent intellectual energy and that it is the poet's 'duty' to work towards the liberation of the majority of mankind. The incidental conclusion that Gaeldom could provide a cultural world leadership should be read in connexion with MacDiarmid's statement in *Lucky Poet* that it is his concern 'to get rid of the English Ascendancy and work for the establishment of Workers' Republics in Scotland, Ireland, Wales and Cornwall, and, indeed, make a sort of Celtic Union of Socialist Soviet Republics in the British Isles'.

18] *Sacco and Vanzetti:* Nicolo Sacco and Bartolomeo Vanzetti were Italian immigrants executed in the USA in 1927 on a charge of murder, though radicals have consistently maintained that they were martyred for their anarchist beliefs.

Facing the Chair

This poem appeared in *The Scotsman* for 9 November 1968 and was subsequently included in the *Selected Poems* published by Penguin Books in 1970.

It was composed after MacDiarmid had moved to his cottage in Biggar in 1951. 'Facing the Chair' confronts the reader with a measure of responsibility for the existence of inhumanity in the world. The poet implies a causal link between the execution of innocents and 'the unconcern of men and women' (line 9) who are content to live their own lives while others suffer death.

14] *la grande amitié des choses crées:* the harmony of all created things.

Bracken Hills in Autumn

This poem came to light in 1961 when the holograph manuscript was discovered in an antiquarian bookshop in Mayfair by Mr Colin Hamilton who subsequently published it as a pamphlet (Edinburgh, 1962). MacDiarmid tells me it constitutes a 'memory of my Border youth' and in *Lucky Poet* he says of that youth:

'My earliest impressions are of an almost tropical luxurance of Nature – of great forests, of honey-scented heather hills, and moorlands infinitely rich in little-appreciated beauties of flowering, of animal and insect life, of strange and subtle relationships of water and light . . . I have been "mad about Scotland" ever since.'

from 'In Memoriam James Joyce'

In Memoriam James Joyce was published in 1955 and rapidly gained a reputation as MacDiarmid's most difficult poem. It is at times multilingual and stridently propagandist but passages like the present excerpt stand out all the more brilliantly for that. MacDiarmid wrote this passage after hearing of the death of Yeats in 1939 and it serves here to define his own artistic credo.

ROBERT GRAVES

In the fifth of his Clark Lectures Robert Graves stated his attitude to poetry in his usual no-nonsense manner: 'Personally, I expect poems to say what they mean in the simplest and most economical way; even if the thought they contain is complex.' For Graves simplicity means an unostentatious mastery of traditional English verse-forms and economy means a minimum of verbal ornament and absence of rhetoric. His own poetic practice conforms to his precepts and he has managed in his best poems to produce works of great beauty that are timeless because they eschew topicality and embrace the permanent.

Graves is a formidable polemicist erudite enough to intimidate many of his enemies. It is likely that he needed a wall of scholarly authority to defend that most fragile of things: love-poetry, his chosen idiom. Graves is a eulogist of women, believing them to embody inspiration and eternal truth, at least when possessed by the White Moon Goddess. Although he has warned that 'poetry should not be confused with autobiography' there are elements in his life that have shaped his attitude.

Graves's submissive attitude led Randall Jarrell to argue in the *Yale Review*

XLV (Winter, Spring 1956) that the White Goddess was a literary tribute to the personality of Laura Riding. The concept is central to Graves's poetry since the late 1930s. *The White Goddess* was conceived in England during the Second World War, completed in Majorca, and published in 1948. The White Moon Goddess is the Muse, the three stages of womanhood (mother of man, his mate, and his mourner) and the Goddess of the Heavens. At a time when 'the Moon is despised as a burned-out satellite of the Earth' Graves worshipped the Woman in the Moon. Poetry, to Graves, is religious invocation of the White Moon Goddess and he believes that indifference to her means creative death.

In a 1960 'Postscript' to *The White Goddess* Graves argued that 'No Muse-poet grows conscious of the Muse except by experience of a woman in whom the Goddess is to some degree resident.' Whether by increased familiarity with his theme or whether because in his second marriage Graves found a Goddess of flesh and blood, his love-poetry becomes less theoretical and more satisfying:

> 'Your slender body seems a shaft of moonlight
> Against the door as it gently closes.'
>
> 'The Visitation'

For a poet who has claimed – in his essay 'How Poets See' – a mainly tactile apprehension of phenomena ('a perfect memory-sense by touch') that is a remarkably vivid visual image.

'My main theme', Graves wrote in the foreword to *Collected Poems* of 1965, 'was always the practical impossibility, transcended only by a belief in miracle, of absolute love continuing between man and woman.' And, in a selection of his *Poems About Love* (1969), he reflects on 'the main poetic problem: which is how to restore the lost age of love-innocence between men and women'. Although this is an ambitious theme Graves puts technical safety before emotional sensation. His poems persuade by argument rather than overwhelming by effect. He is sensitive and reflective rather than sensuous and demonstrative.

We know from *Goodbye to All That* that 'My poetry-writing has always been a painful process of continual corrections, corrections on top of corrections, and persistent dissatisfaction'; and from his broadcast 'The Poet and his Public' that 'The poem is either a practical answer to [the poet's] problem, or else it is a clear statement of it; and a problem clearly stated is half way to solution.' In his concern for clarity Graves often asks more questions than he answers and a catechistic technique has become one of his most obvious mannerisms:

> 'Is this joy? to be doubtless alive again,
> And the others dead?'
>
> 'The Survivor'

> 'I watch the door as it slowly opens –
> A trick of the night wind?'
>
> 'The Visitation'

> 'The untameable, the live, the gentle,
> Have you not known them?'
>
> 'Through Nightmare'

'Is it of trees you tell, their months and virtues,
   Or strange beasts that beset you,
   Of birds that croak at you the Triple will?'
                                    'To Juan at the Winter Solstice'

And in 'The Straw', after asking three questions in six lines, he says: 'These questions, bird, are not rhetorical.' Rhetoric 'disgusts' Graves, so this is reassuring, yet at times the proliferation of questions can be a mechanical device stopping the flow of the poetry. And Graves's poetry moves, by argument, from observation to conclusion so that confessions of doubt can be enervating.

In many ways Graves seems to be an anachronism: an astrologer in an age of astronomy, a poetic conservative in a time of revolutionary poetic change. None of this would worry Graves however, as he would willingly let other poets search for mere contemporaneity among the stars so long as he was allowed to work by the spiritual light of the moon.

Mid-Winter Waking

This poem, from *Work in Hand* (with Alan Hodge and Norman Cameron, 1942) is a celebration of the return of poetic inspiration and a declaration of love for a woman possessed by the White Goddess. The poet likens himself to a seed prematurely flowering in the 'warm airs that blow/Before the expected season of new blossom' (lines 8–9). In his *Swifter Than Reason* Douglas Day classifies Graves's work into four poetic periods: the Georgian; the war years; the post-war years and association with Laura Riding; and, finally, the discovery of the White Goddess – the essence of femininity – as Muse. It is with this final and richest period that we are concerned in this anthology and 'Mid-Winter Waking' signals the prolific period that followed.

Graves favours syllabic rather than accentual lines – the last line of each stanza here is strictly decasyllabic – and he uses only one rhyme per stanza, matching the third with the fifth lines (principalities/ both my eyes; airs that blow/ lambless go; Spring with me/. . . where to see).

1] *long hibernation:* presumably the Laura Riding years when he was formulating his poetic position.
12] *her hand:* the hand of the woman in whom the Goddess resides.

The Glutton

This poem appeared as 'The Feast' in *No More Ghosts* (1940) before being renamed 'The Glutton' for the *Collected Poems* of 1955. Graves has always had a profound distaste for sex as a purely mechanical means of sensual gratification. In his Foreword to *Poems About Love* he wrote that 'Although aware that man–woman love began as sexual courtship [poets] cannot regard its physical consummation as more than a metaphor for love itself.' Here he creates the metaphor of the love-beast to represent Lust personified, a creature eaten by primitive people.

The Door

This poem, from *Poems 1938–45*, attributes ecstasy to the presence of the Goddess-lover and despair to her absence. When she enters the poet's world is suddenly gloriously expanded; when she leaves the door bangs maddeningly on darkness. The Door itself symbolises a block on the vision which can be removed by love. Cf. 'The Visitation':

> 'Drowning in my chair of disbelief
> I watch the door as it slowly opens'

Through Nightmare

This poem, from *Poems 1938–45*, credits the female mind with the capacity to reach into a fabulous world of timeless truths. Graves advises the sleeper to accept the insights and visionary information gained in the 'lost and moated land' (line 14) she penetrates even though she has to go through nightmare to get there. And though the sleeper is a gentle person in everyday life the dream-experience is evidence of the hidden depths of the feminine principle.

12] *disjointedly:* when a sleeper dreams there is rapid eye movement.

She Tells Her Love While Half Asleep

This apparently straightforward love-poem, from *Poems 1938–45*, describes how the effect of a tender declaration of love is like the stirring of Spring in the earth (cf. 'Mid-Winter Waking'). For Graves, almost any situation has mythical connotations and he uses the song in his novel about Jason and the Argonauts, *The Golden Fleece* (1944): Orpheus sings it to the Argonauts and identifies the 'She' of the title as his lost Eurydice.

To Juan at the Winter Solstice

This is the key poem on the White Moon Goddess theme in *Poems 1938–45*. According to Graves the Sacred King (Sun-King) is killed by his beloved White Moon Goddess each summer solstice and is reborn each winter solstice. This cycle of life and death is implicit in all myths and thus, argues Graves, all myths are variations on the theme of the Sacred King and the White Goddess. In *The White Goddess* he writes:

> 'The test of a poet's vision, one might say, is the accuracy of his portrayal of the White Goddess and of the island over which she rules. The reason why the hairs stand on end, the eyes water, the throat is constricted, the skin crawls and a shiver runs down the spine when one writes or reads a true poem is that a true poem is necessarily an invocation of the White Goddess, or Muse, the Mother of All Living, the ancient power of fright and lust – the female spider or the queen-bee whose embrace is death.'

Title] Juan is the poet's seventh child. The winter solstice is the birthday of the Sacred King.

1] *one story:* the Sacred King as divine victim of the White Goddess.

7] *of trees:* it was by deciphering an enigmatic thirteenth-century Welsh poem *Cad Goddeu* (The Battle of the Trees) and the significance of its tree-alphabet that Graves rediscovered the White Goddess theme.

9] *the Triple will:* the White Goddess is a Triple Goddess:

> 'As Goddess of the Underworld she was concerned with Birth, Procreation and Death. As Goddess of the Earth she was concerned with the

three seasons of Spring, Summer and Winter: she animated trees and plants
and ruled all living creatures. As Goddess of the Sky she was the Moon, in
her three phases of New Moon, Full Moon and Waning Moon' (*The White
Goddess*).

10] *the Zodiac:* its slowly turning cycle contains the symbolic sequence of life,
death and rebirth.

11] *The Boreal Crown:* the constellation *Corona Borealis.* This, the crown of
the North Wind, is the Sacred King's royal purgatory after death, the place
where he awaits resurrection, thus the 'Prison of all true kings' (line 12).

13] *ark again to ark:* at the winter solstice the Sacred King is reborn as a
child floating in an ark.

14] *woman back to woman:* as Triple Goddess, woman gives birth to man,
mates with him, and mourns him after his death.

15] *each new victim:* the Sacred King, as divine victim of the Goddess, must
follow this predetermined pattern – 'The never altered circuit of his fate'
(line 16).

17] *twelve peers:* the signs of the Zodiac.

19] *the Virgin:* Aphrodite, the Love-Goddess, a facet of the White Goddess.
Aphrodite (Gr. 'risen from sea foam') was associated with the sea and often
depicted with a symbolic fish-tail.

22] *a leafy quince:* in her Aphrodite–mermaid incarnation the Goddess
always holds a quince as a love-gift which she gives in exchange for the
Sacred King's life. Thus he 'barters life for love' (line 24).

25] *the undying snake:* according to Orphic and Pelasgian mythology the
Goddess created Ophion, 'the cosmic snake', from Chaos and then mated
with him to form the world, his coils forming the sea.

27] *whose chops with naked sword:* Jason, the Argonaut, sailed in the ocean's
'chops' in search of the Golden Fleece, planted the serpent's teeth, and
seized the Fleece from the teeth of a many-coiled dragon.

28] *black water:* after the seizure of the Fleece, the Argonauts sailed round the
Black Sea in whose reeds they became entangled before battling with the
pursuing Colchians.

32] *The owl hoots:* the hooting owl, announcing the approach of death, is a
facet of the Goddess.

32] *the elder:* the tree of doom, associated with witches and supposed to have
been the Crucifixion tree. Its white flowers make it another aspect of the
Goddess.

33] *Fear:* because the owl hooting from the elder means that the Goddess is
ready to claim her royal victim.

39] *great boar trampled down in ivy time:* October, the ivy month, is the month
of the boar. Myth after myth shows the Sacred King being killed by a boar in
October. The boar is the beast of death, and the year's 'fall' is in the month
of the boar.

40] *her brow:* Graves considers Botticelli's *Birth of Venus* to be an 'exact
icon' of the Goddess as Aphrodite. 'Tall, golden-haired, blue-eyed, pale-
faced, the Love-goddess arrives in her scallop shell' (*The White Goddess*).

42] *nothing promised:* the inversion here means that whatever the eyes promise the Goddess can provide.

The Survivor

This poem, from *Poems and Satires 1951* (1951), alludes to Graves's experience on the Somme, of being reported dead and then surviving the war. It also alludes to the breakup of his first marriage and to his second marriage to a younger woman. Graves is asking how far happiness can be salvaged from a physically or emotionally crushing experience.

1] *To die:* cf.:

'Late that night, Colonel Crawshay came back from High Wood and visited the dressing-station; he saw me lying in the corner, and they told him I was done for. The next morning, July 21st [1916], clearing away the dead, they found me still breathing and put me on an ambulance for Heilly, the nearest field hospital' (*Goodbye to All That*).

7] *the others dead:* cf. 'Then [Colonel Crawshay] made out the official casualty list – a long one, because only eight men were left in the battalion – and reported me "died of wounds" (*Goodbye to All That*).

11] *the double suicide:* the mutual feeling of loss and despair experienced by a couple being separated or divorced. Cf. 'Call it a Good Marriage'.

Counting the Beats

Traditionally, man is supposed to be sad after sexual intercourse, but in Graves's poem, from *Poems and Satires 1951*, he is optimistic about the permanent value of a satisfying love. The woman, on the other hand, is full of anxieties about the approach of death which, she feels, reduces the brief ecstasy of sex to absurdity. This is the dialectic of sex, the dichotomy between female concern and male expedient.

Graves's craftsmanship here makes a fluent theme fit a deceptively simple form. With few variations the poem has a syllabic count of 4.6.10.5. while the first three lines of each stanza are identically rhymed and the final lines of each stanza rhyme with each other.

7] *bleeding to death of time:* Graves is very precise in his imagery and this particular image is literally true, for the blood being pumped through the heart measures the passing of time and when it stops time stops for a particular individual. Cf. the description of rapid eye-movement in the last stanza of 'Through Nightmare'.

6] *slow heart beats:* slow because the moment of ecstasy has passed and the lovers reflect together.

11] *the huge storm:* death.

Questions in a Wood

This poem, from *Poems and Satires 1951*, reminds us how uncaring sex, lust, nauseates Graves, who insists that physical union is but one aspect of love. He cannot accept that his own physical expression of love is the same for the parson and his pallid spouse or the hangman and his whore. Then he remembers that without a shared physical love unhappiness will, like a 'blue hag', destroy them both. It is a theme further treated in 'Call It a Good Marriage'. I remarked, in the introduction to these notes, that Graves is fond of asking questions. This poem is entirely composed of questions. It is written throughout in an *abab* quatrain alternating iambic tetrameter with iambic trimeter.

3] *the same vows:* the marriage vows.

4] *the same door:* the vagina. For them this door is an entrance to a physical ecstasy that soon passes. For Graves the entire personality of woman is a door that opens onto a visionary world, as he shows in 'The Door' and 'The Visitation'.

Dialogue on the Headland

As in 'Counting the Beats', this poem – from *Poems 1953* – shows the woman concerned with an enduring love and the man wrapped up in the ecstatic moment, convinced that 'Whatever happens, this goes on' (line 25). Presumably we are to imagine the lovers walking on the headland after making love nearby.

Spoils

This poem from *Collected Poems 1959* contrasts the tangible spoils of war with the emotionally charged mementos of a love-affair and the word 'spoils' is used to mean both 'booty' and 'things spoiled'. Such is the power of love-charged objects that any attempt to hide them merely makes them more insistently present in the mind.

Call It a Good Marriage

By way of contrast to his poems condemning lust, this poem, from *Collected Poems 1959*, comments on the tragedy of a marriage made out of social compatibility rather than the whole gamut of love.

The Face in the Mirror

This is a self-portrait from *Collected Poems 1959*. After presenting himself as someone of rather eccentric physiognomy Graves asks himself why he can presume to 'court the queen' – that is, woo the Muse and make love to the woman in whom the Muse resides. The syllabic count is 11.11.6.11.11. with the central line of each three stanzas rhyming and being sandwiched between a rhymed quatrain.

The Visitation

This poem, from *More Poems, 1961*, presents the beloved as an object of natural beauty and as a manifestation of the White Moon Goddess. The poem can be read and appreciated without reference to the Goddess; Graves has achieved an autonomous lyric that nevertheless repays deeper study. The poem is both a description of his beloved and a confession of amazed delight as a poet at being chosen once more by the Goddess.

4] *a shaft of moonlight:* the lunar ray of the Goddess.

11] *heather-flow:* 'The heather is the midsummer tree, red and passionate, and is associated with mountains and bees. The Goddess is herself a queen bee about whom male drones swarm in midsummer' (*The White Goddess*).

Hedges Freaked with Snow

'Hedges Freaked with Snow' is the third of 'Three Songs for the Lute' from *New Poems 1962* (1962). Appropriately, considering the instrument it was conceived for, it is a love-poem of deep melancholy.

Song: Dew Drop and Diamond

Perhaps the finest of a series of songs from *Poems 1965–1968*. Graves had discovered that he prefers the soft reflective type of woman to the intellectually sharp and brittle sort.

Fact of the Act

This poem, from *Poems 1965–1968*, is poetic advice to a young virgin who dreams of her first engagement in the act of love. Graves warns her that, far from being 'Honey-sweet' (line 12), the act of love is a primitive reminder of the dawn of man and a confrontation of flesh that questions just how far personality transcends physical gratification.

6] *holm-oak:* 'the evergreen oak which rules the waning part . . . in Cornwall the compound *glas-tann* ("green sacred tree") meant evergreen holm-oak . . . The holly rules the eighth month, and eight as the number of increase is well suited to the month of the barley harvest, which extends from July 8th to August 4th' (*The White Goddess*).
21] *the locked gate:* the state of virginity.

Within Reason

This poem, from *Poems 1965–1968*, resuscitates the meaning of the decayed metaphor 'within reason'. By exploring her mind and body the beloved has literally moved 'within reason' to attain a serene wisdom. Though available to women this wisdom is denied to literary men who vicariously probe others' minds beyond the realm of reason. Graves, a literary man himself, has the humility to accept the wisdom of the beloved and asks only to share it.

WILLIAM EMPSON

The earliest poems of William Empson lie outside the period defined by the title of this anthology but, despite his early undergraduate celebrity as a critic-poet, and the reference in Leavis's *New Bearings*, he did not emerge as a force in English poetry until 1950 when John Wain contributed an essay, 'Ambiguous Gifts', to the fortieth and final number of *Penguin New Writing*, which praised Empson's intellectual power and technical control and ended:

'For the plain fact is that many of the reputations which today occupy the poetic limelight are such as would crumble immediately if poetry such as Empson's, with its passion, logic, and formal beauty, were to become widely known. If the day ever comes when poems like "This Last Pain", "Manchouli", "Note on Local Flora", are read and pondered and their lessons heeded, it will be a sad day for many of our punch-drunk random "romantic" scribblers. But I suppose it never will.'

Wain supposed wrong, for his essay instigated a fashion for Empson's poetry and the Movement poets, who were announced in *The Spectator* in 1954 prior to their appearance in Robert Conquest's anthology *New Lines* of 1956, were pleased to pay him homage as founding father.

The early poems, in *Poems* (1935), combine intellectual excitement and scientific imagery in a novel way. Empson's poetic master was Donne, and his theoretical mentor I. A. Richards, who had said in *Science and Poetry* (1926) that the really meaningful contemporary poetry would 'be such as could not have been written in another age than our own. It must have sprung in part from the contemporary situation.'

The contemporary situation that Empson found himself in was scientifically inclined and determined to replace metaphysical speculation by empirical rigour. Russell and Wittgenstein had made Cambridge a centre of logical and linguistic analysis. G. E. Moore had instructed I. A. Richards in the close examination of propositions and statements. And Richards, with *Principles of Literary Criticism* (1926) behind him, encouraged Empson to exercise his analytical gifts on imaginative literature. As *Seven Types of Ambiguity* (1930) showed, Empson was a master of the art of scrutinising the structural and linguistic elements of poetry.

Because *Seven Types of Ambiguity* was published five years before *Poems*, it has been assumed that Empson wrote his poems to illustrate his critical theory of ambiguity. Certainly his own poems do contain ambiguities, puns, allusions, syntactical complexities, and he has admitted, in his notes to *The Gathering Storm* (1940) that 'a sort of puzzle interest is part of the pleasure that you are meant to get from the verse'. But Empson's early poems are not abstruse exercises, they are deeply considered statements combining the Metaphysical manner of Donne and the anti-metaphysical matter of modern science.

Technically Empson's poetry is in two manners: the work in *Poems* is syntactically convoluted, the work in *The Gathering Storm* (1940) is lucid and, at times, utterly plain. In conversation with Christopher Ricks, in the Empson number of *the Review*, Empson preferred to distinguish between his two books thematically rather than stylistically:

'The first book, you see, is about the young man feeling frightened, frightened of women, frightened of jobs, frightened of everything, not knowing what he could possibly do. The second book is all about politics, saying we're going to have this second world war and we mustn't get too frightened about it.'

In the same conversation Empson said his best poems were 'all on the basis of expressing an unresolved conflict'. The presentation of contradictions is at the heart of his poetry and much of its so-called difficulty comes from his own reluctance to come down on one side or the other.

Because this lack of facile commitment is more obvious in the later poems Empson has been accused of a failure of nerve. The surface-texture of the Metaphysical poems was taken to be their substance and when the later poems emphasised content at the expense of form Empson exposed himself to his critics. The injustice of this is soon evident when we consider the depth and honesty of the poems in *The Gathering Storm*. The early Empson disguised his fears in an often impenetrably difficult style. The older Empson preferred to take his own advice, 'learn a style from a despair', and discard the stylistic protection of the early manner.

In *Science and Poetry* Richards had contrasted the beguiling and emotive pseudo-statements of poetry with scientific statements of fact. The early Empson had attempted to combine the two, so that in the same poem we find 'our bullet boat light's speed by thousands flies' and a girl who 'Milks between rocks a straddled sky of stars' ('Camping Out'). He almost always uses metre (almost always iambic pentameter) and rhyme (almost always a restricted number of rhymes) because he believes, as he said in *Seven Types of Ambiguity*, that

'The demands of metre allow the poet to say something which is not normal colloquial English, so that the reader thinks of the various colloquial forms which are near to it, and puts them together . . . It is for such reasons as this that poetry can be more compact, while seeming to be less precise, than prose.'

Though deeply English, Empson has resuscitated exotic forms like the villanelle (which Dylan Thomas used magnificently in 'Do not go gentle into that good night').

The avoidance of extremes is a negative message, perhaps, but in Empson's poems it takes on a positively dynamic force. It is this power to persuade through the irresistible beauty of his verse that makes Empson a minor poet of great contemporary importance. There is, after all, only one of him.

To an Old Lady

From *Poems* (1935). The old lady is the moon; this suppressed identification allows the poet to address the planet in an extended metaphor which is like a long-drawn out 'conceit' in the Metaphysical poetry of the seventeenth century. Rocket-travel to the moon is rejected as a pointless intrusion; since we have no shared religious beliefs to take with us to another planet, we come merely as intruders, not missionaries. She is to be respected as perfectly other. The comparison with the old age of a virgin woman gives much of the imagery a sexual connotation.

1] *Ripeness is all:* From *King Lear* v. ii. The idea carries on in 'wasted' (line 2), 'failing crops' (line 20), 'inaccessible' (line 22).

5] Other planets have names of divinities; earth does not. This implies that earth has no divine power, is inhabited by unbelievers. We have therefore no religious ground for a leap to the moon, would be clumsy intruders.

13–16] The comparison takes over: the old maid's womanly gifts are used in old age on domestic trivia. The antithesis is like Pope in style.

17–20] The planet revolves regularly in its orbit, as the old maid leads a life of settled precision. 'Confine' is a suppressed reference to 'confinement' – giving birth. Empson notes 'the unconfined surface of her sphere is like the universe in being finite but unbounded, but I failed to get that into the line'. The waxing of the moon is like a pregnancy which never brings forth; is related to tides, and to the cycle of fertility in women's bodies ('her sole control').

20–5] The sun is source of life, and the moon shares the sun with the earth. But she appears when he is hidden: they bring nothing to birth in her.

Camping Out

Empson's note to this poem from *Poems* reads: 'The intention behind the oddness of the theme, however much it may fail, was not to be satirical but to show indifference to satire from outside.' Toothpaste from a girl's mouth, spat into a lake, makes the reflections of the stars expand: a God-like gift because daylight has made the real stars invisible. As the girl straddles the pool of toothpaste stars she is reflected like a Madonna with a circle of stars around her head. Our ability to think imaginatively at the speed of light transforms the stars into aspects of the divine. Empson's metrical expertise is shown in his ability to sustain this complicated insight into perception by using only two rhymes per stanza (*aabaaab*).

1–3] Empson's note reads: 'She gives the lake its pattern of reflected stars, now made of toothpaste, as God's grace allows man virtues that nature wouldn't; the mist and pale (pale light or boundary) of morning have made it unable to reflect real stars any longer.'
8] *soap tension:* Empson's note reads: '*Soap tension* is meant to stand for the action of surface tension between more and less concentrated soap solutions which makes the specks fly apart.'
12] *light's speed:* the velocity of light through space is 186,000 miles per second.
13] *their frame unties:* Empson's note reads: '*Their frame unties:* if any particle of matter got a speed greater than that of light it would have infinite mass and might be supposed to crumple up round itself the whole of space-time – "a great enough ecstasy makes the common world unreal".'

Arachne

Empson has a predilection for exotic verse-forms and this poem, from *Poems*, shows him using the *terza rima* with characteristic panache. 'Arachne' presents the world as a bubble of antitheses – birth/death; one/many; reality/illusion; solidity/emptiness; bird/fish; god/beast – on whose surface man must continually dance like a spider, not breaking the surface. This bubble needs a minimum of two molecules to survive, as the world needs a minimum of two people, and as the female spider needs the male. Empson paraphrases the poem thus:

'Man lives between the contradictory absolutes of philosophy, the one and the many, etc. As king spider man walks delicately between two elements, avoiding the enemies which live in both. Man must dance, etc. Human society is placed in this matter like individual men, the atoms who make up its bubble.'

Title] Arachne is the Greek word for spider. Empson adds that 'Arachne was a queen spider and disastrously proud.' In Greek mythology Arachne was a Lydian maiden who challenged Athena to compete with her in needle tapestry and who was metamorphosed into a spider for her arrogance.
1] *his caves:* Empson's note reads: 'The caves of cavemen are thought of as by the sea to escape the savage creatures inland.'
5] *bird and fish:* by metaphorically naming man as a spider, Empson gives his

imagery real substance, for a spider has, as a matter of life and death, to avoid bird and fish.

6] *pin-point extremes:* an allusion to the old metaphysical question, how many angels could dance on a pin-point?

8] *Tribe-membrane:* the bubble contains society.

8] *mutual tension:* Empson's note reads: 'The spider's legs push down the unbroken surface of the water like a soft carpet, which brings in the surface-tension idea. The bubble surface is called land, the thin fertile surface of the earth, because the bubble is the globe of the world.'

14] *Hydroptic soap:* Empson's note reads: 'The water saves the soap because the soap alone couldn't make a bubble.'

Letter 1

This is the first of five verse-epistles in *Poems*, all of them using scientific imagery to intensify a declaration of love. It was one of the ambitions of Cambridge critics like I. A. Richards (Empson's theoretical mentor) and F. R. Leavis to eliminate vague romantic gestures from poetry and to substitute verbal precision and intellectual muscle. Empson, with his mathematical training, was the poet best equipped to put this into practice by presenting even his most basic feelings in an idiom that tested the reader's capacity to think analytically.

The poem is in four seven-line stanzas (*ababbcc*) that are remarkably self-contained. Thus the 'Letter' reads like four scientific propositions with just enough in common to suggest they all illuminate the same problem. The construction of a solution is left up to the reader.

2] *The eternal silence:* Pascal's phrase; he had been terrified by that silence, and looked for God as comfort.

3] *net-work without fish:* Empson's note reads:

'The network without fish is empty space which you could measure, lay an imaginary net of co-ordinates over, opposed in verse 3 to the condition when two stars are not connected by space at all; these are compared to two people without ideas or society in common, hence with no "physics" between them.'

9–10] *glances/Through gulfs:* light through space; and the communication between people.

12] *the thread:* Empson's note reads: 'The *thread* was meant to be "the unlikely chance that we never learn to talk to them by radio and thus find out that they are not wise".'

17–18] Empson's note reads: 'Lacking a common life-blood shared from one totem (showman because tragic hero) they [i.e. the two people without ideas or society in common] are connected by no idea whose name is derived from "physics".' Physics is about bodies, in the general sense.

19] *non-Euclidean predicament:* it was the non-Euclidean geometry of Einstein that led to a new model of space.

21–8] The sun, like other stars, converts hydrogen to helium in a perpetual series of nuclear explosions. If it expanded to become a red giant the heat would burn out life on our planet. That is, we need to be related together in an orbit, our love for each other; not to fly apart or burn each other up.

24] *your circumambient foreboding:* Empson glosses this as meaning 'the empty space round him which connects us to him and which you fear'.

Legal Fiction

This poem, from *Poems*, examines, as J. H. Willis puts it in his monograph on Empson, 'another of man's illusions, the legal fiction that he who owns the soil also owns the sky above and the depths beneath'. In a kind of geometry, imaginary lines are projected upwards as 'long spokes' (line 1) to heaven, and down to the centre of earth, where they meet in the 'Pointed exclusive conclave' (line 10). This is then brilliantly compared to the expanding lighthouse beam, and the dark central cone of the candle's shadow. Helen Gardner, in her anthology *The Metaphysical Poets* (1957), defined a conceit as 'a comparison whose ingenuity is more striking than its justness, or, at least, is more immediately striking'. Here Empson invents a striking conceit by comparing the mind to a piece of private property and applying legalistic rights to it.

Empson's love of the pun is exemplified in these four tightly-packed quatrains: 'short stakes' (line 1) are both unambitious wagers and poles hammered into the ground; 'real estate' (line 2) is both property and authentic realm; owners are both property-owners (damned to an exclusive – both rarefied and fashionable – hell) and imaginative individuals. Empson's love of antitheses is also in evidence in the ingenious oxymorons: 'high flat' and 'nomad citizen' (line 3). By dressing up his thought in such glittering linguistic clothes Empson both dignifies the concept of ownership and, by showing the superiority of imagination to legislation, satirises the narrow legalistic concept of property.

This Last Pain

Empson's notes record that 'The idea of ["This Last Pain" from *Poems*] is that human nature can conceive divine states which it cannot attain.' J. H. Willis glosses the poem thus:

'Man's despair, and Empson's, is the "last pain" of mental or spiritual anguish, far worse than the physical. In Christian theology, as Dante and Boethius knew, it is reserved for those damned souls who are able to understand, but not to experience, the ultimate, beatific bliss of God. In secular terms such bliss resides in a system of values or beliefs which are no longer possible. Modern man is painfully conscious of his desires and tortured by his frustrated expectations. Cut away from his beliefs by scientific, rationalistic knowledge, man is faced with the problem of retaining empty values and of pretending that they mean something. The agonizing reality of contemporary life can only be faced with stylish despair, with an "edifice of form", which may or may not lead to salvation but may transform the pain to something resembling grace.'

6] *her happiness:* the soul's happiness.

7] *He's safe:* man is safe.

9] In his *Tractatus Logico-Philosophicus* (1921) Wittgenstein said: 'Was denkbar ist, ist auch möglich' (3. 02). Empson translates this literally for the ninth line of his poem.

10] *had not dreamt of you:* humorous refutation of Wittgenstein, for 'you' occurred although not conceived by Wittgenstein. This brilliant wit is probably the most startling feature of the early Empson.

11] *But wisely:* Empson's note reads:

'*But wisely:* "it is good practical advice, because though not every ideal that can be imagined can be achieved, man can satisfy himself by pretending that he has achieved it and forgetting that he hasn't". This touches Wittgenstein neither as a philosophical argument nor as a personal remark . . .Wittgenstein is relevant only because such feelings have produced philosophies different from his.'

13–20] Empson glosses these lines thus: '"As the crackling of thorns under a pot, so is the laughter of a fool." A watched pot never boils, and if it boiled would sing. The folly which has the courage to maintain careless self-deceit is compared to the mock-regal crown of thorns.'

19] *from pan to fire:* Empson is fond of exploring the possibilities implied by proverbial wisdom. Here he restores substance to the expression 'out of the frying pan into the fire' (meaning from discomfort to disaster) and uses the fire as an image of hell. The same thing is going on in the fourth stanza where he plays on the proverb 'a watched pot never boils'.

22] Of this line Empson says: 'By the second mention of hell I meant only Sheol, chaos. It was done somewhere by missionaries onto a pagan bonfire.'

32] *phantoms may keep warm:* Empson probably had in mind Emily Dickinson's definition of art as 'a house that wants to be haunted'.

Homage to the British Museum

This is one of the most straightforward items in *Poems* and as such anticipates the pointed conversational lucidity Empson was to employ in his second collection *The Gathering Storm* (1940). The poet describes a wooden deity with other tiny deities clinging to it, like lice. Very confidently he contains or supports many local creeds. What we have, instead of belief, is a museum where dead beliefs are collected. 'The way out' is both the way out of the museum, and the way forward into a new world-view; but 'we have no road.'

6] *Lice:* pun possibly intended on 'lies'.

15] *pinch of dust:* normally the poet would take religion with a pinch of salt but, as this is a museum, he finds dust more appropriate. 'Our pinch of dust' is also ourselves when dead.

Aubade

This poem from *The Gathering Storm* (1940) shows Empson moving away from the contrived ambiguity of his early Metaphysical style and into a wider subject-matter (with adumbrations of international war taking the place of the scientific framework) and developing a greater clarity of expression: the realistic description in the opening stanza could hardly be more straightforward. In a conversation with Christopher Ricks in *the Review* Empson said that this poem

'is about the sexual situation. When I was in Japan, from 1931 to 1934, it was usual for the old hand in the English colony to warn the young man: don't you go and marry a Japanese because we're going to be at war with Japan within ten years; you'll have awful trouble if you marry a Japanese, and this is what the poem is all about.'

As usual Empson oversimplifies in conversation and G. S. Fraser is not being merely ingenious when he says, in *The Modern Writer and His World* (1953, revised 1964), that 'The earthquake stands in the poem for the general insecurity of modern society – which opens under our feet in wars, slumps, and revolutions, so that our human courage seems unable to face it.' The poem alternates a five-line stanza (*aabab*) with the refrain 'It seemed the best thing to be up and go', and a tercet (*aba*) with the refrain 'The heart of standing is you cannot fly.' These apparently contradictory statements are brought together in the last stanza which utilises both and offers a revolutionary synthesis of their antitheses.

Title] An aubade is a musical announcement of dawn, a sunrise song. It is used ironically here, as the lovers are woken by an earthquake.
1] *the quake:* the Tokyo earthquake of 1931.
15] *solid ground for lying:* implies both a steady surface for repose or love, and justification for mendacity.
18] *he:* relative of the Japanese girl.
31] *the same war:* the Manchurian Incident. In 1931 the Japanese occupied Manchuria and set up the puppet state of Manchukuo. It collapsed with Japan's defeat in 1945.
35] *call no die a god:* worship the avoidance of taking chances.
36] *two aliens:* the English speaker and the Japanese girl.

Ignorance of Death

This poem from *The Gathering Storm* shows Empson in his most casually conversational mood and has all the virtues of his prose-style. There is the easy ability to pass from one subject to another, the sardonic wit ('Communists however disapprove of death/Except when practical' (lines 5–6)), the black humour (about necrophiliacs). Although Empson feels 'blank upon this topic' (line 19) he nevertheless does enough damage to successive dogmatists of death (religious, psychological, political) to kill their arrogance and leave the reader feeling blank from so much refutation. Although the poem is unrhymed the word 'death' is used three times as a line-ending.

Missing Dates

This poem from *The Gathering Storm* is more involved at a personal emotional level than any of the early puzzle-poems. 'Missing Dates' is a lament for an enervating waste of talent. Empson uses an exotic form to contain this personal tragedy – the villanelle, a six-stanza form (five tercets and closing quatrain) using the first and third lines as alternative refrains and rhyming *aba*.

1] *the poison:* the metaphorical poison of wasted time or failure, imagined as an infection.
3] *the waste:* the almost palpable waste caused by inactivity remains to poison the blood-stream.

4] *your system:* there is no physical compulsion to waste life, just as a given social system cannot be blamed for individual failure.

5] *the consequence a life requires:* the achievement that justifies life.

7] *bled an old dog dry:* the blood of an old dog was replaced by the blood of a young dog, yet the old dog was only revived for a month. 'Young dog' implies gaiety and sexual potency. Age, then, is the sum of wastage, not physical decay.

10] *the Chinese tombs:* Empson's note cites a legend that 'a fifth or some such part of the soil of China is given up to ancestral tombs'.

13–14] Without creative energy ('fire') the body is lethargic; with only creative energy ('the complete fire') the body is burned out. Yet one must choose either blankness or endless activity because moderation ('partial fires') means slow wastage.

17] *missing dates:* days lost because not used.

Just a Smack at Auden

In a contribution to a television programme on Auden (reproduced in *the Review*, no. 5 (February 1963)) Empson said

'[the pylon poets] were all at Oxford when I was at Cambridge, that's why as a poet myself I was never able to imitate it properly. You had to be in on the movement from the start . . . I agreed with the pylon poets entirely. I've always felt I ought to make that quite plain whenever I had the opportunity.'

Nevertheless in this poem from *The Gathering Storm* Empson makes the leader of the pylon poets feel the thick edge of his wedge of wit. Auden and his followers are satirised as a bunch of schoolboys gleefully waiting for the world to conform to the apocalyptic predictions of their poems. Technically it is a virtuoso performance with all the line-endings rhyming with the boys 'waiting for the end' and with each stanza sustaining an internal rhyme.

36] *Treason of the clerks:* Julien Benda's 1927 essay *La Trahison des clercs* exposed the tendency of politically-minded intellectuals to submerge their pursuit of truth in the interests of propaganda.

Let it go

This poem appeared in *Collected Poems* (American edition 1949, British edition 1955). It is about the impossibility of ever classifying phenomena clearly enough to arrive at certainties. There are so many possibilities and contradictions that to experience them all in a search for truth would lead to madness. Rather than do this Empson is content with uncertainty ('this deep blankness').

DYLAN THOMAS

Thomas's poetry is incredibly dense in metaphor, and in his early work his images are drawn from sexual connotations and the body. In a letter to Pamela Hansford Johnson (November 1933) Thomas wrote that 'every idea, intuitive or intellectual, can be imaged and translated in terms of the body,

its flesh, skin, blood, sinews, veins, glands, organs, cells or senses', and in a
letter to Glyn Jones (March 1934) he confessed his 'own obscurity is . . .
derived . . . from the cosmic significance of the human anatomy'. Consequently Thomas's early poems are extremely physical and organic, usually
dwelling on sexual penetration, but seeing it as universal, as a force of nature:

> 'A candle in the thighs
> Warms youth and seed and burns the seeds of age;
> Where no seed stirs,
> The fruit of man unwrinkles in the stars,
> Bright as a fig;
> Where no wax is, the candle shows its hairs.'

It will be noticed in that extract from 'Light breaks where no sun shines'
that Thomas uses pararhyme (stirs/stars) and assonantal rhyme (age/hairs)
and he was to adopt this practice continually to avoid any predictability of
sound in his poems. More significantly, for his later development, is his use
of the regular syllabic count of 6.10.4.10.4.10. throughout (with the
exception of the irregular penultimate line of the poem). His preference for
the syllabic count instead of accentual verse enabled him to construct his
poems with a scrupulous attention to their aural impact; he was unsurpassed
as a reader of his own, and other poets', poems.

Perhaps because inspiration came so easily in his adolescence, the mature
artist was suspicious of it. More likely he wanted his work to be as durable as
sculpture, a 'monumental / Argument of the hewn voice' as he put it in
'After the funeral' (lines 36–7). Whatever the reason, Thomas's poetry got
more and more formally complex so that his mature poetry is a lattice-work
of cross-association, a delicate embroidery of interweaving internal rhymes.
For example in 'Over Sir John's hill' the first and second lines of each
stanza rhyme with the middle of line five:

> 'Over Sir John's *hill*,
> The hawk on fire hangs *still* . . .
> And the *shrill* child's play'

While this is going on he is sustaining a rhyme scheme of *aabccbdeaedd* and a
syllabic count of 5.6.14.14.5.1.14.5.14.5.14.14. Whether this is due to
the Welsh bardic tradition or the Celtic love of intricate pattern it effectively
refutes those who criticise Thomas for being all heart and no head. It was his
head that kept his heart in the right place.

His use of metaphor in the mature poems is as carefully worked out as the
form. In his elegy for barren women, 'In the white giant's thigh', he speaks
of the women with 'Their breasts full of honey' (line 38) and four lines
later their breasts are referred to as 'the veined hives'. Now simply to have
used an image like 'the veined hives' without preparing the reader *would* be
wilfully obscure, but Thomas always builds up to images like this. He is
very fond, too, of attributing religious significance to natural phenomena and
this is almost a trademark of the mature poetry:

> 'the round
> Zion of the water bead
> And the synagogue of the ear of corn'
>
> 'A Refusal to Mourn'

'he walked with his mother
Through the parables
Of sun light
And the legends of the green chapels'
                                        'Poem in October'

'the sabbath rang slowly
In the pebbles of the holy streams.'
                                        'Fern Hill'

'I open the leaves of the water at a passage
Of psalms'
                                        'Over Sir John's hill'

This is Thomas's way of seeing the presence of God in man's natural environment.

In the *Note* to his *Collected Poems* Thomas wrote:

'I read somewhere of a shepherd who, when asked why he made, from within fairy rings, ritual observances to the moon to protect his flocks, replied: "I'd be a damn' fool if I didn't!" These poems, with all their crudities, doubts, and confusions, are written for the love of Man in praise of God, and I'd be a damn' fool if they weren't.'

Which is not to say Dylan Thomas was a religious poet in the conventional sense. Like Hopkins he felt the world was charged with the grandeur of God, like Blake he could see the world in a grain of sand, and like Donne his love of life reflected his doubts about death. And then, like Edwin Muir, Thomas saw in rural childhood (experienced in summer holidays) an image of Eden. He began his poetic career with a sexual obsession and ended it with a celebration of the innocence of the child's vision of the world.

Finally I would like to mention Thomas's ability to revitalise popular speech-idioms. He could take an expression like 'one foot in the grave' and make it into a phrase like 'muffle-toed tap / Tap happily of one peg in the thick / Grave's foot' ('After the funeral' (lines 2–4)) or he could give new life to the phrase 'black sheep of the family' by using it in a fresh context as in 'Lament':

'But a black sheep with a crumpled horn'

This not only shows the 'old ram rod' of the poem in disgrace but also conjures up an image of a real sheep with a crumpled horn, which in turn is an image of impotence. Ezra Pound defined an image as 'that which presents an intellectual and emotional complex in an instant of time' and again and again Thomas does just that – memorably. He can take common expressions and build new layers of significance on them. The opening of 'In country sleep' with its contrapuntal references to fairy tales is a virtuoso example of this talent.

After the funeral

This poem, from *The Map of Love* (1940), is an elegy for the poet's aunt Ann Jones on whose dairy farm, Fern Hill, Thomas used to spend summer holidays as a child. This 'ancient peasant aunt', as he called her in a letter to Vernon Watkins, died on 7 February 1933 at the age of seventy. Though the theme interested him he did not complete the poem until 1938 when he was staying with his wife's mother at Ringwood, Hampshire. In forty mainly decasyllabic lines the poet rejects Welsh Nonconformist piety and simultaneously builds his own life-enhancing tribute, a 'monumental / Argument of the hewn voice'.

1–2] This image of the mourners as asinine creatures addicted to the conventions of Nonconformist mourning immediately rejects simulated grief.

2–3] Thomas's poetry utilises popular sayings; the satirical use of 'one foot in the grave' castigates the mourners as at least half in love with death.

4] *blinds:* the pun on window-blinds suggests that the closing of eyes is merely routine.

4] *the teeth in black:* satirical suggestion that if the mourners could arrange it they'd even dress their teeth in black.

5] This startling image suggests that the mourners have been spitting in their sleeves (where they ostentatiously wear their hearts) and then rubbing their eyes in it, again to simulate grief.

6] The sound of the spade wakes up the boy Dylan inside the poet, and brings him to his last judgment of his Aunt, hence line 9 'breaks one bone to light with a judgment clout'.

7–9] The poet imagines himself as a boy again, as he was when he spent summers with Ann. In his sympathy for her he enters the coffin, slits his throat to stay there, and sheds dry leaves like a tree losing something old and withered.

11] In his story 'The Peaches' from *Portrait of the Artist as a Young Dog* Thomas describes Ann Jones's parlour: 'The best room smelt of moth-balls and fur and damp and dead plants and stale, sour air. Two glass cases on wooden coffin-boxes lined the window wall. You looked at the weed-worn vegetable garden through a stuffed fox's legs . . . there was a large oil lamp on the patchwork tablecloth, a Bible with a clasp, a tall vase with a draped woman about to bathe on it, and a framed photograph of Annie, Uncle Jim, and Gwilym smiling in front of a fern-pot.' Thomas wants his poem to bring these dead things to life. Thus in line 24 he refers to 'the ferned and foxy woods' and in closing his elegy looks for life from 'The stuffed lung of the fox' (line 39) and birth from 'the strutting fern' (line 40).

12] *this memorial:* i.e. this poem. The poem is his verbal statue to her. In line 27 it becomes 'this skyward statue' and in lines 36–7 'this monumental/ Argument of the hewn voice'.

14–15] To paraphrase: her heart was so overflowing with love that there was enough to drench the arid world of Wales and enough left to exhaust the sun's heat. It is a metaphysical conceit worthy of Donne.

20] *druid:* in rejecting Welsh puritanism Dylan invokes the ancient order of druids to whom the 'bard' (line 21) was sacred.

22] *wood-tongued:* wordless, disinclined to speak in its own praise.

23] Go over the heads of the chapel folk, an image repeated in line 25.

26] *four, crossing birds:* the image of birds flying in the shape of a cross in the sky is contrasted with the claustrophobic heaven of the 'brown chapel' (line 25). It also anticipates his 'skyward statue' (line 27), a poetic monument that reaches to the heavens far above the bleak thought of a corpse in the ground. In Donne's poem 'The Cross' we find this couplet:

'Look down, thou spiest out crosses in small things,
Look up, thou seest birds raised on crossed wings.'

31–5] To paraphrase: Thomas is aware that the woman would, because of her chapel background, be content with the conventional funeral, but this is because her hands 'Lie with religion' (lie in the sense of both repose and mendacity). He transforms her 'scrubbed and sour humble hands' into 'cloud-sopped marble hands' and 'her threadbare / Whisper' into 'this / Monumental argument of the hewn voice'. And as a monument she will remain enormous over her grave until the stuffed fox speaks and the fern lays seeds, in other words until the Last Judgment implied in lines 6 and 9.

A Refusal to Mourn the Death, by Fire, of a Child in London

During the war years Thomas worked on documentary films and in this poem from *Deaths and Entrances* (1946) he passionately records the death of a child. It is simply constructed with a rhyme scheme of *abcabc* and a syllabic count of 10.5.10.10.5.10. spanning four sentences (though, as always, Thomas deviates from the syllabic pattern when he feels it is sonically justified).

1–13] This long sentence asserts that until the end of time the poet will not weep ('sow my salt seed') over the death. By making the darkness 'mankind making / Bird beast and flower / Fathering and all humbling' (a ten-word epithet) Thomas alludes to the creation of the world in Genesis. When the end is come the poet looks forward to a new beginning and a religion present in nature ('the round / Zion of the water bead', 'the synagogue of the ear of corn') when he and the child will be reborn. Hence, of course, the pointlessness of mourning.

19–24] Now the child is dead, those '(life?)long friends' who have vegetated in the earth welcome her to a natural transformation that grows with each generation: 'The grains beyond age, the dark veins of her mother'. The river too is part of this process and accepts it because 'After the first death, there is no other.' This last line has caused much comment from critics who want to know whether it means (1) there is nothing after death (2) after the first death there is immortality (3) after the impact of the first death on earth the others do not matter. While it would be impudent to ascribe one meaning specifically to the line – for if Thomas had wanted he could have specified the authorised version – the logic of the poem does seem to support meaning (2). For the poem is saying he will not mourn the child 'until' the end of the world as we know it. Then, as he enters again a new world, the child will be reborn.

Poem in October

This was one of Thomas's own favourites and has remained one of his most popular pieces. It was completed in 1944 in celebration of his thirtieth birthday and is set in the Laugharne seascape. 'Poem in October' is in seven 10-line stanzas with the syllabic count 9.12.9.3.5.12.12.5.3.9 and further textural unity is achieved by alliteration ('*h*eaven . . . *h*earing . . . *h*arbour . . . *h*eron'), assonantal rhyme (beckon/second) and full rhyme (apples/chapels, burning/turning). The narrative logic of the poem is straightforward. The poet is walking on a drizzly October morning in the fishing village of Laugharne, thinking about his birthday. Suddenly 'the weather turned around' in his mind and he sees the boy he was playing in summer and watching the world with a child's vision of natural beauty.

3-4] *heron | Priested shore:* in Dylan Thomas's poetry the heron is holy. In this poem and in 'Over Sir John's hill' the heron is a priest.

12] *birds of the winged trees:* transferred epithet.

25] *the hill:* Sir John's hill.

40] *the weather turned around:* suddenly in the 'rainy autumn' among the 'Pale rain' he remembers the childhood summers he enjoyed when a child.

48-50] For Thomas religion is manifest in natural objects. In 'In country sleep' he says 'The country is holy' and here the 'green chapels' are the woods (unlike the 'brown chapel' of 'After the funeral') and the parables are perceived in nature not in bible-black books. Cf. these lines with the images in 'A Refusal': 'the round / Zion of the water bead / And the synagogue of the ear of corn'; or 'the nunneries and domes of leaves', 'the rain telling its beads' of 'In country sleep'. Thomas's church is nature.

51] *twice told:* once by the child, then by the poet.

55-6] *listening | Summertime of the dead:* it is not the time of the dead, but its summertime, when nature seems alive and listening to the vision of child-hood, 'the mystery' of line 58.

63] *long dead child:* the poet as a boy. Cf. the 'desolate boy' of 'After the funeral'.

67] *leaved with October blood:* his mind returns from childhood as his eyes see the leaves lying like blood on the ground.

68-70] The hope that he will still be in Laugharne in one year's time.

The Hunchback in the Park

This poem was published in *Deaths and Entrances* though the original idea was drafted as early as 1932. The park is Cwmdonkin Park where Thomas played as a child, and the Hunchback was a real character.

Do not go gentle into that good night

A villanelle for his father who died on 16 December 1952 aged eighty-six and whom Dylan was to survive by only one year. As early as 1934 D. J. Thomas had received treatment for cancer of the throat and the disease transformed him from a dominant, awe-inspiring local figure (the Senior English Master in the Grammar School) into a diffident old man waiting for death. In a letter to a friend, enclosing the poem, Thomas said 'The only person I can't show the little enclosed poem to is, of course, my father, who doesn't know he's dying.' Thomas respected his father and did not want him to accept the inevitability of death so serenely.

The poem has a simple logic. Stanza one asserts that old men should not accept death but should 'rage' against it. Then in the next four stanzas, respectively, the poet gives the examples of 'wise men', 'good men', 'Wild men', 'Grave men' – none of whom 'go gentle into that good night'. There-fore, the conclusion in the final stanza reiterates the initial assertion: D. J. Thomas should – like the wise, the good, the wild, the grave – 'rage against the dying of the light'.

Fern Hill

As a child Thomas spent his summer holidays with his aunt Ann Jones on her dairy farm in Carmarthenshire, Fern Hill. This poem is his most ecstatic, not a memory but a vivid recreation of childhood. It has six 9-line stanzas with an assonantal rhyme scheme of *abcdeabcd* and a basic syllabic count of 14.14.9.6.9.14.14.9.9. Though the final product seems wonderfully affirmative and spontaneous there were more than 200 worksheets of 'Fern Hill' before the poet was satisfied.

3] *dingle:* a favourite word of the poet's (meaning wooded valley or hollow).
4] *Time:* in Thomas's later poetry Time is personified as a Thief who waits to rob the child of his visionary innocence. In 'In country sleep' the Thief is confronted, but in 'Fern Hill' Thomas is grateful to Time who let him 'hail and climb / Golden in the heydays of his eyes'.
7] *below a time:* another example of Thomas's use of popular idioms (once upon a time); here it emphasises the timelessness of the child's vision.
30–6] Like Muir, Thomas recovered Eden ('it was Adam and maiden') in the scenes of his childhood. These six lines have an uncanny resemblance to the mood of Muir's poem 'The Horses' yet I think this is due to coincidence of insight rather than to the influence of one man on the other.
51] *fled from the childless land:* i.e. fled from the timeless vision of childhood; with his awareness of Time the child becomes conscious of his mortality (a theme developed in 'In country sleep').

A Note on In Country Heaven

At the end of his life Dylan Thomas was planning a long poem to be called *In Country Heaven* of which three sections were completed: 'In country sleep', 'Over Sir John's hill', and 'In the white giant's thigh'.

In these poems there is a concern with death: the death of innocence in 'In country sleep', the death of the birds in 'Sir John's hill', and the death of conception in 'In the white giant's thigh'. Thomas, in his *Collected Poems*, put the poems in the order they appear here, though there is no certainty that this would have been the final order.

In country sleep

Though this poem is set in Wales, in the house in Laugharne, it was completed on an Italian holiday in Spring 1947 when the whole family were living in a villa at Mosciano overlooking the Tuscan hills. Section I contains nine 7-line stanzas rhyming *abcbaac* with a basic syllabic count of 12.12.12.12. 4.12.12; section II contains eight 6-line stanzas rhyming *abbcca* with a basic syllabic count of 13.13.13.4.13.13. The poem is a prayer for Thomas's daughter, Aeron, that she might retain a child's vision of the world, that timeless vision of Eden which Thomas tried to recreate in his mature poems (and succeeded in doing so memorably in 'Fern Hill'). He has read the child to sleep and imagines her dreaming of Little Red Riding Hood, Hansel and Gretel, Goldilocks, Robin Hood, Sleeping Beauty, etc. (allusions to these tales are woven into the first section of the poem). He tells her not to fear the frightening aspects of these tales for she is 'shielded by fern / And flower of country sleep' (lines 17–18) and 'The country is holy' (line 39). The real enemy is the Thief, Time, who will make her aware of her mortality and steal her faith in a whole and beautifully ordered world. Therefore he affirms the holiness of nature and finally asserts that she will wake safe from the Thief, her faith 'deathless as the outcry of the ruled sun' (line 111). It is a father's plea that his daughter will not lose the beauty and innocence of childhood.

1] *Never and never:* introduces the mood of the prayer ('For ever and ever') as line 107 'Ever and ever' closes it.

1] *my girl:* the poet's daughter Aeron was born 3 March 1943, so she was four when the poem was completed.

1] *riding far and near:* in her dreams.

2] *hearthstone tales:* the fairy tales (like 'the hobnail tales' of line 10) with which the child has been 'spelled asleep'.

4–16] Allusions to the frightening aspects of fairy tales with those alarming metamorphoses (wolf in a hood, swine into prince, etc.) which the poet tells his daughter to ignore, for she will not end up 'wooed / And staved, and riven'.

17] *shielded by fern:* the countryside is a charm against irrational fear.

21–2] *tolled to sleep by the stern / Bell:* punning again, Thomas alludes to Donne's *Devotions*: 'Any death diminishes me, because I am involved in Mankind; And therefore never send to know for whom the bell tolls; it tolls for thee.' The 'stern bell', which reappears in line 51, is a signal for death.

27–35] To show how holy the country is Thomas piles sacramental image on sacramental image until the wood seems like a cathedral in which everything is blessed: 'angel', 'saint's cell', 'nunneries and domes of leaves', 'three Marys', '*Sanctum sanctorum*' (the holy of holies), 'the rain telling its beads', 'the lord's-table'. In this kind of writing the accumulation of associated images transcends conventional syntax.

38] *the Thief:* Time. I base this identification of the Thief on the evidence of Thomas's imagery in poems like 'Grief thief of time' through variations on that image up to and including 'Fern Hill'.

39] *The country is holy:* the central proposition of the poem, reminiscent of Blake's belief that 'every thing that lives is Holy'.

44–5] *under linen and thatch / And star:* protected three ways, by the blankets, by the roof, and, above that, by the star, symbol of faith.

50–63] The Thief, Time, falls: like snow, rain, hail, mist, dew, leaves, apple seed. The passage also invokes the Fall of Man in Eden and seems to suggest that Time enters into us and makes us aware of the Christian agony 'the yawning wound at our sides', whereas a child's view of Christ is gentle.

64–81] The exclamations, which simulate the sound of nature in the dark wood, warn of the approach of Time. The intense vision of nature given here is the alternative to Time.

88–95] The child in sleep resembles a dead person, and death makes the stern bell toll and lets Time descend on the body; yet the child's heartbeat signifies the persistence of life.

95] *the wound in her side:* an echo of line 62 ('the yawning wound at our sides'), reminding us that Time flowers in the body to make us aware of the agony of life (personified by Christ's crucifixion) rather than its joy.

99–111] The sense of these syntactically difficult lines is that he (i.e. Time) comes to steal the child's faith (which is that Christ comes to her each night in prayer – 'He comes') and to take her faith (which is that Christ comes for his own, 'unsacred', sake to her) in order 'to leave her in the lawless sun', i.e. leave her in a world without order. Time takes away the child's belief that everything is holy. Time introduces doubt into the child's world. Thomas however insists that Christ will come to her every night and will continue to do so, despite the Thief. And because of this her faith will endure. Like the enigmatic ending of 'A Refusal to Mourn' the closing stanzas of 'In country sleep' are open to any number of interpretations, of which mine is but one. In this poem Thomas seemed to be aspiring to the condition of music, a wordless eloquence that would suggest meanings to the reader rather than spell them out.

Over Sir John's hill

As Daniel Jones says in his edition of *The Poems of Dylan Thomas* 'In Laugharne, Carmarthenshire, where Thomas lived, Sir John's hill overlooks the estuary at a point to the east where the river Towy enters it. The whole area is a haunt of water-birds and birds of prey.' The poem is in five 12-line stanzas rhyming *aabccbdeaedd* with a syllabic count of 5.6.14.14.5.1.14.5. 14.5.14.14 (with occasional deviations). In the poem Thomas imagines the hill as a judge (with 'a black cap of jack- / Daws' (lines 14–15)) pronouncing sentences of death on the birds. The 'hawk on fire' (line 2) is the gallows where the birds are executed. As a judge the hill is 'just' (line 15) because the birds have been 'led-astray' (line 43) and the sentence is carried out. However the poet, as witness to the scene, and the heron as priest, ask for mercy because of the songs the birds produced from 'their breast of whistles' (line 43).

2] *hawk on fire:* it hangs in the sunset.

2] *hangs still:* dangles statically and also is still there as hangman. A typically brilliant pun.

3–4] The words 'hoisted', 'drop' and 'pulls' reinforce the image of the hawk as a hangman with his gallows, rope and trapdoor.

7] *swansing:* sing, as swans are said to do, before death.

9] *tyburn:* Tyburn was the historic place of execution in London.

10] *noosed hawk:* develops the imagery of the hawk as executioner.

11] *the fishing holy stalking heron:* in Thomas's poetry the heron is always holy, a priest (cf. the 'heron / Priested shore' in 'Poem in October').

12] *tilted headstone:* the head of the heron-priest bows in acknowledgment of the death.

14–15] The judging just hill dons a black cap to pronounce sentence of death.

15] *gulled birds:* duped birds.

16] *halter:* a rope for hanging criminals. The birds are, of course, 'led-astray'.

19] *the elegiac fisherbird:* the heron.

21–2] Cf. the nursery rhyme

'O what have you got for dinner, Mrs Bond?
There's beef in the larder, and ducks in the pond.

> Crying, Dilly, dilly, dilly, dilly, dilly, come to be killed
> For you must be stuffed, and my customers filled.'

23–4] The poet enters as witness to the execution and sees images of forgiveness in his religion of nature.

40–7] As witness the poet asks for mercy on the birds for the 'soul's song' they produced from 'their breast of whistles'. Though 'led-astray' they deserve forgiveness and a life after death for their songs. It is possible to read into this an autobiographical plea, for Dylan Thomas was a bit of a 'led-astray' bird who achieved immortality through his 'soul's song'.

51] *snow:* the feathers of the dead birds drift down like snow.

57] *and I:* i.e. and I (as well as the heron) make music.

In the white giant's thigh

This poem is an elegy for barren women, in fifteen regular quatrains (*abab*) irregularly arranged. The White Giant is a Welsh landmark said to convey fertility, and Thomas used it as the setting for this poem in which long-dead country women, childless in life, long in their death to conceive. The poet recollects their love-lives and asks them to

> 'Teach me the love that is evergreen after the fall leaved
> Grave, after Belovéd on the grass gulfed cross is scrubbed
> Off by the sun'

2] *conceiving moon:* conceiving because of the menstrual cycle (an image much favoured by Joyce, one of Dylan's favourite modern writers) and because in line 16 we learn that the women loved 'in the after milking moonlight' hoping to conceive.

4] *barren as boulders:* childless as stones.

5] *to labour:* i.e. to labour in childbirth.

5] *lay down:* a pun – they died long ago, also they lay down long ago in sexual embrace though no child came of it.

7] *waded bay:* men and boys wade in the bay and the women pray for their seed to flow into them.

8] Even their tombstones are ruined; they have nothing to survive them.

12–26] A description of the love affairs of the women in winter 'all ice leaved', at the haymaking (again Thomas draws on the sexual connotations of a popular saying: make hay while the sun shines), or after the milking. They were loved by the randy swineherd with their flesh spreadeagled under the roof of his sty, or roughly loved in the orchard.

27–8] An exquisite image meaning that in their ecstasy they were as soft as a lake that ripples like a harp as a stone enters into it. The stone reminds us they are 'barren as boulders'.

29–36] W. Y. Tindall in his *A Reader's Guide to Dylan Thomas* (1962) writes of this poem: 'When the barren girls came hopefully to the Giant, Thomas told me, they expected boys to jump from the bushes, where they had lain in wait, to serve the Giant's promise [of fertility]. Boys and girls did what they could to foster life, but their efforts, however lively and diverting, were fruitless.' Waiting in the bushes they heard the countryside prepare for winter.

37–9] They were used to rough and ready love, like gander and goose, and were bounced in a farm cart ('gambo') in a cowhouse ('shippen').

38] *Their breasts full of honey:* this image prepares us for line 42 where their breasts are 'veined hives'.

42–3] This parenthesis contains the tragic element of the poem. Though the girls were as simple as characters in a child's tale (Mother Goose – associated with the 'gooseskin winter' of line 12 and 'butter fat goosegirls' of line 37) their cupboard was 'barren and bare' and like Jack's Jill they tumbled down but finished with an empty bucket. They bore no children, remained barren as 'a boulder of wives'.

Lament

In this dramatic monologue in five 12-line stanzas (rhyming *abcdabcdefef*) an old man on his deathbed remembers his adolescence (stanza 1), manhood (stanza 2), maturity (stanza 3), old age (stanza 4) and finally laments the fact that he is dying amongst 'all the deadly virtues' (line 60). Like 'After the funeral' it ridicules Welsh Nonconformist morality, though where the Ann Jones poem was elegiac this poem has a bawdy panache and a catalogue of sensual delights.

2] *black spit:* the disgrace of the community. This image is repeated in the second line of each stanza as the speaker becomes 'the black beast', 'the black cross' before he gets his deserts ('serve me right as the preachers warn') in the form of the 'black reward' of a 'Sunday wife'.

3] *the old ram rod:* this describes both the lusty protagonist of the poem and his sexual organ with which he identifies.

4] *gooseberry wood:* in his boyish imagination to find babies under the gooseberry bushes.

7] *Donkeys' common:* Cwmdonkin Park, as *cwmdonkin* is Welsh for donkey common.

10–12] He longed to ruin the respectable wives and leave them in grief. Of course, the poem concludes with exactly the opposite situation when he is married to a 'Sunday wife'.

12] *coal black:* the colour of Welsh sin, or so Thomas would have us believe by the use of the colour at the end of every stanza.

42–8] Exhausted by sex and riotous living he feels the onset of impotence ('crumpled horn', 'limp time') so in desperation he thrusts his soul (which he identifies with his sexual organ with its 'blind, slashed eye') into the darkness to find a companion.

54] *a Sunday wife:* a respectable, God-fearing, neighbour-respecting, chapel-going woman.

57–60] On his deathbed, no longer a threat to the women of the community, he awaits a respectable death as 'all the deadly virtues' surround him.

In my Craft or Sullen Art

Thomas felt his poetry was 'the record of my individual struggle from darkness towards some measure of light' and in this lyrical manifesto he claims that the struggle is for those capable of love.

PHILIP LARKIN

Two statements by the usually-reticent Larkin say much about his attitude, even though they hardly amount to a credo. The first comes from D. J. Enright's anthology *Poets of the 1950s* (1955) and proclaims his belief in literary clarity and uncomplicated imagery:

> 'As a guiding principle I believe that every poem must be its own freshly-created universe, and therefore have no belief in "tradition" or a common myth-kitty or casual allusions in poems to other poems or poets, which last I find unpleasantly like the talk of literary understrappers letting you see they know the right people.'

That, in so many words, is a dismissal of the whole Eliot–Pound–Joyce literary axis. The second statement comes from Larkin's book *All What Jazz* (1970) and explains why he feels obliged to write clearly for an intelligent, literate audience:

> '[the genesis of modernism] is related to an imbalance between the two tensions from which art springs: these are the tension between the artist and his material, and between the artist and his audience . . . in the last 75 years or so the second of these has slackened or even perished. In consequence the artist has become over-concerned with his material (hence an age of technical experiment), and, in isolation, has busied himself with the two principal themes of modernism, mystification and outrage.'

As an emerging poet Larkin remembers himself as 'the immediately post-Oxford self, isolated in Shropshire with a complete Yeats stolen from the local girls' school' and attempting to recreate a Celtic twilight by 'trying to write like Yeats, not because I liked his personality or understood his ideas but out of infatuation with his music'. Certainly his first book, *The North Ship*, came complete with Yeatsian paraphernalia. There is the haunting refrain ('*A drum taps: a wintry drum*'), unashamed self-dramatisation ('My thoughts are children / With uneasy faces'), apocalyptic cadence ('For they are gone from the earth') and sardonic asides ('The battered carcase of a carrion crow'). There is, too, the influence of A. E. Housman, obvious enough when we compare

> 'Heaviest of flowers, the head
>   forever hangs above a stormless bed'
>
> LARKIN, 'Heaviest of flowers'

with

> 'Loveliest of trees, the cherry now
>   Is hung with bloom along the bough'
>
> HOUSMAN, 'Loveliest of trees'

These influences were, however, soon to be replaced by that of Thomas Hardy, from whom Larkin learned to fit his melancholy sentiments into tightly-constructed and deceptively brittle poems. Hardy found a steady rhythm and reverberating rhyme adequate for his message of desolation.

Larkin, with a social desolation all his own, took up this easy manner of dealing with solemn subjects. Paradoxically what his poems reveal is the sense of loss, the way people passively let life happen to them.

Larkin's first recognisably Larkinesque poem is included as a coda to a reprint of *The North Ship* (1966), a poem which he says 'shows the Celtic fever abated and the patient sleeping soundly'. It also shows his fondness for the two-syllable epithet ('the loaded sky', 'A cropping deer', 'an unforced field'), his predilection for real, not mythical, objects ('Drainpipes and fire-escape', 'electric light') and his habit of describing himself in the act of observing ('I thought: Featureless morning, featureless night'). These features have all become part of the microstructure of Larkin's poetry and in his mature volumes, *The Less Deceived* (1955) and *The Whitsun Weddings* (1964), he has consolidated his mastery of the English technical repertoire.

Larkin often moves in areas that might produce maudlin responses: a photograph album, ambulances, hospitals, old age, loneliness, empty marriages. That he makes such a poignant poetry out of such subjects is due to his method of shaping his material so that even the big statements have an elegance that banishes the platitudinous.

'The mass of men lead lives of quiet desperation.' Thoreau's axiom might be Larkin's motto. He sees in working-class life a shabby travesty that ends with the likes of Mr Bleaney in his coffin-like room or draws attention to itself with sad ostentation:

> 'the perms,
> The nylon gloves, and jewellery-substitutes,
> The lemons, mauves, and olive-ochres ...
>   'The Whitsun Weddings'

Nor is his pessimism aroused only by the spectacle of working people. In 'Vers de Société' he shudders at the thought of middle-class life with 'some bitch / Who's read nothing but *Which*'. And as for the literati and poetry and being a librarian:

> 'Get stewed:
> Books are a load of crap.'
>   'A Study of Reading Habits'

What moves Larkin most is the apprehension of a vanished beauty – a deserted church, the splendour of New Orleans jazz. In comparison with such things the present age seems unbearably shabby so that for most people:

> 'Something is pushing them
> To the side of their own lives.'
>   'Afternoons'

For Larkin that 'Something' is the central emptiness of an age when men demolish beliefs like old buildings and put nothing in their place. He teaches us to count our losses that we may appreciate the blessings we still have.

Church Going

Of this poem, from *The Less Deceived*, G. S. Fraser writes, in *The Modern Writer and his World*: 'the Movement's prize poem, Philip Larkin's famous "Church Going", a poem with claims to greatness . . . about an agnostic's reluctant recognition of what the Church has meant'. And in his essay 'Beyond the Gentility Principle' (*The New Poetry* (1962)) A. Alvarez writes:

'The pieties of the Movement were as predictable as the politics of the thirties' poets. They are summed up at the beginning of Philip Larkin's "Church Going":

> Hatless, I take off
> My cycle-clips in awkward reverence.

This, in concentrated form, is the image of the post-war Welfare State Englishman: shabby and not concerned with his appearance; poor – he has a bike, not a car; gauche but full of agnostic piety; underfed, overtaxed, hopeless, bored, wry.'

Because 'Church Going' was the most outstanding poem in that bible of the Movement, Robert Conquest's *New Lines* anthology, it has come to stand as a monument for a poetic fashion. Yet 'Church Going' is more than that, it is a poem with stylistic antecedents in Gray's 'Elegy Written in a Country Churchyard' and thematic antecedents in Matthew Arnold's 'Dover Beach'. That it is nevertheless utterly unlike either of these poems in tone and texture is an indication of Larkin's originality.

The poem opens colloquially to suggest the sceptical mood of the speaker though to prevent any reader mistaking conversational mannerism for careless composition Larkin builds his poem in seven 9-line stanzas rhyming *ababcadcd* with the lines perpetually hovering around the iambic pentameter. As the poem moves to its *ad hoc* solution the language becomes increasingly richer. In place of colloquialisms like 'some brass and stuff' (line 5) and 'one of the crew / That tap and jot' (lines 40–1) we move into a verbal area defined by phrases like 'the ghostly silt' (line 46), 'this cross of ground' (line 47), 'blent air' (line 56). Finally the poem becomes a kind of solution, simulating the provocative power of religious symbols, and the final lines alliterate like the ringing of church bells: 'serious . . . serious', 'recognised . . . robed', 'someone . . . surprising', 'gravitating . . . ground'.

8] *God knows how long:* the irony not only mocks the church, but suggests the initial insensitivity of the speaker.

25] *pyx:* box (in the R.C. church a vessel in which the host is kept after consecration).

30] *simples:* medicinal herbs.

41] *rood-loft:* a gallery over the ornamental partition separating choir from nave.

46] *silt:* fine sediment.

Lines on a Young Lady's Photograph Album

Larkin's characteristic poetic stance is that of spectator rather than participant but in this poem, from *The Less Deceived*, he does involve himself, ironically, in the action. Disturbed at his exclusion from the experiences recorded in the young lady's photographs he steals a photograph as a token of the girl. However, as he has already found photographs to be depressingly factual records of events, this closes the poem on a meaningless personal gesture and directs the reader back to the poem itself which, unlike photography, enriches experience. What moves Larkin, in this as in so many poems, is '*the past*' which reminds him of how much he has missed, of how life passes him by. Romantic poets were heroic figures who swept young women off their feet. The speaker claims no such role. He presents himself, with touching candour, as a man aware of all that he has failed to do, an ordinary man with an extraordinary gift willing even to assume the role of *voyeur* and take a snapshot of a young lady bathing.

Toads

Larkin has spent his working life as a librarian and in this poem from *The Less Deceived*, he suggests that his orthodox social behaviour derives from a personal diffidence. Once again Larkin presents himself as a humdrum, workaday, middle-class, middle-aged man looking forward to nothing but old age and a comfortable pension. The situation is itself rescued from mediocrity by the poet's delightful wit and keen powers of observation. The *abab* rhyme-scheme is deliberately hit-and-miss to create an impression of reluctant resignation.

11] *losels* are wasters; *loblolly-men* are louts.
23–4] This is a deflating swipe at the romantics who chose 'the stuff / That dreams are made on'.

Toads Revisited

This poem from *The Whitsun Weddings* returns to the theme of working for a living. By now Larkin has fully assumed the *persona* of the world-weary observer impressed by precious little and depressed by almost everything. Since 'Toads' he has become more ensconced in his secure job and he firmly rejects the life-style of those who dodge the toad work. Yet the texture of the poem works against the intentions of the speaker. The phrase 'Think of being them' is used twice and Larkin's suggestive language does indeed make us wonder what indeed it would be like to be old or homeless or infirm or cretinous or all of these. Larkin's compassion comes through the poetry and not through the apparent distaste of the speaker.

1] *the park:* Larkin lives near the public park in Hull.
13] *out-patients:* illness is constantly alluded to in Larkin's poems.

Mr Bleaney

This poem, from *The Whitsun Weddings*, deals in pathos rather than tragedy. Disasters simply do not happen to men like Mr Bleaney: they are the ubiquitous but unknown citizens of the Welfare State. Here Larkin deliberately presents a two-dimensional picture of such a man and then suggests a third dimension which may, or may not, have been appropriate to Mr Bleaney. Because Mr Bleaney was simple (so society glibly supposes) Larkin employs almost exclusively monosyllabic rhymes in his quatrains and deals with the narrative side of Mr Bleaney's life in straightforward terms. Then, suddenly, in the last two stanzas the language soars up and suggests a possible world that Mr Bleaney may have glimpsed. The technique is often used by Larkin but seldom with such dramatic impact as here.

1] '*This . . ..* the landlady is speaking.
2] *the Bodies:* In a letter (16 August 1972) Larkin told me:

> 'I was brought up in Coventry, a great car-making town, and there used to be works there which were referred to rather by what they produced than by the name of the makers. "The Bodies" was a fictitious example of this, invented for its macabre overtones.'

3] *thin and frayed:* the parenthetical placing of the epithets makes them refer as much to Mr Bleaney as to the flowered curtains.
27] *one hired box:* macabre overtones of the coffin.

Love Songs in Age

This poem about love songs, from *The Whitsun Weddings*, becomes in itself a poem about love. Typically Larkin shows how the memory of happiness can be the most poignant of all emotions: the further we are from love the more satisfying it appears, but as we get closer, through the poem, then through the widow's songs, to love itself we are confronted with an impenetrable mystery.

Technically this poem is masterly, sustaining fluid and lucid lines through the arbitrary rhyme-scheme *abacbcdd*. It also displays Larkin's essentially visual imagination which can assemble multiple associations round a simple observation.

The Whitsun Weddings

The title poem of his 1964 collection may be Larkin's finest poem. Whereas 'Church Going' provoked discussion, 'The Whitsun Weddings' has evoked admiration. It is a considered statement about the way everyday life is pregnant with disappointment. The poet, late getting away on the public holiday, takes the mid-day train from Hull to King's Cross, London, and relaxes in the heat of his carriage while outside the sun illuminates the debris of modern industrial life; the rows of houses, the streams of cars, the polluted canals, the nondescript new towns, the car factories. This is the setting for young people starting out in life. After taking in this view the poet becomes aware of the wedding groups that perform a ritual of happiness at each station. He describes the groups of working people taking advantage of the holiday to get married. From his sober, uncommitted vantage point the poet can only see a poignant vulgarity. He presents the people vividly but in terms that deliberately suggest the human caricatures on seaside postcards:

> 'The fathers with broad belts under their suits
> And seamy foreheads; mothers loud and fat;
> An uncle shouting smut'

He pictures London as a field and the people as wheat shining in this brilliantly sunny day. Then as the train's 'frail / Travelling coincidence' (lines 74–5) comes into London the sense of excitement felt by the honeymooners is transformed, by the poet, into an image of hope shot up as an arrow and coming back to the earth as a fertilising downpour, both drenching the people and nourishing the wheat. It is an ambiguous conclusion by a poet adept at observing the strangeness at the heart of human relationships: 'the power / That being changed can give' (lines 76–7).

'The Whitsun Weddings' is one of Larkin's richest poems and demon-
strates both his powers of description and his visual imagination. The first
two stanzas are virtuoso examples of Larkin's ability to fit a fluent and telling
passage of descriptive writing into a complicated rhyme-scheme (*ababcdecde*).
He uses the physical fact of sunshine and turns it into an image of hope. Its
presence is emphasised in 'blinding windscreens' (line 3), 'A hothouse flashed
uniquely' (line 16) and, best of all, the 'short-shadowed cattle' (line 14)
(because the sun is above them at mid-day). As the ritual weddings progress
Larkin casts real and symbolic shadows over the events. Not only do the
poplars 'cast / Long shadows over major roads' (lines 58-9) but the couples
become rapidly indifferent to their surroundings. Like the acres of dismantled cars, like the rows of houses, like the blinding windscreens they are
prepackaged and almost interchangeable. And the people in London, like
wheat, represent thousands of couples joined by the pressures of conformity.
The central ambiguity is in the image of married lives beginning on an upward curve, like an arrow, but coming down to earth like a downpour.

9] *The river:* the Humber.

Ambulances

In his best poems Larkin begins with a wealth of description from which
solid basis he moves on to the significance of what he has described. This,
from *The Whitsun Weddings*, is one of his best poems. From the first sentence,
in which ambulances are likened to confessionals, we are aware of the
spiritual issues involved. In an age that has solved the unsightliness of death
by hiding it away (in ambulances, in hospitals) and ensuring that everything,
even death, has its place, there still remains the sense of loss.

Reference Back

'Few things have given me more pleasure in life than listening to jazz',
Philip Larkin wrote in *All What Jazz* and this poem, from *The Whitsun
Weddings*, suggests that Larkin's enjoyment of jazz has much to do with its
instant nostalgia, the way it hauntingly tells of sorrow and loss. Moreover,
Larkin remembers how his mother liked one particular record which he now
associates with her. Thus objects are enriched by layers of personal reference.
Larkin's melancholy is emphasised by the reiteration of the epithet 'unsatisfactory', while the final stanza suggests that it is reasonable to avoid
emotional associations because they bring the beauty of the past vividly to
life and shame the present. The sudden mid-sentence line-breaks imitate the
angular phrasing of traditional jazz.

1] *you:* the poet's mother.
7] *Oliver's* Riverside Blues: Joe 'King' Oliver (1885-1938) was one of the
greatest jazz cornettists.
10] *Chicago air:* Chicago had some of the best jazz recording studios.
12] *The year after I was born:* 1923. On 31 March and 6 April 1923 King
Oliver and his Creole Jazz Band made a historic series of jazz recordings.

Afternoons

This poem, from *The Whitsun Weddings*, shows Larkin drawing pessimistic
conclusions from close observations. He watches young mothers momen-

tarily liberated from the clamorous attentions of their children and places them in a claustrophobic context dominated by the demands of their husbands and household chores. In their flats on the housing estate lie the wedding albums, a record of a promise never fulfilled. Instead of romantic love (which they dreamed about as schoolgirls just as the new schoolchildren do) they have become bored housewives with boring lives. The 'Something' that pushes them away from their dream is the dreary business of living.

Vers de Société

This poem from *High Windows* (1974) shows Larkin's mastery of mood and his ability to change it by linguistic and rhythmic means. The opening is splendidly sardonic and terse and monosyllabic as the poet treats an invitation to a party with contempt. Yet when he begins to write his refusal he is jolted into a consideration of the alternative. Society expects everyman to be sociable, and this pressure makes the poet question his own solitude and the value of contemplative evenings. In the end he decides to conform, and accepts both the invitation and all the social attitudes that go with it. He admits defeat.

Here Larkin produces some memorable lines and vivid images. The 'glass of washing sherry, canted / Over to catch the drivel of some bitch' (lines 9–10) not only indicates a man leaning over but also suggests an obsequious interviewer with a microphone in his hand. There is also the striking synecdoche about emptiness being filled by 'forks and faces'.

Title] verse about social life, embodying social values and tone.
11] *Which?* is a magazine for consumers, containing comparative data for different products and reports on performance.

The Explosion

Introducing this poem from *High Windows* in the BBC broadcast celebrating his fiftieth birthday Larkin said: 'What I should like to do is write different kinds of poems that might be by different people.' Certainly the absence of rhyme is unusual for Larkin, as is the enigmatic way the theme is treated. The poem begins by warning of the inevitability of the explosion (proleptically the poet says it is 'the day of the explosion') which immediately places the miners in a fatally fragile position. So though they curse their bad luck at being out so early in the morning (with its 'freshened silence') they are walking to their deaths with some dignity. Then the explosion. Then the poem cuts into a sermon which, for all its platitudinous gestures of comfort, reminds wives of the husbands they have lost, and the apprehension of this loss invests the dead men with a beauty they were never credited with in life.

16–18] This is the preacher speaking and this is the sort of parody of a churchman the speaker of 'Church Going' felt himself obliged to make.

The Building

If God is dead, religion discredited, and churches obsolete as Larkin has, by no means complacently, suggested in his work, then what does modern man do about death? One answer, examined in this poem from *High Windows*, is to erect modern architectural monuments – hospitals – to keep death in its place. Larkin examines the limitations of this attempt. For one thing, though the building is new and expensive and impressive, human beings persist in being messy: scruffy porters, ripped magazines. This hospital has been constructed for the dying while the living have to put up with nineteenth-century houses in short terraced streets. In this house of death the living are uncomfortable and reduced to self-conscious nervous mannerisms (obsessively drinking tea, or trying to find things to do to ease their fear). In a church people came to confess their sins, in this church-substitute they have come 'to confess that something has gone wrong' (line 22). And they keep a religious quiet because their physical failure is shared with others. Outside, the world and its potential are cut off and so seem more intensely desirable, a 'touching dream' (line 46) sustaining healthy people. The church outside is closed, but here are 'unseen congregations' (line 54) waiting for their death. They know this is inevitable because man has not yet built anything to overcome death – not cathedrals, not hospitals. Both are 'a struggle to transcend / The thought of dying' (lines 60–1). The poem covers some of the area inhabited by 'Church Going' but is without the comfort of the earlier poem.

6] *not taxis:* ambulances.

31] *washed-to-rags ward clothes:* an image that reminds us how many people have died in the same ward clothes.

41] *a locked church:* a contrast to the permanently open and packed hospitals.

CHARLES TOMLINSON

In his celebrated essay 'How to Read' (1928) Ezra Pound distinguished between three kinds of poetry: 'Melopoeia' (musical arrangement of words), 'Phanapoeia' ('a casting of images upon the visual imagination'), and 'Logopoeia' (complicated word-play). The most cursory reading of Charles Tomlinson will show that many of his poems are primarily concerned with the visual imagination and therefore fit the second of Pound's distinctions. When one considers, further, that Tomlinson acknowledges a poetic debt to William Carlos Williams for whom there are 'no ideas but in things' and that he began his creative career as a painter, there is an obvious temptation to classify him as a poet of pure visual description and leave it at that.

However Tomlinson was not forever content to hold a mirror – or, more appropriately, the rippling surface of water – up to nature, and his book *The Way of a World* (1969) showed him so much a master of visual objects that he could arrange them judiciously into his own anti-romantic, particularised aesthetic. His poems became compositions capable of conveying more than the sum of their parts. Thus 'Swimming Chenango Lake' is more than a pleasing description of a man swimming, it is the pictorial and philosophical record of a man struggling against the elemental force of water and achieving a particular victory. And this struggle for single, memorable moments of achievement is what Tomlinson's best poems are all about.

His is not a vision in the normal poetic or political or philosophical sense, because these visions project an ideal world and expect the world to conform to it. Tomlinson begins with the real, objective world and suggests ways we can come to a reciprocal arrangement with it. Everything in Tomlinson's world can be seen and seen clearly, and he is suspicious of appeals to purely subjective emotional impulses. By insisting on fidelity to objects he does not omit his own personality which comes through as clearly as the personality of an impressionist painter.

For all his exotic stylistic mannerisms, Tomlinson is English in his empirical attitudes, and Jonathan Raban was right when he said, in *The Society of the Poem* (1971), that 'At the heart of Tomlinson's poems there is indeed a vein of commonsensical, liberal, philosophizing Englishness; a conviction that both nature and society are essentially intractable, and that the business of the poet is to attend to the details and dynamics of the real.' This is why Tomlinson can bring Scriabin down to earth in a Stoke-on-Trent housing estate, why he can delight at the prospect of grapes ripening over a collapsing city, why he can prefer a driver's view of men to a God's-eye-view of mankind. It is basic to the mainstream of British philosophy that the objective world exists independently from the spectator and Tomlinson's poetry explores the tension between phenomena and the perception of phenomena.

If we consider three poems involving mechanical movement in this anthology we can see how Tomlinson's poems build up general impressions out of solid details but do not presume to speak for others. Thom Gunn's 'On the Move' gets inside the ritual excitement of the black-jacketed motor-cyclists; Philip Larkin watches 'The Whitsun Weddings' from his seat in the Hull–London train but he ends by feeling part of the general situation. Tomlinson, on the other hand, watches the town in 'The Way In' from the safety of his motor-car but finally passes on with one eye on the speed limit. He always keeps his distance from objects and events and, especially, people. His landscapes and townscapes and seascapes are peopled with figures rather than recognisable human beings. It may be an honest appreciation of the impossibility of genuine empathy but it is a diffidence many feel to be unbecoming in a poet.

Tomlinson would no doubt argue that his poems are meant to alert people, not convert them. His poems present significant objects and are themselves satisfying recreations of them. He has a remarkable ability to manipulate a language purged of abstractions. His early poems darted like fish, his later ones advance smoothly with the inevitability of a submarine. Yet perhaps too much has been made of the American influence. He told me

'I admired Moore's diction rather than her metric, Stevens and she released me from the impossibility of finding a foothold in contemporary English verse. Williams (but not until '56) interested me by the way his late cadenced poems brought out emphases traditional metre tidied away. My guiding principle in these cadenced poems is a four stress line (one can shrink to three if there are plenty of other syllables or stretch to six) – a development out of Hopkins's sprung rhythm really.'

He is also fond of Marvell and Wordsworth.

In the concluding poem of *The Way of a World*, 'The Chances of Rhyme', Tomlinson says:

'The chances of rhyme are like the chances of meeting –
In the finding fortuitous, but once found, binding.'

In other words he does not like to set out with a rigid rhyme-scheme and fit his observations into it but likes to let the rhythmic flow come and bring along with it any rhymes it likes. Thus in 'Assassin' line 12 ('October air') rhymes with line 36 ('the roots of the hair') and this use of occasional, unpredictable rhyme is combined with internal rhymes – 'my poems are lousy with internal rhymes' Tomlinson told me – to give his poems inner organs rather than a neat, straight jacket. He is very fond of alliteration and this gives a rugged texture to his verse, appropriate for one who spends so much poetic time watching the wind ruffle the surface of water. Water – with its eternal movement and its transformation of reflected objects – is Tomlinson's stylistic model and the source of his finest imagery. And his finest poems are very fine, full of sustained description and sensuous argument. They are, in the best sense of the phrase, a sight for sore eyes.

The Crane

The title of the book from which this poem comes – *Seeing is Believing* (USA 1958, UK 1960) – aptly describes Tomlinson's early attitudes. With pictorial experience and a distrust of ideology behind him he was determined to eschew abstract sentiment and concentrate on a selective presentation of the objective world. Like W. C. Williams he felt there were 'no ideas but in things', and, again like Williams, wanted to say so in jerky run-on lines to prevent the reader soporifically following a steady rhythm at the expense of the imagery. Yet though the world is seen, it is seen metaphorically. The crane becomes an 'insect, without antennae' which is eventually given semi-human attributes by the anxious spectators who project their own fears onto the towering construction that builds their future.

Steel: the night shift

This poem, from *A Peopled Landscape* (1963), develops some of the tendencies observed in 'The Crane'. Here the poet himself discerns 'a principle, a pulse' (line 7) in man's ability and obligation to control and organise 'these molten and metallic contraries' (line 8) – yet he suspends judgment on the potential of the machine to 'uncreate'. Technically Tomlinson has become more literary, less pictorial, in this poem. There is an excessive use of alliteration to duplicate the repetitive regularity experienced by the steelworkers: 'deepest . . . den' (line 4), 'fire fiercest . . . frontier' (line 5); 'glare / . . . guide the girders' (lines 10–11), etc. And Tomlinson is beginning to use the occasional rhyme to fit the moment though the rhymes are cunningly placed and unpredictable: 'contraries' is separated from 'balconies' by three lines; 'glare' and 'outstare' is an internal rhyme as is 'height' and 'light' – though these combine to make a closing couplet with 'night'.

Gossamers

In this poem, from *A Peopled Landscape*, Tomlinson's mature style is caught in embryo. Tomlinson is now recognised as a poet who continually questions the appearance of the observed world because he knows that the visual expectations of the observer can transform objects. Here the objects are barely-substantial gossamers, yet they become 'certainties that . . . must touch . . . and . . . know'. Everyday objects are being made to carry the philosophical, conceptual burden that Tomlinson perceives in them.

14] *green resistance:* transferred epithet.

The Weathercocks

Although this poem comes from a book called *American Scenes* (1966) Tomlinson associates it with Ozleworth in Gloucestershire where he lives: 'Ozleworth church itself has a fine one on its tower – glinting in winter weather and winter sun: wind, clarity of sky and colours of fields.' Usually Tomlinson has a disciplined and rigorous response to the objects he perceives, but here he indulges in poetic fancy. If the metal weathercocks were real ones they might see by an unreal light the landscape in terms of images. Ploughed fields might seem like continents or 'corduroy lines' (line 14) beneath a changing cloudscape. However this gift of 'mind matter' (line 22) comes from the light of the human imagination and by describing it Tomlinson has demonstrated it.

Swimming Chenango Lake

This poem opens Tomlinson's collection *The Way of a World*, and perfectly embodies the poet's mature style and most characteristic concerns. After working through a primary stage of object-presentation, and a secondary stage of object-interpretation, Tomlinson is now able to move between object and subjective response to object. Illusions and objects mingle, appearance and reality interact. The verse is now informed by a conversational fluidity and the images are not only vivid but placed within a verbal perspective so that each world has its own dimension. Like the leaves on the lake the ripples of the poetry spread outwards: there is the lake, the swimmer's response to it, the poet's response to the swimmer, and, finally, the poem itself which the reader reacts to. This multiplication of meaning gives a substantial presence to the verse in which objects are perceived through several layers of imposed significance. Tomlinson has chosen for his central principle the texture of water because no other surface has the same capacity for transforming objects. A classic philosophical illustration of illusion is the straight stick that appears to bend when placed in water, and Tomlinson has extended this in his description of the water transforming clouds into 'angles and elongations' (line 12) and a bush into 'A shaft of fire' (line 15). Each ripple is a liquid variation on the object whose reflection it distorts and, in the poem, the swimmer tries to 'take hold / On water's meaning' (lines 25–6) as his arms slice into the reflected images. Water, however, *is* and cannot be bounded by semantics. 'Swimming Chenango Lake' is not merely an impressive description, not merely verbal impression of a man swimming, but the record of a particular struggle. A phrase like 'scissors the waterscape apart' (line 22) onomatopoetically suggests water and, by sliding vowels through consonants like muscles through liquid, imitates the physical movement of the swimmer. The language does not merely function as a grid through which we perceive the swimmer – it has an autonomous muscularity that almost sculpts the swimmer's manner out of the verbal matter.

Title] The lake, in upstate New York, is called Poolville Pond. Tomlinson wanted the Indian name and, on learning this was unknown, called it after the now-extinct Chenango Indians who had lived in the area.

29] *The body is heir to:* before the birth the body is surrounded by amniotic fluid.

31] *image he has torn:* his hands have momentarily disturbed the reflection on that part of the water.

46] *obsidian:* a vitreous acid volcanic rock that looks like thick glass.

Prometheus

This poem, from *The Way of a World*, gives the poet's considered response to a radio broadcast of Scriabin's 'Prometheus: The Poem of Fire' (Op 60, 1910) on a thundery summer evening in a Stoke-on-Trent housing estate. In Greek mythology Prometheus stole fire from heaven and gave it to men to promote the useful arts (for which act Zeus punished him by chaining him to a Caucasian rock where an eagle preyed on his liver until Hercules came to the rescue). In Scriabin's symphonic poem orchestra, piano and chorus are combined to convey ecstatic triumph. Tomlinson's note to the poem refers to Scriabin's 'hope of transforming the world by music and rite' and the poem itself opposes Scriabin (and the revolutionary implications of his music) by insisting 'We have lived through apocalypse too long' (line 7). It is the apocalyptic abstractions of art and ideology that inspire men like Lenin and Trotsky to act out their obsessions on the stage of history rather than in the realm of the imagination so that 'History treads out the music of your dreams / Through blood' (lines 44-5). Listening to the music crackle through the static on the radio the poet is too aware of his real surroundings to surrender to the prophetic power of Scriabin's music. Tomlinson is determined to keep us at a distance from Scriabin's 'mock last-day of nature and of art' (line 6) by reminding us of the immediate physical environment (which produces atmospheric interference on the radio) and of his own scepticism about apocalyptic art.

3] *this music:* 'Prometheus: The Poem of Fire' (Op 60, 1910) by Scriabin.

9] *the Finland Station:* in April 1917 Lenin travelled in a sealed train from Switzerland to the Finland Station in Petrograd to direct the course of the Russian Revolution.

11] *Alexander Nikolayevitch:* i.e. Alexander Nikolayevitch Scriabin (1872-1915).

12] *mob of instruments:* as opposed to a mob of human instruments of the revolution.

13] The line effectively reminds us of the poet by his crackling radio and also suggests those who died when Scriabin's musical apocalypse was transformed into a historical reality.

16] *son of a school inspector:* Lenin's father, Ilya Ulyanov, was an inspector of elementary schools in the Simbrisk province.

17] *Tyutchev:* Fyodor Tyutchev (1803-73), a Russian whose early love-poetry was abandoned when he turned to political poems of nationalistic fervour. Charles Tomlinson has published a volume of translations of Tyutchev.

22] *those harmonies:* the post-Wagnerian chromaticism of Scriabin no longer sounds daring or revolutionary to modern ears.

37] 'The Scythians', a poem by Alexander Blok (1880–1921), was published in 1918 as a warning against threats of invasion to Russia. Like Tyutchev, Blok began his career as an outstanding love-poet and eventually wrote political poetry in response to current events. He gradually despaired of the officialdom of the new state.

Assassin

This poem, from *The Way of a World*, deals with the murder of Trotsky on 20 August 1940 in his fortified villa in Mexico City by Ramón Mercader, a Stalinist agent who had ingratiated himself into Trotsky's household. In Tomlinson's poem the speaker is Mercader and it is instructive to compare the dramatic monologue with the actual words of Mercader as cited in Isaac Don Levine's *The Mind of an Assassin* (1959):

> 'I put my raincoat on the table on purpose so that I could take out the ice-axe which I had in the pocket. I decided not to lose the brilliant opportunity which was offered me and at the exact moment when Trotsky started to read my article, which served as my pretext, I took the *piolet* out of my raincoat, took it in my fist and, closing my eyes, I gave him a tremendous blow on the head . . . The man screamed in such a way that I will never forget it as long as I live. His scream was *Aaaa . . .* very long, infinitely long and it still seems to me as if that scream were piercing my brain. I saw Trotsky get up like a madman. He threw himself at me and bit my hand . . . Then I pushed him, so that he fell to the floor. He lifted himself as best he could and then, running and stumbling, I don't know how, he got out of the room.'

The character of Mercader has puzzled historians. Isaac Don Levine sees him as a dedicated, trained murderer relieved of his conscience by his fanatical ideological faith. Tomlinson sees him as a philosophically-inclined extremist determined to batter his way into history by a dramatic piece of existential action.

The quotation at the top of the poem is from Octavio Paz's *Piedra de Sol* (Sunstone).

2] *distractions of the retina:* the extremist's faith is blind.

12] *October air:* the assassination took place in August, but Trotsky is still breathing the ideological air of the October revolution.

15] *rage of the ear:* the extremist's faith is deaf.

18] *the gate of history:* the central image in the extremist's faith is a personified History.

51] *history and necessity:* to its adherents Marxism is an historical necessity and therefore all deeds can be justified by an appeal to the future.

Against Extremity

In place of extremism (with its fanatical refusal to admit good on the other side) Tomlinson desires human communication. In the previous poems from *The Way of a World* ('Prometheus', 'Assassin') the target has been political extremism with its murderous reality; this poem from the same book considers personal extremism and its suicidal tendencies.

4] *That girl:* Anne Sexton, a poet obsessed with suicide, one of whose best known poems is 'Sylvia's Death' which exhibits a loving envy for Sylvia Plath's suicide:

> 'and I know, at the news of your death,
> a terrible taste for it, like salt.'

7] *a friend:* Sylvia Plath, a close friend of Anne Sexton's in Boston.

The Fox Gallery

This poem, from *The Way of a World*, recollects a shared moment of happiness, lovingly recorded as an example of the variety of life. It is in such particular instances that Tomlinson finds an answer to vague and otherwise irresistible abstractions about existence.

1] *long house:* the poet's cottage in Gloucestershire.
2] *you:* the poet's wife, Brenda.

On Water

These quatrains open Tomlinson's *Written on Water* (1972) and express the poet's love of water in whose changing surfaces and 'solid vacancies' he sees an image of the variety of life and the ability of such images to transform objects.

Mackinnon's Boat

Ullinish, where this poem from *Written on Water* is set, is a point on the Inner Hebridean island of Skye. The poet observes two men on a boat bringing in their catch of lobsters. The water is so black that it carries no reflections and, as if to emphasise the primitive conditions, Tomlinson gives a dog's-eye-view of the water. What emerge from the water are not concepts and images – as in the companion-poem 'Swimming Chenango Lake' – but 'Crabs, urchins, dogfish, and star' (line 54) and the captured lobsters. When the men have made their catch they do not reflect, they rest. When they have rested they press on, leaving in their wake a smell of 'diesel, salt, and tobacco' (line 94). Because Tomlinson has returned, here, to an emphasis on things the poem becomes a *tour de force* of visual evocation.

The pervasive tonality is monochromatic with only occasional hints of colour as when one sees 'blue / Such as catches and dies in an eye-glance' (lines 90–1). The figures in this seascape – two men and a dog – do not seek meanings from the sea but a living. Tomlinson finds something impressively solid in their utterly basic response to objects.

5–6] Literally true, and also a hint that the poem is to be a primary response to a scene rather than a philosophical interpretation of it.

The Compact: At Volterra

When he wants to be, as in this poem from *Written on Water*, Tomlinson can be an outstanding essayist in verse, demonstrating that poetry is equipped to take over material normally claimed by prose. The poem opens with topographical, historical and geological details. Volterra stands like mankind, on the edge of crumbling cliffs submitting to the 'slow abyss' (line 7) of erosion. Yet the city has survived historical change: the Etruscans were defeated by the Carthaginians, who were defeated by the Romans, who subsequently experienced their own decline and fall into a 'slow abyss'. Beside the packed streets of the modern city, the erosion of time exposes the cenozoic layer, that geological era associated with the dawn of man. So underneath modern man are the remains of his history and the reminders of his prehistory – all bearing witness to the permanent possibility of destructive change. To dwell on this would be to fall into a 'slow abyss' of insanity. Men survive from day to day by 'unreasoned care' (line 44) for the felicities of the moment. Tomlinson wishes to blow away the smoke of millennial extravagances so that we might see clearly the immediate beauties of the present, and the past, in an air un-polluted by a collective death-wish. Man survives because he refuses to give ground before he must and in the realisation of this lies sanity.

Title] Volterra is a modern town in Tuscany and was once one of twelve cities of Etruria.

1] *crack in the stone:* like mankind, Volterra stands at the edge of crumbling cliffs. Much of Volterra has dropped down into 'the slow abyss' of erosion.

3] *More history:* it shows evidence of prehistory, the cenozoic era.

4] *this place:* Volterra, with its Etruscan gate and Renaissance ramparts.

6] *Caesar and Scipio:* Scipio defeated the Carthaginian general Hannibal in 202 B.C. to end the Second Punic War. Before its own decline and fall into the 'slow abyss' the Roman Empire was in the hands of men like Caesar. They however are insignificant in terms of the time-span that 'the black filament . . . unmasks'.

9] *a compact:* an unspoken agreement between the sun (marking the passing years) and the moon (marking the passing months).

23] *The cenozoic skeleton:* the cenozoic layer exposed by erosion.

26] *fault:* geological fault.

29] *a momentary unison:* if erosion, geological faults, and 'rumours of down-fall' (physical, though implying the connivance of those who desire the apocalypse) combined then the earth beneath the city would collapse.

32] *pergola:* a framework for climbing plants.

Over Elizabeth Bridge

Bridges are links and Elizabeth Bridge links the ostentatious past (Buda) with the efficient present (Pest). Also the memory of the bridge links Tomlinson with a Hungarian friend Ivan to whom he offers a fresh interpretation of a three-year old memory in this poem from *Written on Water*. Standing by the church on the Pest side (right bank) Tomlinson had noticed how the road to the bridge swerves to avoid the church ('a curious sort of courteousness' (line 13)). This analogy of swerving does not, the poet admits, hold in history where those who get in the way of 'progress' are crushed. Yet while politi-cians perish artists are at least survived by their art. Tomlinson is fascinated by the tensions and ambitions and abstractions shared by political man and poetic man and remembers that both died in the city where 'too much happened in too short a time' (line 17). The poem is in six 7-line stanzas with rhymes in lines 2 and 4, and lines 5 and 7.

Title] Elizabeth Bridge is one of six Bridges over the Danube connecting Buda (on the right bank, traditionally associated with church and crown) with Pest (on the left bank, traditionally associated with the apparatus of the state).

9] *A church:* the coronation church on the right bank.

22] *that man:* Imre Nagy who was Prime Minister of Hungary from 1953 to 1955 before being dismissed for failure to ensure industrial growth and for his attitude to the Communist Party. On 23 October 1957 Nagy was re-instated as Prime Minister in the anti-Russian revolution. When Russian forces attacked Budapest in November they guaranteed Nagy's personal safety if he gave himself up. His execution was announced on 17 June 1958.

28] *Rajk:* László Rajk was, as Tomlinson's note points out, 'Hungarian Foreign Minister, executed during the Stalinist period'.

40] *József:* Attila József (1905–37), Hungarian poet whose marxist sympathies were expressed in poems about working-class life and who threw himself under a train after a long period of illness and depression.

During Rain

At first sight this poem from *Written on Water* seems a return to the early Williams-esque pictorial manner, run-on lines and all. However the meta-phorical charge is considerable: the raindrops on the slats ripen and fall like fruit and are then compared to an endless string of pearls marking their own time. Tomlinson is having a reciprocal affair with the objective world – selecting bits of it but investing them with aspects of his own vision.

The Way In

In most of Tomlinson's poems he is the static spectator letting sights assume a dynamic in the field of his vision. In this poem, from *The Way In* (1974), he is on the move, driving into a town in process of reconstruction. What he sees is the old giving way to the new, familiar features being replaced by an anony-mous ugliness, the crash of demolition and the new buildings wobbling in optical illusion (a heat haze). Out of the ruins of the old emerge the old, hoard-ing their possessions and clinging on to familiar objects. To one old couple the ejection from the neighbourhood is like an expulsion from the Garden of Eden – a striking image of the way people cling on to the familiar, however shabby. To the old couple the new buildings might not exist and their empty stare seems to demolish the 'new blocks' (line 34). They are left with the sum of their memories. Before Mnemosyne – Greek goddess of memory and 'our lady of the nameless metals' (line 37) – the poet confesses his own dis-like of the arbitrary architectural additions. Yet on the principle that famili-arity breeds content he grants their appeal to those who will seek refuge in their concrete towers. The poet moves on to the cantilevered road, taking advantage of the changes while registering his 'daily discontent'.

2] *Teeters at thirty:* speed-limit of 30 m.p.h.

7] *this place:* in fact the poet was thinking of Bristol (where he works) though the observations would apply to any town in the grip of reconstruction.

36] *Mnemosyne:* the Greek goddess of memory, mother of the muses.

43] *climbed into their towers:* taken refuge in concrete towers as aloof artists are said to hide in ivory towers.

THOM GUNN

When Thom Gunn made his poetic debut with *Fighting Terms* and *The Sense of Movement* (especially *that*) the literary audience used to comfortable seats squirmed at the prospect of being thrust on the back of a motorcycle by an advocate of will and energy. To some it seemed wrong for a poet to identify himself with mindless toughs and to insist on the element of risk in modern life – it was simply not expected of a young man with a first-class brain and a good education. In their book *Modern Poetry* (1963) C. B. Cox and A. E. Dyson described Gunn as a man who has 'a hate, almost a contempt, for people who are afraid to choose'; and Kenneth Allott, in his *Penguin Book of Contemporary Verse* (1962) found it 'hard to share his uncritical sympathy for nihilistic young tearaways in black leather jackets'.

One of the poems found most objectionable was 'Lines for a Book' (from *The Sense of Movement*) which praised 'all the toughs through history'. What was forgotten, or ignored, was that by choosing (and remember the significance of choice for Gunn) to say this in rhyme and metre Gunn was showing which side he was on. However much he admired the panache of the Black Jackets his own sensitivity transformed a desire for empathy into an expression of sympathy.

Early critics were so anxious to seize on the poet's mannerisms they forgot to grasp the philosophical essence of his poems. Gunn was attempting to salvage some aspects of tenderness from all that 'deliberate human will'. He was aware of two aspects of man – the instinctual, animal aspect; and the reflective, human aspect. If he observed more of the former than the latter then it would have been dishonest of him not to say so.

In a note on *Moly* Gunn wrote, *apropos* the myth of Circe turning men into pigs:

'We can all take on the features of pigs – or what humans interpret as those features – we all have in us the germs of the brutal, greedy, and dull. And we can all avoid becoming pigs, though to do so we must be wily and self-aware . . . we do not have to become pigs, we do not have to be unmanned, we are as free to make and unmake ourselves as we were at the age of ten.'

This concern has always been present in Gunn's poetry. In the early work he was more inclined to show man as a bit of a swine, but the recognition of that has allowed him to win a real victory for sensitivity in his more recent poetry – the revelation of beauty is all the more impressive because the poet has worked so hard to achieve it. He may have begun by riding with the Hell's Angels, restlessly on the move, but he has now settled to a more serene state under the influence of American colleagues like Allen Ginsberg and Gary Snyder.

'We are as free to make and unmake ourselves as we were at the age of ten.' That remark reflects the existential element that has persisted in Gunn's thought. According to existentialist theory existence precedes essence: man is free to choose his role and reject the norms of society. Gunn would agree with Sartre's Orestes who says, in *The Flies*, 'I *am* my freedom.'

One of Gunn's heroes, Albert Camus, was asked in an interview – reproduced in *Lyrical and Critical* (1967) – whether his insistence on the absurd might lead people to despair. He replied:

'Accepting the absurdity of everything around us is a stage, a necessary experience: it should not become a dead end. It arouses a revolt which can become fruitful. An analysis of the concept of revolt could help us to discover notions capable of restoring a relative meaning to existence, although a meaning that would always be in danger.'

Gunn himself, introducing the *Selected Poems of Fulke Greville* (1968), wrote:

'What is important is not so much the perception of absurdity, which to a certain kind of thinker is inevitable, as how one conducts oneself after making that perception. Camus' great contribution is less in the analysis of the sickness into which we are born than in the determination to live with that sickness, fully acknowledging it and accepting it as the basis for our actions.'

However Gunn also says in the same essay: 'a poem must be more than the ideas it contains. If it cannot validate itself without one's having to make historical allowances, then it is not likely to be very good.'

So we begin and end with the poetry, noting that Gunn has explored various formal possibilities thoroughly if cautiously. Gunn began displaying many of the metrical wares associated with the Limited Company calling themselves 'the Movement' (he was one of the nine poets in Robert Conquest's *New Lines* anthology of 1956) – there was the tread of well-worn iambic feet, the development of theme through rhymed stanzas, and the rhythmic caution. With *My Sad Captains* (1961) Gunn began to swap his English iambic accent for the more open sound of syllabic poetry. And he acknowledges that 'syllabics were really a way of teaching myself to write free verse'. He has not, however, abandoned metre and when he returns to it he uses it with an un-iambic, spoken fluidity as in the beautiful poem 'Sunlight' which concludes this selection of his work.

The Wound

Of this poem, from *Fighting Terms* (1954) Thom Gunn writes: 'I think this is the best poem in my first book. There's a lot of Shakespeare behind it, not only *Troilus and Cressida* but *Coriolanus* also. At this time I think I was hiding irritation beneath the heroic, or maybe trying to translate it into the heroic.' (All the quotations from Thom Gunn in these notes are taken from correspondence with the poet.)

The poem is tightly constructed round an *ababa*-stanza but by the judicious use of enjambement (heal / About; in turn / On; out / Each day) Gunn avoids metrical rigidity. Nevertheless all but two of the line-endings are monosyllables whose finality slows up the flow of the poem: Gunn is here still a brilliant apprentice, not yet a master craftsman (understandably so, considering he was still an undergraduate when the book was published). The narrator of the poem experiences a world of possibilities inside his head. He imagines himself as Paris, as Neoptolemus, as a Greek, as a Trojan. He chooses his sides, is not chosen by them: 'I was myself' (line 16).

1] *my head:* Gunn fancies this to be 'a dream part of myself'.
10] *Neoptolemus:* the son of Achilles.

On the Move

From *The Sense of Movement* (1957). Gunn believes this to be 'the poem where I most expanded my range' and adds 'The landscape is of the San Francisco Peninsula. There are certainly touches of Stevens and Yeats in the poem. This was to be only one of a series of poems, something like Marvell's Mower poems.' For the philosophical content of the poem Gunn was indebted to J. P. Sartre's lecture of 1945, *L'Existentialisme est un humanisme.* (tr. P. Mairet, *Existentialism and Humanism*, 1948). In his lecture Sartre argues that one respects the freedom of others by making one's own freedom: 'We will freedom for freedom's sake, in and through particular circumstances. And in thus willing freedom, we discover that it depends entirely upon the freedom of others, and that the freedom of others depends upon our freedom.' Few readers would credit the Boys of Gunn's poem with much capacity for respecting the freedom of others but Sartre is again relevant:

'The existentialist frankly states that man is an anguish. His meaning is as follows: When a man commits himself to anything, fully realising that he is not only choosing what he will be, but is thereby a legislator deciding for the whole of mankind – in such a moment a man cannot escape from the sense of complete and profound responsibility. There are many, indeed, who show no such anxiety. But we affirm that they are merely *disguising their anguish or are in flight from it*' (my italics).

Gunn's Boys have found, in their gratuitous action, only a 'part solution' (line 25) because their direct and demonstrative expression of energy only accounts for the immediate present whereas a truly existential act adds a dynamic dimension to the personality. Then again they express themselves through a mechanical 'created will' (the motorcycle (line 34)). Were the Boys all animal instead of 'half animal' (line 27) they could rely on their instinct but their humanity, however latent, intervenes:

'They strap in doubt – by hiding it, robust –
And almost hear a meaning in their noise.'

'Almost hear': that is one of the crucial points of the poem. In the 1950s the poem was often cited as a sociological document of the period. In perspective it is possible to see that Gunn was creating a subtle poem with anguish and not aggression at its heart.

5] *instinct:* a key concept in Gunn's poetry. Animals, for Gunn, are uncomplicated creatures who are true to their instinct while men cannot respond to instinct because they have been civilised.
21] Our natural, animal being is governed by the will.
22–4] Just as man creates his machines so he can 'manufacture' his personality ('soul'). Remembering the existential axiom that existence precedes essence Gunn is saying that man can be master of his fate if he avoids merely habitual action.
27–8] One is not damned because the non-animal part of us blunts natural instinct.

30] *valueless world:* meaning a world without accepted values, *not* a worthless world.

34] *the created will:* the motorcycle as a mechanical metaphor of volition.

38–40] Whether or not we approve of it the choice of the Boys is something positive – their uniform and manner consciously rejects conventional social criteria – and has a certain ritual beauty. The cadence of the last line is Empsonian, cf. 'The heart of standing is you cannot fly' from 'Aubade'.

Vox Humana

This poem, from *The Sense of Movement*, was Gunn's second piece in which the lines are syllabic (seven to each line) rather than accentual, though he has retained the loose rhyme-scheme *abccba*. Taking his cue from Donne, Gunn elaborates his own experience of a thought by personifying Choice and making it the narrator of his poem. Thus we are given the image of Choice being something perceptible and perpetually available. Those who ignore the opportunity to choose will 'remain blurred'. Those who confront Choice will determine their own future.

Title] Literally the human voice. Gunn may also have been thinking that in the organ the vox humana is a reed stop capable of suggesting the human voice.

1] *Being:* this can be taken both nominally or verbally.

2] *I:* the personification of Choice.

8] *least resistance:* least likely to conform to social norms.

In Santa Maria Del Popolo

'Here at last', Gunn says of this poem from *My Sad Captains*, 'I begin some kind of critique of the Heroic.' Gunn lived in Rome, on a studentship, before going to California in 1954. The poem is set in the Church of Santa Maria del Popolo, Rome, whose Cerasi Chapel contains two paintings by Caravaggio (1573–1610): *The Crucifixion of St Peter* and *The Conversion of St Paul*. Gunn concentrates on the latter, a masterpiece of *chiaroscuro* and dramatic composition, which shows Paul prostrate with his arms raised upwards before his horse. At first the poet is unable to read the painted shadows because of the real shadows and, when this leads to a confusion between reality and illusion, he wonders whether the painter saw more than the capacity for change in everyman. Then, turning from the Cerasi Chapel, the spectacle of poor women in desperate prayer reminds him that people are, after all, partly determined by circumstances and that gestures come more easily to painted saints than to real sinners.

For this poem Gunn returned to the iambic pentameter and a strict rhyme-scheme *ababcdcd*.

9–10] There are three figures in *The Conversion of St Paul*: the foreshortened saint, the horse, and, almost hidden by the horse, the groom.

20–2] Gunn refers to two other Caravaggio paintings: *Mary Magdalen* (Rome, Doria Gallery); and *The Cardsharpers* (location now unknown).

23] *was strangled:* Caravaggio's life was turbulent. In 1606 he murdered a man in a quarrel; in 1608 he was imprisoned; in 1609 he was gravely wounded; in 1610 he died of malaria, alone, on a beach near Grosseto.

The Byrnies

This poem from *My Sad Captains* is, says Gunn, 'My own myth about the origins of conceptual thinking.' A band of primitive warriors stop before something unknown, and as they do so only the chinking of their chainmail sounds familiar. Before them they see a growing forest which cuts some of the sunlight from them. Although they are ready to face a familiar enemy ('the nicker's snap, and hostile spear' (line 20)) they are bewildered by the huge dark obstruction before them. Then, as they look at each other, they see that the sunlight has not deserted them but gleams in their chainmail. Therefore they associate their protective chainmail with safety. Thus they classify their new experience. What Gunn's myth implies is that the world begins as a mass of undifferentiated phenomena which only gradually becomes assimilated as new impressions are related to familiar convictions.

3] *byrnie:* O.E. word for a chainmail shirt.
4] *the constant Thing:* Gunn writes 'the "Thing" is constant by contrast to the inconstancy, the mutability, the changeableness, the duplicities of the human being'.
20] *nicker:* O.E. word for water-monster.

My Sad Captains

Of the title-poem of his 1961 collection Gunn says 'A good sad serious poem that rounds off this part of my poetry, poetry in much of which I emphasise the will as an end in itself. From now on, a bit more flexibility.' The title comes from a speech by Antony in *Antony and Cleopatra*:

> 'Come,
> Let's have one other gaudy night: call to me
> All my sad captains, fill our bowls; once more
> Let's mock the midnight bell.'

(III. xiii)

The poet, aware of a personal change, bids farewell to his poetic past and those who most influenced him in it. There were the friends and the famous ('with historical/names' (lines 3-4)) – Gunn suggests such as Stendhal, Camus, Shakespeare, von Stauffenberg. He remembers them as men of intensity, those who formed the pantheon to which he dedicated his poetry of will and 'hard energy' (line 18). Like 'Vox Humana' it is in septasyllabic lines – this time rhyming *abcabc*.

The Goddess

This poem, from *Touch* (1967), is Gunn's 'invocation to the Muse'. The muse is Proserpina, the fertility goddess, who is, for Gunn, also Goddess of energy and Muse. He imagines her as an elemental and irresistible force blasting its way up from the earth's centre, through the ocean depths (where 'eyeless fish' would meet her) and ubiquitously and indiscriminately expressing itself. This time the septasyllabic lines are unrhymed.

Touch

Gunn considers the title-poem of his 1967 collection 'My first successful free verse poem of any importance.' Here the poet traditionally associated with action, energy and will shows his capacity for tenderness.

Pierce Street

This poem, from *Touch*, refers to a street in San Francisco where two painter-friends of Gunn's lived in 1965. They had painted figures round the walls of one room. The poet describes a visit to the house and tells how he found it devoid of people and peopled with illusions – painted figures 'twice life-size' (line 22). These, he concludes, are the soldiers of the imagination that preserve creative power by their existence. Art survives its creators. Here Gunn uses the iambic pentameter with a rhyme-scheme *abacbc*, lines 4 and 5 in each stanza constituting a single metrical unit but typographically arranged to reveal the internal rhyme.

Rites of Passage

Of this poem, from *Moly* (1971), Gunn writes:

'I'm very pleased with the way I've used myth here . . . the boy may be growing antlers *really*, or he may be hallucinating them. Father–Grey-Top-Old Man is his father, whom he contemplates castrating at the end of the poem. But the references are very wide – one suggestion for the poem came from a line I heard Ferlinghetti read at a poetry reading (about growing horns) another from Jim Morrison's song 'The End' (first LP by The Doors, about 1967). But there's also Zeus and Cronos in it, and all sons against their fathers.'

At first reading the poem recalls an earlier one, 'The Allegory of the Wolf Boy' (*The Sense of Movement*), which was also concerned with metamorphosis. However in the earlier poem the change was tragic, stressing the impossibility of urban man reverting to the purely instinctual level. Here the change is presented joyously by the speaker of the poem. He rejoices in the animal power the transformation gives him – a power to take revenge on his past, represented by his father.

The Messenger

From *Moly*. A poem dealing with perception. The messenger cannot dismiss the flower by naming it and attempts to penetrate its meaning by looking at it, by imitating its shape, by listening to it. This kind of lyrical utterance shows Gunn stripping his language of the philosophical and stylistic assumptions associated with his early poetry. The poem speaks for itself taking the reader step by step, stanza by stanza, into a world of phenomena temporarily freed from our expectations.

1] *turning angel:* In Greek and Hebrew myth an angel was a messenger.

Sunlight

This poem, from *Moly*, says Gunn, 'Came as a result of the chant to the sun by Ginsberg, Snyder, &c. at the end of the first Human Be In in Jan 1967'. It continues the process of purification in Gunn's poetry: he is no longer seeking effects but is seeking to write poems that contain the information they explore. Although some way from the philosophical complexity of 'On the Move' this poem is but deceptively simple. At its heart is the scientific fact that the sun is a star that will eventually exhaust itself:

> 'The system of which sun and we are part
> Is both imperfect and deteriorating.'

Yet there is an intuitive knowledge that transcends the accumulation of facts and it is this that the poet invokes.

TED HUGHES

In an essay on the chronology of his first wife's poems in *The Art of Sylvia Plath* (1970) Ted Hughes says: 'It's my suspicion that no poem can be a poem that is not a statement from the powers in control of our life, the ultimate suffering and decision in us. It seems to me that this is poetry's only real distinction from the literary forms that we call "not poetry".' The emphasis on suffering is characteristic of a poet who seems convinced that the first creative artist, God, made a ghastly mess of things when he created a world in which the powers of darkness had an immediate and unfair advantage over the powers of light. Poetry, for Hughes, is not song but ringing statement and his development as a writer has been a movement away from a poetry of observation to a poetry of potent statement and unanswerable narrative power. Perhaps, like his roosting hawk, Hughes always knew what he was looking for but, being all-too-human, could not go 'direct / Through the bones of the living' ('Hawk Roosting').

Hughes's persistent obsession with the animal kingdom began when he spent much of his childhood on the bleak wilds of Yorkshire. He seems to have decided, from the extant evidence, that men are handicapped by their rationalistic, reflective approach to problems and noticed that animals simply react while men search in vain. Animals have a purpose built into their bones. Man has yet to find one. Hughes was clearly fascinated by the instinctive point of view and wanted to give it a voice. In the title-poem from *The Hawk in the Rain* (1957) he compares himself – a 'Bloodily grabbed dazed last-moment-counting / Morsel in the earth's mouth' – unfavourably with the hawk whose 'wings hold all creation in a weightless quiet'. Henceforth he wanted to be on the side of the predatory angels and see things with their instinctive eyes.

The hawk sees everything from a great height and Hughes quickly assumed a God's-eye-view, or hawk's-eye-view, which would let him present the world as an absurd perpetual motion machine of earth moving in an infinity of black. It is a creative perspective he has never abandoned. In 'Roarers in a Ring' he watched 'the world . . . whirling still / . . . in the bottomless black / Silence' (lines 33–6). In 'Skylarks' he speaks of 'The mad earth' (line 59). In 'Song of Woe' he tells how 'the earth rolled slowly away . . . / Into non-being' (lines 36 and 38). From this cosmic vantage-point the activities of men are seen in clear patterns. Hughes sees the movements of individuals rather than their motives. And Hughes tends to judge people, from his hawks' height, on their actions alone. Explanations do not interest him. His vision reduces human beings to a Lilliputian scale so that he is able, as it were, to describe the ants that crawl over this lump he can grasp up in his mind's hand. While men search 'The night snows stars and the earth creaks' ('The Howling of Wolves', *Wodwo*). His perspectives are enormous and enormously confident. Hughes's iconography does not merely contain animals. He is on intimately familiar terms with their Creator and capable of saying 'God is a good fellow, but His mother's against Him' ('Logos', *Wodwo*), or 'Adam ate the apple. / Eve ate Adam' ('Theology', *Wodwo*). We are persuaded that he *knows*.

Hughes has, then, a Miltonic sweep, a massive certainty of visionary utterance that lets him dispute the state of the world with God. It is a vision that excludes personal tenderness – the exception here is his poem for his daughter in *Wodwo*, 'Full Moon and Little Frieda' – and avoids dispensing his sympathy, for if Hughes were to come down to land on earth he might lose the powers that possess him. It is unusual in a self-styled common-sensical age to come across a possessed poet but Hughes is utterly serious about his cosmology. In an interview with Egbert Faas in *London Magazine* (January 1971) Hughes defined his position thus:

'Any form of violence – any form of vehement activity – invokes the bigger energy, the elemental power circuit of the Universe. Once the contact has been made – it becomes difficult to control. Something beyond ordinary human activity enters . . . When the old rituals and dogma have lost credit and disintegrated . . . the energy cannot be contained, and so its effect is destructive – and that is the position with us . . . If you refuse the energy, you are living a kind of death. If you accept the energy, it destroys you. What is the alternative? To accept the energy, and find methods of turning it to good, of keeping it under control – rituals, the machinery of religion.'

As his themes so clearly show, Hughes has decided to accept the energy and to try and control it in his poetry. To do this he had to be sure of his technical power, of his ability to shape the energy into communicable patterns, and there is no question but that he has assimilated many disparate influences in an effort to make his own voice echo with the power of the past. Shakespeare is his favourite author, *Sir Gawain and the Green Knight* his favourite poem. Some of his own poems are haunted by other poems and poets: 'The Hawk in the Rain' by Dylan Thomas's 'Over Sir John's hill'; 'An Otter' by Gerard Manley Hopkins; 'Song for a Phallus' by W. H. Auden's 'Victor. A Ballad'; 'Gog' (part II anyway) by T. S. Eliot. But more than anything else there is the influence of the Bible. 'You spend a lifetime', Hughes has said, 'learning how to write verse when it's been clear from your earliest days that the greatest poetry in English is in the prose of the Bible.'

Probably Hughes's greatest poetic strength is his use of rhythm. It is a mimetic rhythm capable of recreating animal movement or suggesting human desolation. There is the darting euphony of Part I of 'An Otter'; the sinewy motion of 'Second Glance at a Jaguar'; the thundering clatter of Part III of 'Gog'; the light rapidity of 'Skylarks'; the anguished sob in the refrain of 'Song for a Phallus'; there is the parallelism of 'Lovesong'. Whether conjuring up monosyllabic madness in 'Hawk Roosting' or polysyllabic suffocation in 'Lovesong' Hughes is a master of the sound-picture.

Given this mastery of rhythm many followers of Hughes were appalled at the austerity, the catalogue-of-assertions-technique, of *Crow* (1970). I think the explanation is that Hughes has desired to become more and more biblically basic and has learned to do without unnecessary ornament. When images are needed they are used to illuminate a dark passage and relieve the monochromes. Few poets would begin poems 'Once upon a time there was a person' which is now a standard Hughes opening. Few poets, however, could control a modern folk-idiom that is both stylistically transparent and philosophically dense. A poem like 'Song of Woe' can be read both as a magical fable and as a Buddhist allegory. Eliot said – in 'Reflections on *Vers libre*' (1917) – that 'Swinburne mastered his technique, which is a great deal, but he did not master it to the extent of being able to take liberties with it, which is everything.' In *Crow*, and the poems since, Hughes has managed to do what Swinburne could not.

Despite the consistent elements in his cosmology – the failure of Creation, the botched genesis of man and woman, the comparative strength of the powers of darkness – Hughes seems in recent poems like 'Song of Woe' to deal with a tortuous kind of serenity but a serenity nevertheless. He is now, it seems, in control of, not at the mercy of, his energies. The certainty of utterance says so. What is also certain is that Hughes will continue to develop – however mature the tonality and range of his poems seem to be even now – and that he has not yet defined his own nature to his own satisfaction.

Meanwhile there is the proliferation of rhythm to enjoy, the thematic range to admire, the iconography to investigate, and the dark revelations to attend to. Ted Hughes is one of the few poets willing to be judged by the rigorous standards we apply to poets of the past. He treats, not topical matters, but the same themes that obsessed Seneca and Shakespeare and Chaucer. He does not, therefore, really fit into the contemporary scene and that, no doubt, is the way he wants it.

Roarers in a Ring

This poem, from Hughes's first book, *The Hawk in the Rain* (1957) shows that, from the beginning, it was a gross oversimplification to classify Hughes as an 'animal poet'. Here, the rural elements are certainly observed: the snow-covered moor, the starved fox, the peat fire, the low-beamed inn. Yet the inn and the references to Wenceslas and Christmas Eve evoke, of course, the nativity, which is what Christmas Eve is supposed to be about, but which the farmers in the poem celebrate as a pagan Bacchanalia. Not only that, but they hysterically avoid even the slightest hint of solemnity. Then, the morning after, each experiences his own drunken fall of man. Although these elements are present they are used not satirically but to give an extra dimension in which we can see the activities of the farmers. The poet himself is not excessively solemn but uses vivid images – 'Faces sweating like hams' (line 6), 'The moor looked like the moon' (line 26) – to contrast the genuine warmth inside with the chill outside. And there is something amiable in the sheer ability of the farmers to keep the laughter going round and round 'in a Ring'. So the poem is both a description of an event, and a provocative celebration of the nativity. Technically the poem opens in the manner of a

Christmas carol – 'Snow fell as for Wenceslas' – and graduates to the ballad manner:

> 'The air was new as a razor,
> The moor looked like the moon,'

and the open syntax of the closing quatrain suggests both the falling farmers' last glimpse of the world, and the earth itself falling, like a spinning drunk, into a 'bottomless black / Silence'.

Title] The Ring is the drinking circle the farmers make in the inn. The notion of endless circular motion reappears throughout the poem as in 'tossed a ball' (line 10), 'the ale went round and round' (line 17), 'the world . . . Went whirling still' (lines 33–4). It explains and interprets the dizziness of the drinkers.

Hawk Roosting

In his *London Magazine* (January 1971) interview with Egbert Faas Hughes said of this poem from *Lupercal* (1960):

'The poem of mine usually cited for violence is the one about the Hawk Roosting, this drowsy hawk sitting in a wood and talking to itself. That bird is accused of being a fascist . . . the symbol of some horrible totalitarian geno-cidal dictator. Actually what I had in mind was that in this hawk Nature is thinking. Simply Nature. It's not so simple maybe because Nature is no longer so simple. I intended some Creator like the Jehovah in Job but more feminine. When Christianity kicked the devil out of Job what they actually kicked out was Nature . . . and Nature became the devil.'

In Hughes's poems the difference between animals and men is that while men search for meanings, animals instinctively know what they are and what they are after. They react, they do not reflect. If they did reflect they might state their case in the terms of 'Hawk Roosting'. The hawk feels he is sufficiently omnipotent to dispense with arguments, but asserts that 'the one path of my flight is direct / Through the bones of the living' (lines 18–19). Life has a purpose for such a creature, even if it is entirely destructive and at the expense of others.

The quatrains use occasional rhymes and half-rhymes – feet/eat; slowly/ body – and skilfully contrast monosyllabic with polysyllabic lines:

> 'I sit at the top of the wood, my eyes closed.
> Inaction, no falsifying dream'

16] *manners:* both behaviour and etiquette.

An Otter

The otter is an evolutionary oddity – an aquatic carnivore with webbed feet and a furry body. In 'Hawk Roosting' the hawk did the talking, in 'An Otter', from *Lupercal*, the otter does the moving. The otter is in search of a lost world, a realm where he can find an identity who is 'neither fish nor beast' (line 2), 'Of neither water nor land' (line 11). There is a marvellous manipu-lation of sounds to suggest the movement of the otter. The drag of 'Under-water eyes' (line 1) is followed by the rapid spurt of 'an eel's / Oil' and this mimetic rhythm is sustained throughout Part I of the poem. The otter is alive and constantly moving, looking, hiding, hunting, swimming, wandering – the mimetic rhythms tell us so. However, the otter is also hunted in the summer, an English pastime. So in Part II the poem moves into quatrains to suggest the solid human movement, the steady march of hunters and the otter's ability to keep still when he has to. To hunters the only beautiful otter is a dead one, yet the linguistic and rhythmic virtuosity of Part I has already convinced us that it is movement that makes the otter magical.

2] *Oil of water:* proverbially oil and water don't mix, but they come together in the contradictory otter who is 'neither fish nor beast'.

Second Glance at a Jaguar

In *The Hawk in the Rain* Hughes included a poem called 'The Jaguar'. It is in quatrains and describes a crowd at the zoo mesmerized before the jaguar's cage, while the animal is 'hurrying enraged / Through prison darkness'. The poem indicates the human absurdity of placing such an instinctively expansive creature in a cage, and concludes:

> 'His stride is wildernesses of freedom:
> The world rolls under the long thrust of his heel.
> Over the cage floor the horizons come.'

In the 'Second Glance at a Jaguar' from *Wodwo* (1967) Hughes has moved from outside the cage into the world of the jaguar. The poet is no longer spectator, but celebrant of the jaguar's power. As in Part I of 'An Otter' Hughes employs mimetic rhythm to evoke the jaguar. The rhythm is like a motor, propelling the jaguar forward, magnificently capturing its tormented perpetual motion. A phrase like 'He swipes a lap at the water-trough as he turns' (line 13) is more than description, it is a sound-picture of the action. There are only five period-stops in the thirty-three lines and the open-ended similes and metaphors pile on top of one another in an attempt to capture all the essentials of the jaguar. He is 'Skinfull of bowls' (line 1), 'Gangster' (line 23), and is compared to 'a cat going along under thrown stones' (line 4), 'a thick Aztec disemboweller' (line 7), 'a prayer-wheel' (line 29). All these images of violent motion describe the jaguar, but it is the rhythm that defines him. And if the jaguar has been captured in words, he has not been caged. In 'The Jaguar' he was trapped in the cage of the quatrains, in the 'Second Glance' he breaks out of it on the impetus of his insistent movement and we imagine, with him, what it is like to wade in his natural surroundings.

27] *the rosettes, the cain-brands:* the jaguar's skin is marked with black rosettes, here compared to the marks of Cain, Adam's son, the world's first murderer.

Gog

In this poem, from *Wodwo*, Hughes shows his ability to renew and reassemble powerful mythical material and his capacity to contrast different types of rhythm. In the *London Magazine* interview he said: 'I wrote another jaguarish poem called "Gog". That actually started as a description of the German assault through the Ardennes and turned into the dragon in Revelation. It alarmed me so much I wrote a poem about the Red Cross Knight just to set against it with the idea of keeping it under control . . . keeping its effects under control.' In Revelation 20: 2 'the dragon, that old serpent, which is the Devil, and Satan' is bound and cast into a bottomless pit for a thousand years. After the thousand years he is to be 'loosed a little season' upon Gog and Magog, the nations of the earth deceived by Satan. Then he is to be 'cast into the lake of fire and brimstone'. In Part I of 'Gog' Hughes describes, in the first person, the letting-loose of the dragon Satan who pounds through Gog and Magog 'Over the sounds of motherly weeping' (line 20). He then returns to 'a pool' (line 21), the lake of fire and brimstone. Part II describes the aftermath in Gog of the dragon's season on earth. In Revelation 20: 9 'fire came down from God out of heaven, and devoured them'. Or, as Hughes puts it, 'The sun erupts . . . the creatures of earth / Are mere rainfall rivulets' (lines 25, 27–8). In Revelation 20: 13 'the sea gave up the dead which were in it; and death and hell delivered up the dead which were in them'. Hughes sees everything, thus, as the mirror of death. Part III describes the coming of the Red Cross Knight. In Book I of Spenser's *Faerie Queene* the Red Cross Knight is St George, patron saint of England, Champion of Holiness. His first exploit is to attack 'a dragon, horrible and stern' which, of course, Hughes links to the dragon in Revelation. The Knight kills the dragon which is half-woman, half-monster. Hughes adds octopus-like features to the dragon, perhaps because when the Red Cross Knight kills her 'A stream of coal black blood forth gushed from her corpse.' Hughes imagines the Knight emerging from the devastated earth to herald the return of Christ. He sees the dragon wearing the Holy Grail as a helmet. To rescue this symbol of Christ, this womb from which Christ will emerge, the Red Cross Knight will have to overcome the dragon with the woman's smile and the tempting coils. And if Christ is to survive he, too, will have to overcome the smile of illusion. The poem ends with battle about to commence. It is a remarkable piece of writing. In Part I the rhythms are solid and heavy and pounding – 'My feetbones beat on the earth' (line 19). The tone is massively egotistical, as befits a Satanic dragon: 'I woke', 'I ran', 'My mouth', 'my error', 'My skull', 'my song', etc. In Part II, by contrast, the narrator does not intervene but keeps his distance from the scene. Objects abound: 'The sun', 'The moon', 'a skull', 'The stones', 'the vast bubble', etc. The effect of this catalogue of catastrophe is to evoke desolation. Part III has Hughes and his mimetic rhythms in full gallop. The repetitions and parallelisms bring the Red Cross Knight to life, thundering across the earth. Structurally the poem is a triptych showing Destruction (Part I), Desolation (Part II), Resurrection (Part III). Yet the outcome of the Resurrection is not certain and this reflects the pessimism that pervades *Wodwo* and will come to dominate *Crow*.

1] '*I am Alpha and Omega*': a phrase God uses several times in Revelation.
43] *wound-gash:* such combinations are common in Anglo-Saxon poetry.
47] *helm:* O.E. 'helmet'.
54] *the octopus maw:* cf. 'her filthy maw' *Faerie Queene* I. i. xx.
55] *the rocking, sinking cradle:* Hughes sees the Satanic dragon playing a part in the birth of Christ.
59] *Coriolanus:* hero of Shakespeare's play of that name.
59] *right through Rome:* part of the Red Cross Knight's battle, in Spenser, is against Duessa, the Roman Catholic religion.

Skylarks

The songbirds of this poem are real skylarks, meticulously observed, though the poet permits himself – '*as I see them*' (line 55) – to imagine them as birds with conscience, birds singing for their place on the wall, clearing their throats to clear their conscience. Normally Hughes favours long, weighty lines, but here he shows ability to shape verse for the occasion. The arrangement and sound of the lines follows the skylark from the ground, up into the sky, and then comes back to earth. There is an extended use of liquid, mellifluous sounds in the alliterative variations on 'l': 'Leaden / Like a bullet' (lines 15–16), 'milling the shingle' (line 30), 'the lark labour' (line 36), 'silently and endlessly' (line 50), 'those flailing flames / That lift from the fling of a bonfire' (lines 60–1), 'Claws dangling full' (line 62), 'flare and glide' (line 76). The effect of this is to conjure up, onomatopoetically, the song of the bird.

A Childish Prank

Crow (1970), from which this poem is taken, is really Genesis-according-to-Ted Hughes. In the Old Testament 'God created man in his *own* image, in the image of God created he him; male and female created he them.' And he put them in the beautiful Garden of Eden – beautiful to Him, though it included 'every thing that creepeth on the earth'. Hughes seemed to feel that Man and Woman had little chance from 'the beginning', what with the forbidden fruit and the serpent. He sees God's first conception as a ghastly error, for He had really created a world fit for the destructive. The first victory is won by the serpent, for example. Hughes sees this as a world where nobility was, inevitably, out of place. 'In the beginning was Scream' Hughes says in 'Lineage' and, given this situation, it is appropriate that Crow should find himself more at home on earth than man could. Crow is the other side of Creation – the very word has a harsh cackle when compared to the flowing sound of 'Creation' – and Crow's activities mock God for his foolish attempt to create a beautiful world out of darkness. There were several reasons for choosing the crow as a spokesman for Destruction. In a letter (27 February 1973) Hughes wrote me: 'Crow, as the bird of Bran, is the oldest and highest totem creature of Britain . . . England pretends to the lion – but that is a late fake import. England's autochthonous Totem is the Crow. Whatever colour of Englishman you scratch you come to some sort of Crow.' But crows are not confined to England (they inhabit every bit of land on earth apart from Antarctica). The crow is a cunning, predatory bird that feeds on dead and putrid flesh and, when carrion is scarce, will eat afterbirth or attack ewes in labour, pecking out their eyes. It is the most intelligent of birds and the evidence shows that it uses its intelligence to exploit the weak and helpless. As R. K. Murton says in *Man and Birds* (1971): 'Predacious habits and black plumage, burnt by the fires of hell, long ago made the crows prophets of disaster.' Hughes has incorporated these real and legendary features into his Crow and also given him a voice to speak with and a situation to crow over: the basic human situation created by God. God is the ally of Creation, Crow the ally of Destruction. God's basic error was in not eliminating darkness when he created the earth. The earth is God's dream, Crow is God's nightmare. And the nightmare triumphs over the dream.

In 'A Childish Prank' Crow improves on God's handiwork by inventing sex. He bites the Worm in two and stuffs one end each into Adam and Eve who are thus inexorably brought together. Sex thus becomes a pain that unites men and women regardless of their volition. God wanted a world where man would use his free will to resist temptation. Crow's universe is deterministic.

Hughes's ability to construct a new myth – however malicious or satirical – is a measure of his maturity in *Crow*. He is now writing a positive poetry, a poetry of propositions and statements of finality.

7] *the Worm:* the serpent of *Genesis*.

Song for a Phallus

Crow does not simply appear; he also sings, or crows. In his *London Magazine* interview Hughes said of Crow:

'The idea was originally just to write his songs, the songs that a Crow would sing. In other words, songs with no music whatsoever, in a super-simple and a super-ugly language which would in a way shed everything except just what he wanted to say without any other consideration and that's the basis of the style of the whole thing.'

Crow chooses to crow over one of the most murderous and destructive legends in man's history: the story of Oedipus who killed his father Laius and married his mother Jocasta. In 1967 Hughes had been invited by Peter Brook to adapt Seneca's *Oedipus* for production at the National Theatre. This is his own personal version – or, more exactly, Crow's version – of the Oedipus legend. Freud used the Oedipus myth as the basis of his Oedipus Complex which claims that all boys, from three to five, go through a 'phallic stage' in which sexual feelings towards the mother produce a corresponding dislike of the father who they fear will castrate them for their desire. Crow is enough of a Freudian determinist to sing of the phallic stage in a grown man, and the refrain 'Mamma Mamma' is a childish cry of desire. In the Greek legend Oedipus was a patricide. In Crow's version he becomes a matricide as well and ends by splitting his mother open so he can curl up inside her bloody womb.

Hughes's use of the ballad stanza is robust and deliberately 'super-ugly'. There is a precedent for the Freudian ballad in Auden's 'Victor. A Ballad' which uses phrases like 'Have you ever had a woman?', 'Victor's a decent fellow', 'God, what fun I had with her.' The influence is obvious enough. Hughes goes beyond Auden in respecting the vernacular origins of the ballad and he gloriously uses language that is everyday at the moment.

7] *a Dickybird:* the modern oracular message – 'a little bird told me'. A normally childish phrase, though sinister in the mouth of the super-bird Crow.
13] *stropped his hacker:* sharpened his razor on a leather strop.
23] *tied its legs:* Oedipus's heels were pierced and tied together when he was left on Mount Cithaeron as a baby. 'Oedipus' is Greek for 'Swollenfoot'.
48-9] The Sphynx's riddle was 'What goes on four feet, then two, then three, and is weaker the more feet it has?' When Oedipus correctly answered 'Man' the Sphynx threw herself down from her rock.
69] *on or:* the rhyme 'bucket' (line 67) obviously leads the reader to expect

'fuck it' at this point. This sort of innuendo is common in modern ballads, viz. army songs or music hall numbers.

71–4] cf.   'He stood there above the body,
            He stood there holding the knife;
            And the blood ran down the stairs and sang,
            "I'm the Resurrection and the Life".'
                                        AUDEN, 'Victor. A Ballad'

Lovesong

Having invented sex in 'A Childish Prank' Crown now proceeds to catalogue the activities and consciousness of the modern successors of Adam and Eve. It is no surprise that the lovers in the 'Love-song' from *Crow* inhabit a sexual battlefield, not a domestic love-nest. This Crow's-eye-view of a human relationship strips it of its traditional beauty and presents it as a monotonous, monochromatic ritual. Crow sees the lovers as two furious protagonists and 'love' as a destructive force. It is the mechanical side of sex as might be seen by a totally clinical observer making notes towards the definition of lust. The poem eschews lyricism for a poetry of cruelty, a poetry of vicious imagery: 'She bit him she gnawed him' (line 4), 'Her looks nailed down his hands' (line 9), 'Her embrace was an immense press' (line 16), 'His smiles were spider bites' (line 18), 'His words were occupying armies' (line 20), 'His whispers were whips and jackboots' (line 24), etc. The poem systematically alternates the suffocating attributes of each protagonist and, at the end of the furious battle, they have simply succeeded in changing places. It is a pessimistic crow over man's basest impulses. God, in Genesis, wanted man to 'cleave unto his wife: and they shall be one flesh'. Crow describes, with quasi-fascist relish – 'whips and jackboots' (line 24), 'the grinding of locks' (line 27), 'Their screams' (line 37) – how this works out in practice. Crow wants to remind God that man is totally without nobility, that he is a failure, that his activities are nasty, brutish, ritualistic and maniacal. And, of course, his images imply the evidence for his case: Crow is in the unique position of being able to see the world whole and he constantly reduces individuals to typical aspects of general patterns. The poem should ideally be read in the context of the *Crow* sequence, but it stands on its own as a description of love by the devil's advocate. Remember that Hughes wanted to write, in *Crow*, 'the songs that a Crow would sing'. This is such a song.

38–9] Crow has already used this image in line 76 of his 'Song for a Phallus'.

Song of Woe

The text of this uncollected poem is reproduced from Keith Sagar's monograph on Hughes. Sagar says of it: 'This seems to me the furthest Hughes has gone. It is very close to St John of the Cross: "Hence the soul cannot be possessed of the divine union, until it has divested itself of the love of created beings."' It is even closer to *The Tibetan Book of the Dead*. In 1960 Hughes had been invited by the Chinese composer Chou Wen-chung to write a libretto based on *The Tibetan Book of the Dead* (and he did, though there was no financial backing for production). He came to know the text very well as is obvious from this poem. The original title of *The Tibetan Book of the Dead* is the *Bardo Thodol* which means 'liberation by experience of the after-death'. The death is the death of the ego and this involves transcendence of the world and the self. In the *Bardo Thodol* there are three stages of transcendence. First, beyond the world and the self (*Chikhai Bardo*). Second, confrontation with the self (*Chonyid Bardo*). Third, rebirth (*Sidpa Bardo*). Hughes's poem describes 'a person' mounting precisely these stages to attain a spiritual rebirth. In lines 1–30 he renounces the world, in lines 33–8 he renounces the self (*Chikhai Bardo*); in lines 39–44 he confronts the self, 'His howling transfigured double' (line 44) (*Chonyid Bardo*); in lines 45–9 he is reborn (*Sidpa Bardo*). Which is not to say that Hughes has moved from Crow's critique of God to Buddhism. As he points out in his *London Magazine* interview the story has universal application:

'Once fully-fledged [the Shaman] can enter trance at will and go into the spirit world . . . he goes to get something badly needed, a cure, an answer, some sort of divine intervention in the community's affairs. Now this flight to the spirit world he experiences as a dream . . . and that dream is the basis of the hero story. It is the same basic outline pretty well all over the world, same events, same figures, same situations. It is the skeleton of thousands of folktales and myths.'

To emphasise the folk-element in his version, Hughes begins 'Song of Woe' with one of his now-standard openings: 'Once upon a time / There was a person.' This had been developed in evolving the verbal austerity of *Crow* where many poems begin casually: 'There was this terrific battle', 'There was this hidden grin', 'There was this man' and, in 'A Bedtime Story', 'Once upon a time there was a person.' Yet there is always a poetic control informing the basic simplicity: 'Like the legs of a stag in wet brambles' (line 9), 'like a curtain over the finale / Of all things' (lines 12–13), etc. Hughes has moved beyond obvious technical virtuosity to concentrate on verbal austerity and narrative impact. He also appears to have moved beyond the poetry of cruelty to a poetry of spiritual depth. Nevertheless, the natural stylistic tendencies remain constant. In the first poem in this selection he had 'the world . . . whirling still . . . in the bottomless black / Silence through which it fell'. In 'Song of Woe' 'the earth rolled slowly away / Smaller and smaller away / Into non-being' (lines 36–8). The God's-eye-vision has been retained, but it now sees things with a more understanding eye.

SYLVIA PLATH

Although Sylvia Plath was born in Boston she can, like her fellow-American T. S. Eliot, be justifiably included in a book of English verse. She studied at Cambridge, married a Yorkshireman, had her children in London and Devon, spent the three most creative years of her life in England. And, of course, she died tragically in England. Her outstanding poems in *Ariel* (1965) draw on things she had seen and events that had happened to her in England and it is on *Ariel* that she will be judged as a poet. Her first book, *The Colossus* (1960), with the influences of John Crowe Ransom and Theodore Roethke showing, is a promising book but hardly a great one. Indeed Sylvia Plath herself dismissed all her poems written before 'The Stones' (i.e. before Autumn 1959) as juvenilia, and 'The Stones' was the last poem she wrote in America.

Ted Hughes, in an essay in *The Art of Sylvia Plath*, has described how the juvenilia were written: 'She wrote her early poems very slowly, Thesaurus open on her knee . . . as if she were working out a mathematical problem, chewing her lips, putting a thick dark ring of ink around each word that stirred for her on the page of the Thesaurus.' The breakthrough of 'Tulips' came in March 1961. Hughes says she 'wrote this poem without her usual studies over the Thesaurus, and at top speed, as one might write an urgent letter. From then on, all her poems were written in this way.'

Her message was indeed urgent. It was to the effect that some things in life are worth dying for. She drew on the background of her father's death, her own attempted suicide, her experience of mental distress, the concentration camps, decay, destruction. As she said in an interview with Peter Orr reproduced in *The Poet Speaks* (1966): 'I believe that one should be able to control and manipulate experiences, even the most terrifying, like madness, being tortured, this sort of experience, and one should be able to manipulate these experiences with an informed and an intelligent mind.' The poems posthumously published in *Ariel* (and indeed in *Winter Trees*, 1971) fulfil her criteria by dealing with intensely personal concerns in a technically clinical way. She said that her poems were long and skinny like herself, but like her too they are powerfully perceptive and brilliant.

In the writing of these poems she was influenced by certain poems of Anne Sexton and by the precedent of Robert Lowell's *Life Studies* (1959) where experiences of mental strain are confessed and confronted. Lowell himself, however, recognised that her poems were more than the sum of their influences when he wrote, in a letter to M. L. Rosenthal cited in *The Art of Sylvia Plath*:

'Maybe it's an irrelevant accident that she actually carried out the death she predicted . . . but somehow her death is part of the imaginative risk. In the best poems, one is torn by saying, "This is so true and lived that most other poetry seems like an exercise", and then can back off and admire the dazzling technique and invention.'

Exactly. While Sexton and Lowell wrote their confessional poems as an auto-therapeutic act Sylvia Plath meant every word she wrote and it is this intensity that gives the poems their stature.

'Dying is an art' writes Sylvia Plath in the macabre 'Lady Lazarus'. So is poetry, and her own poems demonstrate that art at its most powerfully personal. Its rhythms are fast, her symbols are consistently convincing. Take her use of colour. In 'Suicide Off Egg Rock', from *The Colossus*, Sylvia Plath talks of

'his blood beating the old tattoo
I am, I am, I am.'

and this existential appreciation of blood is often at work in the poems where red is a symbol of energetic life. In 'Poppies in October' there is the woman whose 'red heart blooms through her coat so astoundingly'; in 'Tulips' Sylvia Plath's own heart 'opens and closes / Its bowl of red blooms'; in 'Daddy' she speaks of her 'pretty red heart'. Red is warm and alive and full of blood and palpably there. Opposed to the virility of blood is the sterility of white. White is clinical and cold and appears in the poems as the perfection of death. In 'Tulips' the patient enjoys the serenity within 'white walls'; in 'Berck-Plage' the dead man has a 'wedding-cake face'; in 'Edge' we have 'Each dead child coiled, a white serpent'. And hovering over this white perfection are the black shadows in which lurk the horrors of life. Black is destructive and menacing and one escapes from it by seeking the whiteness of death. There is the merciless 'black boot' in 'Berck-Plage'; 'Daddy' is 'So black no sky could squeak through'; in 'Years' God is seen in a 'vacuous black'. And yet along with her fascination for the white finality of death went an obsession with staring into the black shadows. 'I like black statements' she said in 'Little Fugue'.

And in 'Kindness' she said 'The blood jet is poetry, / There is no stopping it.' Rhythm is the life-blood of poetry and Sylvia Plath's rhythm is like a heart beat, fast in excitement, steady in calm – a 'heart-rhythm' as John Frederick Nims called it in his contribution to *The Art of Sylvia Plath*. That existential heart-beat 'I am, I am, I am' could be technically transcribed as 'iamb, iamb, iamb'. In addition to which there is Nims's suggestion that the soundness of iambic pentameter is due to the fact that on average there are five heart-beats to each normal breath. Yet if the underlying rhythm is iambic, the form of the poems is unconventional. Stanzas are used as typographical patterns, but the sense breaks out from the stanzaic pattern. For example 'Berck-Plage' is written in couplets, but they are wide open, not closed:

> 'Tubular steel wheelchairs, aluminium crutches.
> Such salt-sweetness. Why should I walk
>
> Beyond the breakwater, spotty with barnacles?
> I am not a nurse, white and attendant'

As Sylvia Plath said, her poems were intended for 'the ear, not the eye' and they certainly endure with a haunting refrain. She felt herself surrounded by the violence of everyday life and communicated these feelings with a startling clarity. Tulips are 'explosions' ('Tulips'), there is 'Viciousness in the kitchen' ('Lesbos'), human skin is 'Bright as a Nazi lampshade' ('Lady Lazarus'). Ted Hughes has said that 'Her reactions to hurts in other people and animals, and even tiny desecrations of plant-life were extremely violent. The chemical poisoning of nature, the pile-up of atomic waste, were horrors that persecuted her like an illness – as her latest poems record.' Her theme is the terrifying vulnerability of the hyper-sensitive human in a terrifyingly hostile world from which the only escape is death.

She could hardly have composed her poems so exceptionally well had she not had a powerfully apt command of metaphor. It is this that proclaims her artistry and it is this that should warn us against being excessively autobiographical in the treatment of her work (as if the poems were sick patients). Her personal agony was like an open wound but she had enough self-control to put a pinch of salt on it from time to time. The self-dramatisation never becomes self-pity because there are so many metaphorical objects to cling onto in the sea of suffering. 'My body is a pebble' ('Tulips'), 'The lines of the eye . . . / Boomerang like anchored elastics' ('Berck-Plage'), 'Stars . . . bright stupid confetti' ('Years'): these striking images are the muscular basis of the poems. And her poetry abounds in such images, proclaiming itself as poetry, not the random confessions of a woman tottering on the brink of suicide.

Her life – or, more exactly, her death – has become inextricably linked with the poems and the enormous interest in her work stems in part from literary necrophilia. This is understandable if largely inexcusable. In Sylvia Plath's case there are more nightmares than beautiful dreams, certainly, but her work will survive her legend because it is something all of us can share. Oscar Wilde may have put his talent into his work and his genius into his life: in Sylvia Plath's case the converse obtains.

Some of her finest poems came in the nine-month period before her death, like a birth. Let us be sure to come to them with a mind to be made up not as part of the morbid 'peanut-crunching crowd' who gaped at 'Lady Lazarus'.

Tulips

'Tulips', from *Ariel* (1965), was the first poem in which Sylvia Plath found her way into a territory that was recognisably her own, a vast brainscape haunted by the objects and people she responded to. 'Tulips' belongs to March 1961, and records some tulips she had in the hospital where she was recovering from an appendectomy. The tulips are a bloody intrusion of life into a white, deathly quiet realm where the poet has found peace. Peace is white – 'how white everything is' (line 2), 'these white walls' (line 4), 'two white lids' (line 9), 'white caps' (line 12), 'white swaddlings' (line 38) – and the tulips explode into this clinical snowscape and remind the poet that she is alive and her heart is beating. It had been her desire to escape into an oceanic anonymity – 'I have given my name . . . up to the nurses' (line 6), 'I have wanted to efface myself' (line 48) – but the tulips bring her back to life, as the photograph of her husband and child cling onto her like 'little smiling hooks' (line 21). The tulips, 'too excitable' (line 1) and 'too red' (line 36), are raw for life and make straight for her heart which she feels opening and closing like a tulip.

The poem has no set rhyme-scheme but there are many assonantal corres-pondences in the line-endings: explosions/surgeons; pillbox/hooks; trinkets/tablet; fuss/noise; me/sea. This keeps the poetic flow, like a heart, in the right place. There is also a profusion of similes which give a textural density to the poem and contribute to its fluency: 'Like an eye' (line 9), 'like a black pillbox' (line 19), 'like a Communion tablet' (line 35), 'like an awful baby' (line 38), 'like a loud noise' (line 52), 'like dangerous animals' (line 58), 'like the mouth of some great African cat' (line 59), 'like the sea' (line 62).

1] *The tulips are too excitable:* an arresting use of the pathetic fallacy to indi-cate the mood of the speaker.

1] *here:* hospital.

5] *I am nobody:* In some of her late poems Sylvia Plath sees people as merely the sum of their physical parts and the point of this phrase is that she has been able to escape, momentarily, at least from her body.

10] *Stupid pupil:* one of the vivid puns that occur in the late poems.

15] *as water:* Sylvia Plath grew up near the sea and sees water as a vast source of wonder and potential violence. The imagery is continued in lines 27, 53, and 63. It is this ability to sustain her imagery that testifies to the craftsman-ship that makes the impact of the poems so lasting.

Berck-Plage

In his 'Notes' on the chronology of the poems Ted Hughes writes of this poem from *Ariel*:

'In June, 1961, we had visited Berck-Plage, a long beach and resort on the coast of France north of Rouen. Some sort of hospital or convalescent home for the disabled fronts the beach. It was one of her nightmares stepped into the real world. A year later – almost to the day – our next door neighbour, an old man, died after a short grim illness during which time his wife repeatedly needed our help. In this poem that visit to the beach and the death and funeral of our neighbour are combined. It belongs to July 1962.'

This is one of the few poems where the poet herself is not the central charac-ter and it is, for that reason, uniquely successful. The Plath colour-scheme is beautifully controlled throughout the work: the dead man with his 'wedding-cake face' (line 55) and his 'powdery beak /. . . so whitely unbuffeted' (lines 63–4); the sinister man in black, the priest, a 'black boot' (line 19) of a man, a 'high, dead, toeless foot' (line 21). At the beginning of the poem he is a shadowy, surrealistic figure, but at the end he is rooted in reality. While 'the melt of shoe-blacking' (line 120) jolts the mind back to the 'black boot' it simultaneously describes a real scene. The influence of Dylan Thomas is present in the poem in phrases like 'eyelids and lips / Storming the hilltops' (lines.117–18) and 'the barred yard' (line 119) and the theme itself can be profitably compared to Dylan Thomas's treatment of death in 'After the funeral'. Though the couplets are syntactically open they are occasionally joined by half-rhymes: these/distress, faces/iris, party/cart, vessel/dull, opening/thing. In many of Sylvia Plath's poems reality becomes a nightmare. In this poem the logic is reversed. It opens with a nightmare and dissolves into a real scene. It is one of her most sustained poems and one that stands superbly without any biographical elucidation.

5] *I have two legs:* this anticipates both the 'black boot' (line 19) and the 'Tubular steel wheelchairs, aluminium crutches' (line 39).

9] *half their old size:* reduced by perspective, though again it prepares for the half-people of Part III.

31] *O white sea-crockery:* cf. 'I think the sea swallowed dozens of tea sets – tossed in abandon off liners, or consigned to the tide by jilted brides.' Sylvia Plath, 'Ocean 1212-W' (see *The Art of Sylvia Plath*).

40] *Why should I walk:* effective use of the line-ending after the references to wheelchairs and crutches.

44] *These children:* the disabled children in the hospital. 'Normal' children appear at the end of the poem.

44] *hooks:* cf. 'Tulips' where 'Their smiles catch onto my skin, little smiling hooks.'

56] *now:* i.e. now he is dead.

73] *like a green sea:* which takes the mind back to the opening, a typically skilful constructive device.

77] *Full of dresses and hats and china:* this takes the mind back to the 'white sea-crockery' of line 31.
100] *limb stumps:* cf. line 39.
124] *round black hats:* top-hats.

Lesbos

Apart from its great intrinsic value, this poem from *Winter Trees* (1971) – a collection of poems from the *Ariel* period, those nine months before the suicide, assembled by Ted Hughes – illustrates the pitfalls of reading too many biographical details into Sylvia Plath's work. The woman in the poem has a daughter and a baby boy, like Sylvia Plath. Then there is the title. Lesbos was the island where Sappho and Alcaeus lived and Sylvia Plath could hardly have failed to see a parallel between the two Greek poets and the husband-and-wife team installed in Devon. Sappho – whose father was killed, who was devoted to her daughter – was hypersensitively feminine; Alcaeus was aggressively masculine. Between them they founded a lyrical school of poetry in the Lesbian vernacular. So far, this tells us something of the elements that germinate in a poet's mind before the birth of the poem. Now the poem itself takes over. Lesbos is also famous as the nominal birth-place of Lesbianism and the speaker of the poem – *not* a self-portrait of Sylvia Plath, but one of her artistic projections – is speaking intimately to another woman. The speaker is a self-confessed 'pathological liar' (line 7), full of hatred, and the other woman is a once-beautiful actress full of patronising good advice: drown the baby, drown the kittens, have an affair. The speaker, although surrounded by Hollywood-style domestic debris, reminds the actress of her own life. She has the memory of her beauty, her career, and one beautiful night with the speaker. Then there is the reality of a comfortable home from which her Jewish husband flees into the arms of a bitch or his mother rather than put up with the actress's suffocating 'soul-stuff' (line 77). With all this reality separating them they are unlikely to meet, even in nirvana. The poem is packed with occasional rhymes and written in a conversational, clipped manner. It is full of deliberately unpoetic phrases like 'The bastard's a girl' (line 16) and 'there's a stink of fat and baby crap' (line 33) and these elements isolate the speaker from the actress in her 'Zen heaven' (line 92).

3] *all Hollywood:* all artificial, like a film-set.
36] *two venomous opposites:* the speaker in her kitchen, the actress in her Zen heaven.
52] These exclamations show the influence of Lowell and Anne Sexton both of whom frequently strive for similar effects.
92] *Zen heaven:* nirvana.

The Bee Meeting

In *The Savage God* A. Alvarez says of this poem from *Ariel*:

'in that strange, upsetting poem "The Bee Meeting", the detailed, doubt-less accurate, description of a gathering of local bee-keepers in her Devon village gradually becomes an invocation of some deadly ritual in which she is the sacrificial victim whose coffin, finally, waits in the sacred grove. Why this should happen becomes, perhaps, less mysterious when you remember that her father was an authority on bees; so her bee-keeping becomes a way of symbolically allying herself to him, and reclaiming him from the dead.'

That certainly is one way, though an excessively biographical way, of looking at the poem. Otto Plath, Sylvia's biologist father, did indeed write an authoritative book on *Bumblebees and their Ways* (1934) and Sylvia Plath herself kept bees in that Devon village. However the poem is an artistic whole, not a private fantasy, and its theme is vulnerability. The villagers are protected, 'all gloved and covered' (line 4) while the speaker is in 'my sleeveless summery dress' (line 3), 'nude as a chicken neck' (line 6). She feels excluded and because no one told her she asks: 'does nobody love me?' (line 6). Even when dressed for the bees she is still isolated, being led by others certain of their roles (secretary of bees, rector, midwife). She goes through a beanfield and sees something unknown, an 'apparition in a green helmet, / Shining gloves and white suit' (lines 28–9). The image of this knight in shining armour – white being the Plathian colour of death – does not comfort this damsel in distress. She stands rooted to the spot as the villagers hunt the queen bee and the young virgins dream of a victory. But the queen is spared and there is instead a white coffin (*white* again) waiting for the speaker who is to be sacrificed instead.

The poem is a superbly modulated presentation of menace in which archetypal dream/nightmare figures appear among the butchers and the post-men. The knight, the sacrificial virgin, the murderess, all transform the reality of the bee meeting into a visionary nightmare.

3] *I have no protection:* this feeling informs most of Sylvia Plath's late poems, the feeling of vulnerability.
11] *the man in black:* as in 'Berck-Plage' and 'Daddy' the man in black stands for the destructive forces she was aware of. The blackness is rapidly spreading because 'Everybody is nodding a square black head' (line 13).
20] *scarlet flowers:* red is her colour for life.
28] *This apparition:* the archetypal knight in shining armour who, in dreams comes to the rescue of damsels in distress, but who cannot help them in the nightmare of reality.
52] *Pillar of white:* therefore, proleptically, already dead.

Daddy

In a note prepared for a BBC broadcast of her poems (but never given) Sylvia Plath said of this poem from *Ariel*:

'The poem is spoken by a girl with an Electra complex. Her father died while she thought he was God. Her case is complicated by the fact that her father was also a Nazi and her mother very possibly part Jewish. In the daughter the two strains marry and paralyse each other – she has to act out the awful little allegory once over before she is free of it.'

This should be borne in mind before attributing an entirely autobiographical significance to the poem as A. Alvarez seems to do in his contribution to *The Art of Sylvia Plath* when he says 'she seemed convinced, in these last poems, that the root of her suffering was the death of her father, whom she loved, who abandoned her, and who dragged her after him into death. And in her fantasies her father was pure German, pure Aryan, pure anti-semite.' This is simply to treat the poem as a pathological outburst. It is anything but. Otto Plath was a bee-keeping biologist and, though Sylvia Plath's poetry *can* be entirely autohistrionic, in this instance she was writing a dramatic monologue which, of course, she intensified by drawing on personal experience. The poem is an act of verbal assassination on the father-figure who is eventually killed vampire-style by having a stake driven through the heart of his heart-lessness. The rhymes revolve around an *ooh!* sound – 'do', 'shoe', 'Achoo', 'blue', 'you', 'two', 'Jew', 'glue', 'screw', 'through' – which simulates human anguish by sounding like a cry of grief.

2] *black shoe:* black is the colour used throughout for the fascist father-figure. Cf. 'a swastika / So black' (lines 46–7); 'the blackboard' (line 51); 'the black man' (line 55); 'A man in black' (line 65); 'The black telephone' (line 69); 'your fat black heart' (line 76). This effectively contrasts with the bright colours associated with life: 'bean green over blue' (line 12); 'my pretty red heart' (line 56).

4] *poor and white:* because deprived of the light.

26] *barb wire snare:* this introduces the concentration-camp imagery and prepares the reader for the references to 'Dachau, Auschwitz, Belsen' (line 33).

49] *boot in the face:* although a brutally abrupt image it has been cunningly placed after the earlier shoe/foot imagery: 'black shoe' (line 2); 'one grey toe' (line 9); 'your foot, your root' (line 23). Eventually it is used to conjure up a satanic image of 'A cleft in your chin instead of your foot' (line 53).

58] *I tried to die:* here Sylvia Plath is using her own early attempt at suicide and no doubt remembering also her own attempt to get back to the beloved father she had lost at the age of eight.

Lady Lazarus

At first sight this poem, from *Ariel*, is the most obviously autobiographical in this particular selection. Sylvia Plath had twice attempted suicide. Her third attempt would end her life a few months after the composition of this poem. Thus the lines

> 'Dying
> Is an art, like everything else.
> I do it exceptionally well'

have been taken as her personal, suicidal credo, her manifesto of destruction. However the poem does not depend for its power on the fact that its predictions were confirmed by her death. The poem is allegorical and, with biblical allusions to the dead Lazarus, projects a modern female Lazarus who looks into the heart of life and sees the face of death. The body is terrifyingly vulnerable in the hands of men in black (Nazis), and even doctors remind her what members of that profession did in concentration camps. The poem suggests that to survive intact in the modern world – with its horrific past and uncertain future – one would have to be insanely insensitive. She was not such a one. The rhymes are repetitive to give the poem a cyclical movement and suggest the impossibility of any way out of the vicious circle of life – except death.

Title] Lazarus lay dead in a cave before Christ raised him. At the age of twenty Sylvia Plath attempted suicide by digging herself into a hole in a cellar and taking fifty sleeping pills. This is the autobiographical basis of the poem though, as I have suggested, it does not invalidate the poetic power of 'Lady Lazarus'.

10] *the napkin:* In John 11 : 44 Lazarus is described: 'he that was dead came forth, bound hand and foot with grave-clothes: and his face was bound about with a napkin'.

31–3] According to A. Alvarez's *The Savage God* this tercet was originally followed by a fourth line: 'I may be Japanese': thus modernising the concentration-camp imagery and bringing in Nagasaki and Hiroshima.

65] *Herr Doktor:* the doctor becomes, in the nightmare vision, a concentration-camp doctor.

INDEX OF FIRST LINES